THE LAST QUEEN

The
LAST
QUEEN

Elizabeth II's Seventy Year Battle
to Save the House of Windsor

CLIVE IRVING

PEGASUS BOOKS
NEW YORK LONDON

THE LAST QUEEN

Pegasus Books, Ltd.
148 West 37th Street, 13th Floor
New York, NY 10018

First Pegasus Books cloth edition January 2021

Library of Congress Cataloging-in-Publication Data is available.

ISBN: 978-1-64313-614-1

10 9 8 7 6 5 4 3 2

Printed in the United States of America
Distributed by Simon & Schuster
www.pegasusbooks.com

To Mimi Irving, my wife and collaborator throughout most of the period covered in this book, whose research and perceptive guidance were indispensable

CONTENTS

PREFACE

Queen Elizabeth II is the longest-reigning monarch in British history and will likely be the last Queen of England. No British monarch has faced such an extended and turbulent period of change. The Queen adapted as best she could, but often seemed out of touch. The advisers who served her did not help. Throughout her reign, egregious family secrets threatened to break cover. Behind the throne, two sides of the royal bloodline competed for influence. And the lives of her heir and second son have become the stuff of scandal. It sometimes seemed that the monarchy would not survive, but somehow it did.

My personal perspective on the Queen is shaped by the coincidence that my career as a journalist has run parallel with the years of her reign. During that time, fawning and obsequious coverage and automatic public deference gave way to aggressive and intrusive worldwide scrutiny. Royal journalism became the most profitable stream of celebrity journalism, and the royal family assumed the role of a compulsively viewable soap opera. Consequently, it became difficult to see the Queen's life clearly and fairly because of the way it was conveyed in the terms and language of the tabloid circus that now always follows the family. This book is partly the story told from the inside of that conflict, of its toll on the monarchy, and of the real stories that lie hidden behind the noise.

PART ONE

CHAPTER 1

THE ACCIDENTAL QUEEN

WINDSOR CASTLE, 19 MAY 2018

The wedding of Prince Harry and Meghan Markle is as glorious as any in the long line of British royal pageants. The gushing TV commentators from every corner of the world all agree that nobody does it better than the British royal family. Even the weather cooperates, with peerless blue skies, and Windsor Castle provides a spectacular backdrop, part *Game of Thrones*, part Camelot. It certainly has the qualities of a fairy tale – a narrative layered with legend, fantasy, tragedy, intrigue and resilience.

However, the real star here is not taking the vows but instead sits in a pew, brightly dressed and wonderfully behatted. The Queen has outlived even the venerable Victoria in her duration on the throne and is now a monarch who seems to be above reproach.

I have covered the royal family as a reporter and critic for decades. Now I am reporting on the wedding for the Daily Beast, based in New York, and I marvel:

St. George's Chapel Windsor became, for the first time in its long history, host to a new kind of rainbow coalition, ranging from doddery old dukes to the exuberance of a gospel choir rocking the place with 'Stand By Me.' And all of this was pure Diana … Metaphorically, Diana burned down the penitential structure that had attempted to restrain her. Harry and Meghan will now enjoy and represent the spirit of that brave rebellion.

It is a thought that seems to strike many onlookers: Princess Diana, the bewitching beauty who died as 'the People's Princess', seems to be the absent but spiritual architect of this apparent transformation in the appearance of the House of Windsor and this joyous display of love and ancient ritual. But Prince Harry knew the underlying reality: some time before, he said that being king or queen is a job that nobody in their right mind would want. His brother William, however, had no choice; his turn would come, while Harry and his new bride would have to try to find their own place in the system. Of course, neither was there any choice available to Queen Elizabeth II, and it would be pointless to ask her if she ever regretted it. But at that moment in St George's Chapel, she could reflect that she had carried the monarchy through many rough patches and that it was still intact. She must also have known that she was probably the last queen her country would ever see.

* * *

The Queen's accession to the throne was accidental. It came about because her father was obliged to replace Edward VIII when he abdicated, and Princess Elizabeth, as the elder of George VI's two daughters, automatically had the same fate as her father thrust upon her. However, the origins of this disruption to the intended line of succession lie much deeper in Windsor family history than the abdication itself. They are embedded in the peculiar character of that family and they influenced the life of the young Elizabeth both before and well into her reign.

It is important to realise that the reality of royal family life in the first decades of the twentieth century was never permitted to be seen by the public. Indeed, it was never admissible as a concept. It would be too glib to talk of a cover-up in the sense of how we understand that term today, as a conspiracy to control information and conceal a scandal. The belief was that the monarchy could be sustained as an institution only if it appeared at all times to be above reproach: in order for it to exist, it had to be a fantasy.

Edward VIII's abdication began the undermining of that fantasy. Much has been written about the abdication. It is always portrayed more as a constitutional and political crisis than as a serious moral failure within the royal family, but that is fundamentally what it was. And that failure, in the first place, was the inevitable result of a wretched atmosphere created in Buckingham Palace by George V, while he was head of the family, and by the weaknesses of his wife, Queen Mary. As a result, the character and behaviour of the King's four sons played out in such a way that the abdication ended up as a choice between two of them. One was unfit to be the King, one had the Crown thrust upon him.

Edward, the Prince of Wales, was born in 1894; Albert, the Duke of York (later George VI), in 1895; Henry, the Duke of Gloucester, in 1900; and George, the Duke of Kent, in 1902. (A fifth son, John, died at the age of thirteen in 1919.) The King and Queen were disastrous parents. George V was a bluff and dull man who frequently seemed to feel trapped in a role that he was plainly ill equipped to carry out. He rose quickly to anger and his sons were in fear of his rages. Sometimes at meals he was so rude to the Queen that she would leave the table, followed by the children. The Queen had no maternal instincts and, according to one courtier, 'was one of the most selfish human beings I have ever known'.

As they grew up, the young princes found themselves among a

generation permanently scarred by the ravages of the so-called Great War, with a pervasive sense that the war had been about nothing other than the senseless feuds of Europe's royal houses, a bloodbath that should never be repeated and that pitched Europe into economic distress. Of the four, the most restive and reckless was the direct heir, Edward, the Prince of Wales.

In contrast to the grim life the princes led inside Buckingham Palace, there was a wild and hedonistic atmosphere to be savoured in the city immediately surrounding the palace. London in the late 1920s and early 1930s had some of the flavour of Weimar Berlin: a raucous libertine social scene; an upper class fearful of revolution; dynamic and radical cultural movements in literature and the arts; a rising agitation from the working class suffering severe hardship in the Great Depression; and an extreme political party that adopted the uniforms and insignia of the European fascist regimes. All four bachelor princes moved in circles where there was a general view that Soviet Russia posed a greater threat to capitalism (and themselves) than the Nazis, an opinion reinforced for the royal princes by the intimate memory of their Romanov cousins, whom they had known as children, being assassinated in a cellar by the Bolsheviks.

Of the four sons, the second, Albert, was the first to marry, in 1923, and to find the satisfaction of a settled life with a woman who was everything that his mother had not been – a caring mother and a lively partner. Elizabeth Bowes-Lyon had the granite virtues of a Scottish background and no affinity for the louche ways she saw in two of her husband's brothers, Edward and George, the Duke of Kent. In fact, as Edward himself cut a swathe through London society with serial affairs, his youngest brother was living far more dangerously.

By all accounts, George was the cleverest and most glamorous of the princes. He was an aesthete with an interest in the arts, design and the theatre. These pursuits introduced him to a far more bohemian crowd than the royals usually encountered. He played the piano, spoke French and Italian and, like Edward, had developed a foppish interest in men's fashions that gave him the style of a dandy-about-town. He was also bisexual, avidly promiscuous and addicted to morphine and cocaine. In the absence of any parental interest, it fell to Edward to offer what persuasion he could to rehabilitate George and clean up the mess of his life. That seemed to be achieved in 1934 when George married the gorgeous Princess Marina of Greece and Denmark. They ran a salon in Belgravia that attracted the leading creative talents of the time – a more aristocratic and frivolous assembly than the contemporary Bloomsbury Group. But the marriage was a façade. George was still living recklessly in his own secret world. And he watched his elder brother become equally reckless when he met and was beguiled by a new lover, Mrs Wallis Simpson, a liaison that was dangerous beyond anything that George had enjoyed.

3 DECEMBER 1936 ...
THE ARRIVAL OF THE TABLOIDS

The newly crowned Edward VIII and Mrs Wallis Simpson were living together in Fort Belvedere, a faux-Gothic castle on a hill that bordered Windsor Great Park. Edward had previously entertained two other mistresses at Fort Belvedere, a discreet love nest that he preferred to Buckingham Palace and that was away from the public eye. But his affair with Mrs Simpson, an American with a colourful past, was about to tip the country into the great crisis that would end with his abdication.

On this morning, the King waited anxiously for Mrs Simpson to appear for breakfast. He recorded the moment in his memoir: 'Wallis entered the drawing room. In her hand she had a London picture newspaper.

"Have you seen this?" she asked.

"Yes," I answered. "It's too bad."'

And the King lamented, 'The world can hold few worse shocks for a sensitive woman than to come without warning upon her own grossly magnified countenance upon the front page of a sensational newspaper.'

The 'sensational newspaper' was the *Daily Mirror*, the paper to which every modern tabloid owes its DNA. In fact, in the long and fraught history of the relationship between the media and the Windsors this can truly be seen as a watershed moment, a tipping point. It was the first time the monarchy had faced the full exposure of a scandal, led by the tabloids. When Wallis Simpson picked up that day's issue of the *Mirror*, she felt a dismay that many other royals after her would come to know, all the way up to the tragedy of Princess Diana in the 1990s. (Edward's reference to Wallis's 'grossly magnified countenance' was hyperbole. The *Mirror* had used a studio portrait commissioned by Mrs Simpson, albeit blown-up.)

The national newspapers at the time were owned mostly by a small clique of self-made men whose fortunes had been made with ink and whose peerages had been paid for by political patronage. They had the influence to support or destroy political careers, but until now the press barons had on the whole protected the monarchy as a necessary institution. Though they regarded the royal family as a useful source of harmless news that boosted circulation, they had also acted to keep minor royal scandals out of their papers – that is, until this scandal became too big to stifle.

Edward had met Mrs Simpson in 1931, while she was still married. She presided over a London salon where, according to the King's own later recollections, the conversation was 'witty and crackling with the new ideas that were bubbling up furiously in the world of Hitler, Mussolini, Stalin, the New Deal and Chiang Kai-Shek'. Hitler's 'new ideas' attracted the future King, out of a mistaken belief – popular at the time – that fascism would turn out to be a form of social engineering that would be good for Europe. His new mistress, unbeknown to him, was already on familiar terms with fascists. She was an intimate of the gregarious German ambassador in London, Joachim von Ribbentrop. Edward's delusion that fascism could be congenial was matched by Ribbentrop's delusion that the British upper classes did not really want war with Hitler and would be able to persuade the whole country to follow suit – an idea that Mrs Simpson's salon encouraged and that Edward would eventually imbibe.

None of this was reported in the London newspapers when Mrs Simpson was granted a divorce in 1936, on the grounds of her husband's adultery. The case was heard in provincial Ipswich and the King made a deal with the press lords that they would bury the story. As Edward noted later, 'It was the miracle I desired – a "gentleman's agreement" among editors to report the case without sensation.' The agreement held for a while, although American newspapers were not party to the deal and sent reporters to nose around Mrs Simpson's new London home. They were seen off by a police sergeant and two constables, but this little drama only heightened the reporters' appetite for a story, and they soon discovered that the King had given Mrs Simpson a $125,000 emerald necklace.

It seems extraordinary to us now, but there was so little exchange of gossipy news across the Atlantic that the British public could remain totally ignorant of what was going on. Meanwhile, the American papers soon got wind of the most sensational development: the King had made up his mind to marry Mrs Simpson. On 16 October, the *New York Journal* had splashed 'KING WILL WED WALLY'.

Hidden from the public, a furious conflict of loyalties had raged between politicians, the press lords, the leaders of the Anglican Church and palace courtiers. One newspaper, *The Times*, was regarded as way above the common herd and custodian of the nation's integrity and the arbiter of royal behaviour. Geoffrey Dawson, the paper's editor, had significant influence with the Prime Minister, Stanley Baldwin, and was appalled by the prospect of the marriage. Baldwin felt the same way, but in the face of an erupting scandal, the two men remained silent. A government minister later noted that no 'quality' newspaper wanted to be first to break the story – the establishment felt that the government should give the lead, and *The Times* would not speak without the government's assent.

The *Mirror*, without that constraint, was looking for a cue to break the story, and it came on 1 December when the Bishop of Bradford reprimanded the King in public, saying in a speech to his Diocesan Conference, 'I ask you to commend him to God's grace, which he will so abundantly need … if he is to do his duty faithfully. We hope that he is aware of his need. Some of us wish that he gave more positive signs of his awareness.' On 3 December, the edition of the *Mirror* that had so distressed Edward and Wallis came off the presses at 3.53 a.m. The paper's editor-in-chief, Harry Bartholomew, had arrived in the middle of the night and remade the front page, wearing an overcoat over his pyjamas. The final of five editions, it was printed so late that it was seen only in London and the surrounding Home Counties; readers elsewhere were left ignorant of the crisis.

The text, under the headline 'GOD SAVE THE KING', seems from this distance flavoured with pomposity and false bravado. It read:

Until this week the *Daily Mirror* rigidly refrained from commenting on or publishing news of this situation. We have been in full possession of the facts but we resolved to withhold them until it was clear that the problem could not be solved by diplomatic methods. This course we took with the welfare of the nation and the Empire at heart. Such is the position now that the nation, too, must be placed in possession of the facts.

Bartholomew, who had a brilliant gift for sensational journalism, had had enough of Fleet Street's collective self-censorship and brought the *Mirror* out in support of the marriage, more from an innate distaste for the hidden hand of the ruling political class than out of any fealty to the King. In the large black type that he pioneered, Bartholomew spoke as if he represented the voice of the nation: 'THE NATION IN-SISTS ON KNOWING THE KING'S FULL DEMANDS AND CONDITIONS'.

This kind of language and the directness of the way it addressed the monarchy and the government was new – and shocking to the ruling caste.

One of the most conflicted players in the crisis was Winston Churchill, who was at the time regarded as a maverick without prospect of future power. He believed as strongly as anyone in the role of the monarchy, and for this reason he backed the King – but he thought Edward was suffering a temporary passion and he did not support the marriage to Mrs Simpson. Along with his close friend Lord Beaverbrook, the owner of the *Daily Express*, he believed that if Mrs Simpson could be scared away from England, the King 'would retire to Windsor Castle. Close the gates. Pull up the drawbridge. Challenge Mr. Baldwin to throw you out if he dares.'

But who, exactly, would do the scaring? Measures were, in fact, taken to frighten Mrs Simpson. Bricks were thrown through the windows of her apartment and vitriolic, threatening letters were sent. Asked many years later if he had personally thrown a brick through her windows, Churchill replied, 'No, but Max [Beaverbrook] did.' Beaverbrook denied it but said it was possible that somebody from the *Daily Express* had done so. 'It was all a lot of fun,' he said. Like many details of the abdication crisis, that particular anecdote took a long time to emerge, surfacing only in 1985 in the diaries of Sir John 'Jock' Colville, one of Churchill's closest aides during the war and the palace press secretary when Queen Elizabeth came to the throne.

The *Mirror* may have thought it was in complete possession of the facts, but that was far from the case. Nor did it have any ability to make royal lives more transparent, cheeky and insubordinate though it may have been. Edward's abdication provides a revealing prologue to future problems that would be caused by the gap between what the public thinks it knows about the monarchy and the reality. At that time, nobody holding power, secular or sacred, believed that it was important or even decent for the public to know anything about the inner life of the monarchy. Had it been possible, it would have been shocking.

Moreover, there was no serious journalistic commitment to making any significant change. The insolent tone of the *Mirror*'s new tabloid vocabulary was just noise – there was never any intention of backing it up with serious reporting. Nor were the proprietors and editors ever close to toying with or supporting republicanism; they remained instinctively supportive of the Crown.

Some years afterwards, an editor of the *Mirror* recalled the suppression of coverage of Edward's relationship with Mrs Simpson, and warned, 'A newspaper that wishes to retain the confidence of its readers should be ruthless and remorseless in revealing all the news it can get.' Many editors today would happily accept those words as a reasonable mission statement, but few then ever really matched up to it.

Royal historians have generally been kinder in their portraits of the Windsors than any reporter should be. This is not to say that they are all hagiographers (although some of them are) but rather that the royal family has been remarkably diligent in controlling their archives and protecting their skeletons. In the 1950s, when James Pope-Hennessy wrote an acclaimed biography of Queen Mary (knowing full well the nightmare of the marriage), the proofs were submitted to Sir Alan Lascelles, known as Tommy, a long-serving and omnipotent courtier who guarded the Windsors with the avidity of the ravens who watch over the Tower of London. Lascelles approved: 'Is there anything in the book that could offend, or distress, The Queen herself, or any members of her family? – Answer, No, nothing. It is throughout written in perfect taste – the book of a gentleman, rare in these days…'

Well, yes, if you equate being a gentleman with being party to a cover-up. Censored and bowdlerised biographies drain the life from their subjects. Amazingly, we are still discovering things about Queen Victoria that make her seem far more human than the figure depicted in those rebarbative public statues of her that remain in cities across her former empire – for instance, we now have ample evidence that she enjoyed a very healthy sex drive.

Edward's abdication was a serious distraction for both the government and the people at a time when Hitler's aggressive plans were clear and Britain was ill-prepared to meet them. Against this background, the King cut a woeful figure. He was self-absorbed, petulant and uxorious to a fault. The secret service knew of Mrs Simpson's liaison with the German ambassador, and they also knew that the King was attracted to the authoritarian style of rule as manifested by Mussolini and Hitler, as were many around him.

To be fair, the taste for appeasement in the 1930s was shared – for a while, at least – by both the honourable and the dishonourable, patriots and traitors. But none of this really lessens the odium that is now justifiably attached to the Duke of Windsor, as Edward became after the abdication. His character fell far short of what is necessary in a monarch – and especially of what would be required of a monarch in a war to save western civilisation.

It's important to remember that none of the Duke's flirtation with fascism was public knowledge at the time, nor for many years afterwards. For decades following the abdication, the royal family's advisers ensured that any details of the Duke and Duchess's meetings with the Nazis while they were travelling in Europe were purged from public records. As we will see, by the end of the war, Churchill was so concerned that the monarchy would be harmed if the Duke's treachery were revealed that he assigned civil servants to comb the German archives for any damning documents and remove them.

When the new King, George VI, moved into Buckingham Palace in 1937, both the country and the monarchy required calm. Prince Albert deliberately chose the regnal name of George to signal continuity with his father, subtly implying that his brother had been an aberration. The British press was more than ready to welcome to the Crown this wholesome-looking family, with its pleasant mother, Queen Elizabeth, and two charming daughters, Elizabeth and Margaret, then aged ten and six.

The family had lived away from the limelight and the traumas of the palace, at 145 Piccadilly, a grand eighteenth-century mansion on the fringe of Mayfair. Despite its twenty-five bedrooms and a ballroom, it was considered relatively modest for a royal residence. To the press, the new royal family presented a perfect picture of the refurbishment of the monarchy; scandal involving them seemed unimaginable.

On being parachuted on to the throne, the King had complained to his cousin, Lord Louis Mountbatten, 'I never wanted this to happen. I've never even seen a state paper. I'm only a naval officer, it's the only thing I know about.'

As it turned out, the King needed a lot of tutoring in world affairs. We have recently learned that in September 1939, shortly after the outbreak of war, he asked Churchill (who was by then serving as First Lord of the Admiralty) whether it would be better for Britain to side with Germany against Bolshevism. This clearly echoes the thinking of his brothers and might seem shocking: it certainly undermines the standard view of George VI as a sound patriot untainted by his predecessor's attraction to tyrants. But in view of what we now know about George V's sons, and the atmosphere in which they grew up, perhaps it is not anomalous after all. Prince George, the Duke of Kent, was as forgiving and tolerant of Hitler as Edward, perhaps more so. And so it is entirely possible that Edward, rather than being an outlier, has been deliberately used as a convenient scapegoat to draw attention from the opinions of the other princes. The Duke of Kent was spared ignominy when he was killed in 1942 in an air crash in Scotland while serving in the RAF. Someone who had served a long time in the Windsor court said of him, 'I always said what luck he died a hero's death, otherwise…' The 'otherwise' hangs in the air ominously and hides a lot, as we shall discover. Churchill's anxiety to remove the damning evidence about Edward from the German records after the war could well have been fuelled by his personal knowledge of the similar opinions of the Duke of Kent and his memory of what the King had said to him in 1939. Had this history come out, it would have been a devastating blight on the House of Windsor.

As the German blitzkrieg was unleashed on France, the Duke and Duchess ended up in a villa in the Portuguese resort of Estoril, not far from Lisbon. Aware that German agents were reaching out to the Duke to enlist him as a possible King-in-waiting should Britain fall, Churchill ordered that he should be bundled off to the Bahamas and to the sinecure position of Governor General. Nonetheless, in Britain's darkest hour, Churchill was forced to endure complaints from the Duchess about being trapped in a colonial backwater. I found a note in the National Archives that was personally typed by the Duke, asking Churchill for permission for the Duchess to go to New York to do some shopping. Churchill forbade it.

* * *

The phantoms of that time, with many lingering questions about loyalty and allegiances within the royal family, continued to dog Elizabeth

II as late as 2018, when her father's conversation with Churchill about whether communism was a greater threat than fascism was revealed in a new biography of Churchill by Andrew Roberts. The Queen seemed to be subtly responding to this in her Christmas message when she reminded us of her father's service fighting the Kaiser:

> My father served in the Royal Navy during the First World War. He was a midshipman on HMS *Collingwood* at the Battle of Jutland in 1916. The British fleet lost fourteen ships and 6,000 men in that engagement. My father wrote in a letter: 'How and why we were not hit beats me.'

In fact, the real story was more dramatic than her version of it. Her father had been sick in his quarters when the *Collingwood* came under heavy attack by torpedo fire, but leapt out of bed and went directly to command the response from a gun turret. He ended a letter to his father, George V, with jingoistic enthusiasm: 'It was certainly a great experience to have been through and it shows that we are at war and that the Germans can fight if they like.'

CHAPTER 2

THE WAYWARD SISTER

To those of us able to remember it, the Britain in which Elizabeth came to the throne in February 1952 was a grim place. The war had drained the Treasury and exhausted the nation. The euphoria of a great victory was short-lived. Churchill and the Tories were thrown out of office. A Labour government under Clement Attlee attempted a mammoth task – to create a welfare state, with radical changes to health care and education, while still maintaining the apparatus of a global empire. Six years of war were followed by nine years of austerity, including food rationing. All fit men were conscripted into the military at the age of eighteen to serve two years of national service. Many of them went to war – dealing with an insurgency in Malaya and, more deadly, serving in the hot surrogate of the Cold War, the Korean War.

The winter of 1946–47 was the most severe for fifty years. The Thames froze at Westminster. The nation's fuel supplies ran low and coal had to be rationed. Later in 1947, the wedding of Princess Elizabeth and Lieutenant Philip Mountbatten brought some light relief after the months of misery. Nominally as a wedding present, British communities abroad sent hundreds of tons of non-perishable food to Britain. It was Elizabeth's choice to distribute it as she saw fit. Under her direction, it was sent to the kitchens of Buckingham Palace and carefully sorted into food parcels that went out to widows and pensioners, each with a personal note from the princess.

So one thing that should frame any assessment of Elizabeth's long reign is the perception that she – as much as any of her subjects – has made the journey from that grim condition of Britain and that concept of British imperial power to a time when there are few if any remnants of that world. She must remember. To her it must seem like two different planets. And she must remember this at a different level from most people, because as an inexperienced young woman she was thrust into the role of personally embodying the nation in all its pretensions, however absurd. She had no choice. Who could not remember something like that?

On the surface, Elizabeth's coronation in 1953 seemed like a great moment of national harmony. Although barely 2 million homes had television sets, more than 20 million people watched the ceremony broadcast by the BBC. Gathered around the small, hazy, flickering black and white projections of a cathode ray tube, people felt they were part of a rare moment of national communion, similar to the celebrations held in every city, town and village to celebrate Admiral Nelson's victory at the Battle of Trafalgar 150 years earlier, when beacons were lit on every chain of hills to send forth the news.

The vision of a young queen passing through a sacred medieval ritual for the first time in the full view of all of her subjects was as compelling as it was novel. Televising the coronation was a radical step in palace policy. It promised an enlightened intention to make the monarchy more approachable. It was a spectacle that gripped the world with its anachronisms and its magic.

Another and more cynical view of this is that Elizabeth was being used by politicians in what would now be called a rebranding exercise, under the rallying rubric of A New Elizabethan Age. Her youth and beauty were obvious. She was perfect for the part. The coronation was stage-managed to be a carefully controlled display of extravagance at a time when millions were living in under-heated homes and carefully planning every meal within the rationing regime.

One of the architects of the display was Churchill, Prime Minister once again after his post-war banishment. Against the advice of the Minister of Food, he ordered that sugar and sweet rationing should be ended in time for the coronation. The ministry warned that chaotic shortages would follow, but they were overruled.

The nation did seem to be on a sugar high, as the Queen was swept up in a carnival designed to reinforce the great imperial narrative and make her people feel good. She rode from Westminster Abbey in a gold coach first used by George III in 1762, although her escort was based in military barracks that were freshly painted but a squalid slum inside. There followed a review of the Royal Navy's fleet, a great ball at Windsor Castle, replete with fireworks, and at the Royal Opera House in Covent Garden the premiere of *Gloriana*, a suitably unctuous concoction by Benjamin Britten dedicated to the monarch.

Elizabeth's reign had opened with a box office hit on a scale that Hollywood could only dream of. There were other balls, banquets and parties displaying an extravagance that had not been seen since before the war. When it came to putting on a show, it seemed that even in straitened circumstances no country could do this kind of thing with more élan. It was part Cecil B. DeMille, part Ruritanian romance and part Noël Coward, with a dress code out of P. G. Wodehouse.

Three years later, the promise of a New Elizabethan Age had lost any conviction. The edifice of imperial power disintegrated with the debacle of the Anglo-French invasion of Egypt at Suez, at a cost to the Treasury of more than £300 million and a great deal of prestige and moral authority. But the warnings of a sugar shortage were false. There were plenty of sweets.

* * *

During the broadcast of the coronation, a few sharp eyes noted what seemed like a remarkable moment of intimacy between two of the wedding guests, as the Queen's younger sister, Princess Margaret, removed a fleck of dust from the uniform of a royal aide, Group Captain Peter Townsend. This suggestive glimpse of affection gave a fleeting clue that there was a ticking time bomb in the palace. The British press did not draw attention to the incident, even though editors knew full well what it signified. By contrast, in America and Europe a liaison between the two had been suspected for some time and hinted at in gossip columns. Sharman Douglas, the daughter of the American ambassador in London, was a close friend of Margaret and warned her that the episode in the Abbey had been covered sensationally in New York. In some ways, the charade of Edward and Mrs Simpson was being replayed, with the British public left unaware of a story that was titillating millions of people abroad.

For the Queen, the affair would be a first trial by public scrutiny that could be damaging to her. What could be more sensitive and personal than to see her young sister's private life suddenly caught in the glare of worldwide attention? And yet the moral framework that dictated the outcome was not the Queen's to decide. Even worse, the Queen was torn between being two different people: the supportive elder sister and the monarch, who by tradition as the head of the Church of England was supposed to uphold the strictest codes of behaviour. Her response was not made any easier by the advice of her courtiers, who, on the whole, had no grip on the public mood.

*   *   *

Back in February 1944, with the Allied invasion of Europe only a few months away, a slim and somewhat gaunt RAF officer had been called in to the Air Ministry in Whitehall. Peter Townsend was a veteran fighter pilot who had flown in the Battle of Britain. The rate of attrition for front-line pilots had been high, and Townsend seemed older than his years. He had suffered what would now be recognised as post-traumatic stress disorder and after being promoted to Group Captain had been withdrawn from active service and asked to head a training unit. Then, having made the move, he was summoned by Sir Charles Portal, Chief of the Air Staff, who told him that George VI was looking for a new equerry. Townsend had only a vague idea of what an equerry did, but Portal explained that it was his job to attend to the King from the moment he woke to when he retired. Moreover, the King was dissatisfied with his current equerries, who were traditionally chosen on the basis of family or regimental connections, and he was keen to recruit somebody noted for their fighting record. It was typical of George VI that he wanted the company of people who were familiar with the world beyond the gilded cage of the palace.

Townsend was interviewed by the King, and his life was completely transformed. After the interview, Sir Piers Legh, Master of the Royal Household, known as 'Joey' to a few intimates, was leading Townsend from the royal apartments in Buckingham Palace when they encountered two young women. Legh introduced Townsend to Princess Elizabeth, then seventeen, and Princess Margaret, who was fourteen.

Townsend was so successful at the job that he became indispensable to the family as Deputy Master of the Household. After the King died in February 1952, his widow, now Queen Elizabeth the Queen Mother, asked Townsend to become the comptroller of her new home, Clarence House. Townsend took the post and a few months later was granted a divorce from his wife Rosemary, who was given custody of their two sons. Two months later she married John de László, son of the portrait painter Philip de László.

Townsend's palace duties had placed a strain on his marriage, made worse by the King's illness and death. Princess Margaret had been particularly close to her father, and she and Townsend found solace in each other's company, and fell in love, despite the enormous implications. The London newspapers had voluntarily covered up the affair until the coronation, hoping that the palace would acknowledge it themselves. Commander John Colville, who had served Churchill subtly and skilfully as a Whitehall mandarin during the war, and been appointed private secretary to Elizabeth before she became Queen, was badly miscast as the official contact between editors and the palace, bumbling along hoping the affair would fizzle out, not realising that the situation had become very serious.

Less than two weeks after the coronation, the story broke in Britain. A blistering front-page editorial in *The People* stated:

> It is high time for the British public to be made aware of the fact that newspapers in Europe and America are openly asserting that the Princess is in love with a divorced man and that she wishes to marry him … Every newspaper names the man as Group Captain Townsend.

Taking aim at Colville, *The People* stressed that this story had appeared 'without meeting any official denial'.

To many of the Queen's subjects, rather than being shocking, the affair was a touching romance, and a heart-warming news story. The fact that Townsend was fifteen years older than Margaret was hardly disgraceful; at twenty-three, she was surely old enough to know her own mind. Moreover, Townsend had not been the guilty party in his divorce.

In the palace, Townsend reported to the queen's private secretary, Tommy Lascelles. When Townsend told his boss how deeply he and Margaret were in love, Lascelles said, echoing Lady Caroline Lamb's description of Lord Byron, 'You must be either mad or bad.' Lascelles has been cast as something of a pantomime villain in the TV series *The Crown* – a reactionary who stood in the way of anything at odds with rigid Victorian protocol. He certainly looked the part, with an old-fashioned wardrobe of dark vested suits with narrow trousers, a watch chain, shirts with starched collars and a moustache worthy of a First World War general. His background was typical for his position: he came from a well-connected family where royal service was regarded as a vocation that required humourless discipline. He had also been in palace service long enough to know – and conceal – a lot of scandalous history. Both Townsend and Margaret detested Lascelles; she later said, 'I shall curse him to the grave.'

In his memoir, published in 1978, Townsend said that Winston Churchill opposed the affair, but Colville's diaries, published seven years later, tell a different story. Colville records that Lascelles drove to Churchill's country house, Chartwell, in Kent to tell him that Margaret wanted to marry Townsend. Churchill's first reaction, after Lascelles had left, was to remark that 'the course of true love must always be allowed to run smooth' and that nothing should stand in the way of 'this handsome pair'. Lady Churchill disagreed, and warned her husband that he would be making the same mistake as he had in the abdication crisis by supporting the King.

Her view was shared by much of the country's establishment. They insisted that the Queen should be protected from such scandal and invoked both the Royal Marriages Act, which decreed that until she was twenty-five Margaret needed her sister's consent to marry, and Canon 107 of the Church of England's laws, which forbade divorce. This view prevailed and Townsend was exiled to Brussels to serve as an air attaché at the British embassy.

The Queen had struggled to balance the competing pressures of political, legal and ecclesiastical advice on one side and her feelings for her hot-blooded sister on the other side. When first told of the romance, the Queen and Prince Philip invited Margaret and Townsend to supper at the palace, much in the way that parents concerned about a proposed union would want to test out the seriousness of the couple's feelings. Of course, this wasn't an audition in which Townsend needed to prove his character; he had been serving the family for nearly twelve years. Knowledge of the Townsends went back even further than that: Philip had served on a Royal Navy destroyer under Captain Michael Townsend, Peter's brother. At Buckingham Palace and Windsor, Philip and Townsend had played squash and badminton together. During the supper Philip showed no concern about the couple's age difference, and in his man-to-man style of banter he was more openly optimistic that a way would be found for them to marry than the Queen. 'He was on our side, a real chum,' Margaret said later.

But there was a third voice with influence over the Queen: her mother. Nobody knew Townsend better than the Queen Mother – after all, she had taken him from the palace to oversee her own household. Before that, she had witnessed Townsend's devotion to the King, and the King's pleasure in his company. But this was a memory that influenced what she now felt about the affair – there was no way, she believed, that the King would have approved the marriage of his youngest daughter to Townsend. There is no record of how much weight the Queen gave to the different voices. In the end, she advised her sister that if she waited two years until she was twenty-five, she and Townsend would be allowed to marry. And Margaret believed her.

Thus ended the first act in a two-act tragedy that would dog Princess Margaret for the rest of her life, expose the monarchy to ridicule and embolden the newspapers to begin scrutinising the Crown in a way that was new and far more invasive than anything in recent history.

*   *   *

I gained a far closer view of these events by arriving in London on the eve of Act Two. In the summer of 1955, I took a job as a sub-editor on a tabloid, the *Daily Sketch*, located in the half square mile between the Inns of Court and Ludgate Circus that was referred to collectively as Fleet Street. Rarely has any profession been shaped more palpably by a specific locus than British journalism: since the eighteenth century, this area – first known as 'Grub Street' – had served as the national listening post for everything from political and financial intelligence to scurrilous gossip. From here, pamphleteers like Daniel Defoe and William Cobbett had fired off broadsides against the monarchy and ruling caste. Charles Dickens had been a gumshoe reporter exposing rascals of many kinds. In the late nineteenth century came the first popular daily newspapers, their fortunes rising with the appearance of a new middle class. In 1955, this concentration of the power of print journalism was at its apogee. To a young journalist arriving from the provinces (in my case from a tabloid in Liverpool), it was one of the most mesmerising places in which to pursue a career.

Like many papers of that era, the *Daily Sketch* is now long gone. It was soon clear to me that the staff had the hunger of underdogs, something I recognised from having seen a similar situation in Liverpool. In Fleet Street, the tabloid to beat, the mother of all tabloids, was the *Daily Mirror*. The *sui generis* Bartholomew tabloid that had shaken Edward VIII had evolved into the bestselling paper in Britain, a daily firebrand that, under a visionary editor, Hugh Cudlipp, had allied itself with the Labour Party to become a political force. Bert Gunn, editor of the *Daily Sketch*, is far less remembered now than his poet son Thom, but in 1955 he was an experienced and respected editor with a big problem on his hands. The *Sketch* was superficially similar to the *Mirror* but lacked its mass-market instincts. Gunn had been hired from Beaverbrook's *Daily Express* to breathe new life into it. His idea was to combine the sophistication of the features in the *Express* with the robust 'common man' appeal of the *Mirror*. I was assigned to the features department.

A few weeks after I joined the paper, on 21 August 1955, Princess Margaret reached her twenty-fifth birthday.

Like the rest of Fleet Street, we knew that Townsend had returned from exile and that, with Margaret's birthday approaching, the saga of their relationship was about to be publicly reignited. Townsend was free from the constraints imposed by the palace and was shadowed every day by reporters. Margaret was on a royal tour of the Caribbean, where she was able to read the American papers. Once more, they regarded it as the biggest royal story since the abdication. 'MEG, FLIER WILL WED' was a headline in the *New York Post*, displaying a certainty in the success of the relationship that the couple themselves lacked.

Editors at the *Sketch* were also aware that during Townsend's banishment to Brussels, Margaret had been orchestrating a brilliant charade. There were continual reports of the revels of 'the Margaret set', a crowd of aristocratic hedonists she collected around her, which included a number of male escorts. However, we weren't aware that Margaret and Townsend had been able to keep their affair alive with weekend trysts at the country houses belonging to discreet friends. The birthday came and went, and nothing happened.

Gunn, quoting unnamed sources, said that the Prime Minister, Anthony Eden, who had succeeded Churchill, was opposed to the marriage. He didn't need to underline the hypocrisy of this: Eden was a divorcee who had remarried a much younger woman himself. But all the old players in the palace and the clergy were once more lining up against Margaret and Townsend. Nobody knew what the Queen herself thought, and it seemed clear that the monarchy was heading for a debacle that would sell a lot of newspapers.

CHAPTER 3

ROYAL FAMILY VALUES

Bert Gunn was wrong in his suggestion that Eden was opposed to the marriage. In fact, the Prime Minister had worked out a plan to circumvent the Royal Marriages Act, but nobody outside a small circle of ministers and the palace officials was aware of this. The truth about these events was withheld until the release of official papers nearly fifty years later, in 2004, which is a telling sign of how little Fleet Street ever really knew and how the Queen's own feelings and role were obscured by the inept officials around her.

Eden's proposal was that Margaret could keep her title and her civil list allowance of £6,000 a year and would also receive another £9,000 when she married. The key device was that the Act could be amended to remove her from the succession, meaning that she would no longer need her sister's permission to marry. As Eden explained it to Commonwealth Prime Ministers, 'Her Majesty would not wish to stand in the way of her sister's happiness.'

Eden's hand had been strengthened when Lord Kilmuir, the Lord Chancellor and the government's chief law officer, sent a note to Eden saying that in his view the Act would not even apply to Margaret: 'This Act has no pride of ancestry, is badly drawn and uncertain and embarrassing in its effect.'

The draft of the plan was completed on 31 October, and Eden prepared to tell Parliament that the Royal Marriages Act 'was out of harmony with modern conditions'. Three days later, however, Margaret announced that the marriage was off.

In August, though this was unknown until the release of the papers in 2004, Margaret had written to Eden explaining that her feelings about Townsend were uncertain: 'It is only by seeing him that I feel I can properly decide whether I can marry him or not.' In his memoir, Townsend gives no sign of being aware that Margaret has cooled towards him. He describes being reunited with her in the sitting room of Clarence House: 'As we rediscovered one another, we realised that nothing had changed. Time had not staled our accustomed, sweet familiarity.'

No attempt was made to conceal this meeting from the press, but Commander Colville remained as unhelpful as he had been two years earlier, answering that 'no statement is at present contemplated' and never moving beyond that inflexible position.

The *Mirror* reflected the general opinion: never had the Crown been given such appalling advice. 'If not "at present", then when?' A Berlin tabloid, *Morgenpost*, felt the same: 'The basic error was the unbelievably amateurish fashion in which public opinion was being led by the nose.'

Townsend's recollections suggested that he had enjoyed the drama: 'Each time the Princess and I saw one another or dined with friends, the suspense and the speculation mounted.' The Queen joined the couple for tea at Clarence House in what must have been a tense encounter. Townsend never disclosed what was said. Nor did Margaret. Townsend knew that the Cabinet was being briefed on the Royal Marriages Act but interpreted this as a sign that Margaret would be allowed to marry only 'at crushing cost to herself'.

At the *Daily Sketch*, we were still in the dark about the Prime Minister's efforts on behalf of the couple but sensed that public opinion was growing restless. The people wanted an end to the farce, and a majority wanted the marriage to go ahead. Still nobody knew what the Queen herself thought – or intended. Suddenly that no longer mattered, because she found herself being advised that she had no choice in the matter. An editorial in *The Times* on 26 October argued that the real issue was neither theological nor legal but related to the status of the Queen – millions of people saw themselves reflected in her, and her family provided a role model for them. Given this standard, thundered *The Times*, the vast numbers of the Queen's subjects could not regard the marriage of Margaret and Townsend as marriage at all.

It is doubtful that the Queen agreed. This line of attack invoked a popular attitude that was at least thirty years out of date, and disclosed a view of society that was also way behind that of the Prime Minister. But the paper had effectively spoken for the Queen, whether she liked it or not. At the *Sketch*, we did not know what was really happening in Westminster any more than Townsend, who, on the day *The Times* editorial appeared, went to see Margaret at Clarence House, having drafted a public announcement for her that began 'I have decided not to marry Group Captain Townsend'. A week later, on 31 October, Margaret delivered an amended version, beginning, 'I would like to make it known that I have decided not to marry Group Captain Townsend … Mindful of the Church's teaching that Christian marriage is indissoluble, and conscious of my duty to the Commonwealth, I have resolved to put this consideration before others.'

Margaret's words were probably disingenuous. One of her biographers, Christopher Warwick, said that during the twenty-two years he knew her, she clammed up whenever the Townsend affair was raised, saying, 'It was a long time ago and I have forgotten it.' She was more explicit in 1980 with another biographer, the *Daily Mail* columnist Nigel Dempster: 'If Lascelles hadn't told me that marriage was possible, I would never have given it another thought. The relationship would have been out of the question and Peter could have gone off quite peacefully. Instead we waited for ages and then discovered it was quite hopeless.'

Weighing up all the differing accounts of the affair, Margaret comes across as a skilled dissembler who used the crisis to cast herself in the most sympathetic light. In the established narrative, she was the victim of an establishment stitch-up, an idea that she went along with, though it had, in fact, collapsed. *The Times* had fired off the final salvo of a past generation, but it was enough to unnerve Townsend.

Margaret must have felt gratified when, at the end of that tumultuous week, she opened the *Sunday Times* to find that one of the nation's most esteemed historians, Sir Arthur Bryant, had written a tribute to her. Completely embracing the idea of her noble act of self-sacrifice, he absurdly compared her to British heroes such as Elizabeth I, Thomas Becket, Admiral Lord Nelson, Florence Nightingale and – bewilderingly – Scott of the Antarctic. Margaret's decision, Sir Arthur asserted, 'was an act of history and one that will not be without its effect on the future of our time'.

The role of the thwarted lover was a perfect part for Margaret to play for the rest of her life, but it was based on a fairy tale. Eden's plan that would have allowed her to marry Townsend had required very few sacrifices from her; after all, succession was never going to be an issue as Charles and Anne had already arrived. Over time, even the most conservative of subjects would have come to terms with the marriage, especially since Townsend was a model of propriety.

But Margaret had got over Townsend: absence had not made the heart grow fonder, and when he returned from Brussels, the age difference was more apparent. He was less exciting than some of the people she now knew. She was ready to have some fun, and marrying Townsend would have ended it.

The affair changed Margaret for ever, not by inflicting a wound of love that would not heal but because she had become a world celebrity, and she liked it. Eventually the cost of this level of celebrity would be lethal. In the process, the royal family had been made to look careless in its handling of what was, at its heart, a family crisis, as well as a national one. Afterwards the lives of the two sisters would increasingly diverge. One had escaped the glass cage; the other was indentured to it.

The Queen was certainly harmed – nothing was said to correct the impression that she had sided against her sister. If Margaret herself is to be trusted as a source on what really transpired between the two then her version came years later, again through Nigel Dempster (who could give a masterclass in cultivating sources among royalty and the aristocracy). His biography of Margaret quotes her directly saying, 'In our family we do not have rifts. We have a jolly good row and then it's all over. And I've only twice ever had a row with my sister.' The 'jolly good row' sounds authentically Margaret. She did not specify what those two rows were, but Dempster knowingly proposes that the first was during the final weeks of the Townsend saga and the second was provoked by a later affair that Margaret had with someone the Queen loathed. In fact, the Margaret–Townsend affair serves as a telling precursor of what would be a continuing problem for the Queen throughout her reign: if the palace theory of public information was to provide as little information as possible, we are always as likely to get a false version of events as an accurate one.

The apparatus supporting this theory has been remarkably persistent, with officials sheltering under the protection of the rule that state papers of any sensitivity should not be seen for fifty years, by which time all the parties involved would usually be dead. The family kept its own archives in Windsor Castle and had a similarly restrictive view of controlling their accessibility. And some of the players in the Margaret and Townsend saga, including Margaret herself, locked away large quantities of their own correspondence – with consequences that long obstructed our knowing the truth of events.

The only newspaper that palace officials did respect was *The Times*. It seemed able to play a quasi-institutional role, speaking *de haut en bas* to the nation. Why was it able to play such a decisive role in ending the affair? Amazingly, the paper had never carried a word of reporting on the crisis as it unfolded. To anyone not reading any other paper, the thundering editorial would have been the first mention of it.

The paper's editor was Sir William Haley, who after a career in Manchester as a newspaper editor was appointed director general of the BBC at the age of forty-two and became editor of *The Times* in 1952, at the age of fifty-one. Thus Haley had, uniquely, led the two in-stitutions that held a peculiar place in the cultural and social policing of the country. The BBC was a public service broadcaster of supposed-ly political independence bestriding both radio and television that had earned the affectionate nickname 'Auntie' because of its self-perceived duty to provide an alternative to the vulgarity of popular journalism and entertainment. *The Times* represented in print the same attitude of self-appointed authority.

There was no news on the front page of *The Times*; instead, in eight tight columns, the page was a notice board of small advertisements to which the upper classes turned when they wanted to hire a nanny, a cook or a butler. At the centre of the masthead, above the adver-tisements, was the royal coat of arms, as though the paper served as the monarchy's house journal. Emphasising that authority, each issue carried the daily Court Circular, listing the engagements of members of the royal family, and noting royal appointments.

Haley, in spite of his rapid rise and grasp of institutional power, was virtually unknown to the public – and he liked it that way. His power was strengthened by his relative anonymity. Painfully shy, he was a mystery even to many of his staff, who feared his fanatical attention to detail – he would, for example, ask why his foreign desk had not noted a scoop buried on an inside page of a German newspaper. He was a brilliant administrator of the mandarin type and, like many of the mandarins in Whitehall and at the palace, he was moralistic in a way that by the mid-1950s rendered him totally out of touch with the popular mood towards institutions like the monarchy. Nobody had asked him to blow up Townsend's hopes of marrying Margaret – the thunder came from his own self-righteousness.

The Times was not part of Fleet Street in any sense, although its offices were only a few blocks away from ours. Its editors belonged to clubs in Pall Mall like the Athenaeum, the Reform and the Travellers Club, while Fleet Street editors belonged to the famously boozy Press Club, tucked away on a side street, or the wine bar El Vino, a dark den with its own subtle hierarchy of fellowship. Editors frequently burned out, as capricious proprietors treated them as disposable. Fleet Street was an intense 24-hour meat grinder with a picaresque underpinning, and I loved it.

The *Sketch* had paid inside tipsters everywhere, from Scotland Yard to the Central Criminal Court at the Old Bailey. In Soho, reporters mingled easily with gangsters who ran the whorehouses while paying protection money to the police, and in the East End, thugs like the Kray brothers who ran their own protection rackets had family connections to some of the crime reporters. I noticed that some of these reporters had flashy cars that they could not possibly have afforded with their salaries.

Many of the stories collected from these sources were unprintable, since they involved prominent politicians, judges and other members of the Great and the Good who went slumming for fun, knowing that they were immune from exposure. Listening to these reporters opened my eyes to the hypocrisy of the moral arbiters of the nation and also taught me an important lesson that I never forgot: in a finely stratified society, it is usually the people at the bottom rather than those at the top who turn out to be the most trustworthy sources.

To Colville and many others tasked with keeping the impertinence of Fleet Street reporters at bay, it seemed that things could not get worse than they had been during the Margaret and Townsend crisis. And something had changed. The country was creaking with the pressure of social change, and the palace was no worse in its failure to sense this than the state's other institutions. But there would be no more tacit agreements between press barons to cover up embarrassing events. What was freely reported elsewhere in the world could no longer be so easily excluded from the British public – although British libel laws, more extensive in range and more rigorously enforced than elsewhere, would continue to inhibit Fleet Street editors from reporting on scandals involving powerful people.

Haley's assertion that the royal family represented a kind of sacred standard for the whole nation's family values was not only preposterous; it was an impossible burden to place on them. Colville and Lascelles lived in a bubble of their own making – and they made sure the Queen lived in it, too.

CHAPTER 4

A FEUD BEHIND
THE THRONE

Long before the Queen struggled to deal with the crisis created
by her sister, she was faced with one precipitated in part by her
husband. But unlike the Margaret saga, this one remained private at
the time. Fleet Street knew nothing of it. By now there was an heir
growing up in the palace; Charles was born in 1948 and a sister, Anne,
was born in 1950. With a new generation of Windsors established, the
family name suddenly became contentious.

Late in February 1952, not long after the death of George VI, Prince
Ernst Augustus of Hanover, one of the Queen's many German relatives who remained in regular orbit among the royal family, caused
great alarm at court. He had been among the guests at a house party
at Broadlands, the grand Palladian country home of Admiral Earl
Mountbatten. A highly agitated Prince Ernst reported to Queen Mary,
George V's widow, that during dinner Mountbatten announced that
with the passing of George VI the royal family would now be able to
shed the name of Windsor and become the House of Mountbatten.
As a result of receiving this news, Queen Mary had spent a sleepless
night. The next day she summoned Commander Colville, who had
just become Winston Churchill's principal private secretary, to warn
him of Mountbatten's declaration. Churchill and his whole Cabinet
made it clear they would not tolerate the idea.

No wonder. The family name of Windsor was adopted by a decree of George V in 1917 to sever all association with the Kaiser and that part of the tribe that was waging war with the British Empire. At the same time, the name Mountbatten was concocted to replace Battenberg for those whose European roots, a blend of Russian, Danish, German and Greek royal houses, also needed a new identity. But to suggest that Mountbatten would now supplant Windsor was shocking not only to Queen Mary but to the whole Anglicised side of the family, particularly the Queen Mother.

The internal family and political dynamics of this episode are important because they had a lasting influence on the Queen's life to an extent never apparent at the time. Particularly salient is what these events reveal about how Earl Mountbatten – always known as Dickie to his intimates, even though Richard was not among his actual names – played a singular role during decades of the Queen's reign. In a presidential republic like France or the United States, Mountbatten's military distinction would have made him a natural choice to run for head of state, following the example of two of his Second World War contemporaries, Charles de Gaulle and Dwight Eisenhower. It is ironic that as second cousin once removed to Elizabeth II, Mountbatten had to accept that being part of a constitutional monarchy did not allow that career path. Nevertheless, he assiduously cultivated as much influence and power as he could, straddling both political and royal life in a way that no other figure could.

In 1952, at the time of his attempt to change the family name, Mountbatten was serving at the Admiralty as Fourth Sea Lord, one of the Royal Navy's key commanders. It was a far less significant post than the one that had brought him to international renown during the war, Supreme Allied Commander for South East Asia, where he had reversed the Japanese assault in Malaya and, in a moment that avenged one of Britain's most humiliating military defeats of the war, accepted the Japanese surrender of Singapore.

It was Churchill who gave him the Asian command in 1943, even though Mountbatten had been largely responsible for a disastrous amphibious raid on the French port of Dieppe in 1942 in which 60 per cent of the force, mostly Canadians, were killed or captured. But Mountbatten managed his command of multinational forces in Asia with more skill, relying more on his diplomatic polish and gift for self-promotion than on any military acumen. Handsome and rakish, in this role Dickie achieved a personal wartime fame that he imagined, vaingloriously, equalled that of other great commanders like Montgomery and Eisenhower.

But by 1952 he had lost Churchill's approval. There were two reasons for this, and they merged into one big one. As soon as Churchill lost office in 1945 and before Japan surrendered, Mountbatten became an open supporter of the new Prime Minister, Clement Attlee. Given his strikingly privileged background, this shocked many, but it turned out that, perversely, Dickie saw much merit in socialism. However, Churchill's disaffection went far beyond the alliance with Attlee. The Labour government was in a hurry to dismantle the British Empire, starting with granting independence to India. Attlee appointed Mountbatten as India's viceroy, the man who would wind down what Churchill regarded with strong personal attachment as the empire's jewel in the crown. To Churchill's dismay, it proved impossible to avoid partition and the creation of two independent states, India and Pakistan. Churchill (and others) thought that Mountbatten had been precipitate and too accommodating to Attlee.

Attlee's government fell in 1951, shortly before George VI's death. Churchill was nearly seventy-seven when he returned to Downing Street – too old for the job according to many, including his wife

Clementine. But the cry of 'Churchill is back!' resonated through the land, and abroad, in a way that fed his ego and his confidence.

As Churchill became reacquainted with his military leaders, several of them familiar from the war, there was an incident that did nothing to improve his opinion of Mountbatten. Dickie was invited to a gathering of staff officers and senior civil servants before Churchill sailed to America for a meeting with President Truman. In his diary, Colville wrote that Mountbatten 'talked arrant political nonsense: he might have learned by heart a leader from the *New Statesman* ... He caused much irritation to the Chiefs of Staff. The P.M. laughed at him.' The disaffection was mutual. When Mountbatten was told that the Cabinet had ruled out any change to the royal family name, he said that the Queen's position against it had been forced 'by that old drunk Churchill'.

The hand of Prince Philip in the feud over the family name was very clear. Philip was having trouble accepting the role of Prince Consort. His behaviour suggested that in the five years of marriage before George VI's death he had not grasped the reality of how the burdens of being Queen would change their lives. There were certainly plenty of anachronisms in the palace's daily routines to frustrate him. By his own admission, he saw the machinery of the institution as something he could not challenge. He portrayed himself as a modern man being constrained by courtiers who lived in the past. It became very personal: 'I am the only man in the country not allowed to give his name to his children,' he complained.

However, that seems a strangely anachronistic sentiment in itself. Of all the frustrations confronting Philip as he sought a meaningful role, the wish to revisit the family name was not obviously relevant to the mission of a modern man. What was really so intolerable about a name that the country had grown familiar and comfortable with, a name that had its origins in a Norman castle and was uncontaminated by association with any of the successive dynasties that had claimed the Crown with varying degrees of legitimacy and competence? The royal family tree was creaking with many branches and titles that sounded like some vanished nineteenth-century network of tribes and privilege. It was absurd to have any interest in perpetuating any of it.

But Philip was obsessed. When the government, making concrete his defeat, proposed an official proclamation confirming that the family would remain known as the House of Windsor, he wrote a memorandum of protest to Downing Street. There were suspicions that Mountbatten had had a hand in drafting it. It was tartly rejected.

*   *   *

Philip was born on the island of Corfu on 10 June 1921. His parents were Prince Andrew and Princess Alice of Greece. His given name was Philippos and technically he was sixth in line to the Greek throne. But that was fanciful. The Greek monarchy had shallow roots and never really gained a permanent hold on the country. It was founded in 1832 when Prince Otto of Bavaria became King of a newly independent nation. Otto was so despotic that he had to be deposed in 1862. Between 1924 and 1935 there were twenty-three changes of government in Greece, a dictatorship and thirteen political coups. The royal family went into exile. In 1952, Philip referred to himself as a 'refugee husband', but that was far more true of his immediate family's past history than it was of his own life – thanks largely to the intervention of Mountbatten.

Philip arrived in England in 1930. His four sisters remained in Paris with their mother while his feckless father took off for Monte Carlo with a mistress. For a relatively impecunious family like this, living off the charity of relatives, there was always one pressing issue: marriage. The daughters were respectable and presentable, and their blood was blue enough to avoid marrying outside the golden network prescribed by the *Almanach de Gotha*. There were enough minor princes scattered about Europe to provide husbands, and Philip's sisters did well in that market, all of them marrying well-heeled German royalty, several on good terms with the Nazi Party – a party committed to removing the most threatening revolutionaries of the day, the communists.

At the age of nine, Philip already promised to become a handsome and eligible bachelor, and the family decided that the ideal home for him was Great Britain, where the House of Windsor was the wealthiest and most securely entrenched monarchy in Europe. Mountbatten agreed to become a mentor. He saw in Philip someone who, under his direction, could be fashioned into a new kind of British prince. Soon after he arrived in England, Philip was put in the charge of Mountbatten's brother, George, the Marquess of Milford Haven, and his wife Nadejda, whose family seat was Lynden Manor, a sprawling estate near Maidenhead. They had an eleven-year-old son, David, who quickly became Philip's best friend. From then on, the Milford Havens funded Philip's upbringing.

In Paris, Philip had gone to the American School in Saint-Cloud and spoke fluent French. This was a conventional choice for families who could afford a sophisticated 'international' education. But the education selected for Philip in England would turn out to be far from conventional, although it began unremarkably enough at Cheam, the oldest private school in England, where a relatively small number of boys, fewer than fifty, boarded in a converted Georgian farmhouse. David Milford Haven was already a pupil, and when Philip joined him there, they became inseparable. They were known as the 'Mountbatten boys'. Both were keen on sports, and a badminton court was built for them at Lynden Manor.

But at Lynden Manor, George Milford Haven pursued a private interest that most of his family, including the children, knew nothing about. He was a collector of pornographic books and erotica. He approached the subject with the pedantry of a butterfly collector, in his own hand carefully composing an index ranging over books and photographic albums devoted to sadomasochism, incest and bestiality. There were catalogues describing various sex toys and the techniques for using them. Some of the book titles seemed directed at sophomoric fantasists, like *Les Callipyges*, 'the whole philosophy and secret mystery of luxurious flagellation by former English aristocratic ladies'. ('Former' implies an improbable passage to disgrace.)

A network of pornographic book dealers had long existed to cater for wealthy clients like Milford Haven. Many of the books were produced to the high standards demanded by serious collectors, with the best-quality paper and bindings; the perversions, no matter how bizarre, came with the pretence of academic study and connoisseurship. It was all in keeping with the social compact enjoyed by the eminent and privileged. Depravities that were criminal when enjoyed by the common herd became discreetly permissible for the upper orders. In the Weimar-like fever of London in the 1930s, the Milford Havens, Mountbattens and Windsor princes could – and did – enjoy great latitude in their private pleasures.

Philip's happy and adventurous life in the lushest of the English shires ended in 1933 when he was sent to a school in Germany called Salem, run by Kurt Hahn, on lines very different from Cheam. Hahn promoted a new 'progressive' educational regime in which tests of exacting physical endurance ranked equally with academic attainment. But Hitler came to power in 1933 and Hahn was a Jew. On the face of it, the regime at Salem seemed perfectly Teutonic, at one with the spartan ideals and methods of the Hitler Youth movement. But in September 1933 the Nazis issued a proclamation excluding Jews from 'cultural' posts and in 1934 Hahn fled to Scotland, where on the North Sea coast he founded a new school, Gordonstoun. Philip followed him there.

This rigorous, character-hardening process was part of Mountbatten's design to nurture Philip as a man of action, as a prelude to a career in the Royal Navy. Of the three services, the Navy was the most socially esteemed: known as the Senior Service, it had a pervasive ethos of superiority and wholly embodied the British class system, drawing into its ranks members of the monarchy, including Prince Albert, the future George VI. (Albert's brother Prince George, future Duke of Kent, forced against his will into the Navy by his father, suffered physically and emotionally until finally allowed to change vocations.) Mountbatten's naval career began as a midshipman in 1916 and by 1937 he had risen to captain with command of a destroyer. With a rich wife and high social glamour, Mountbatten saw the Navy as a unique British institution in which he could thrive. Philip was an ideal candidate for him to mentor for a similar career.

Kurt Hahn delivered what Mountbatten hoped for. Philip did so well at Gordonstoun that he became head boy. Hahn reported, 'He was one of those boys who very early rendered disinterested service and who never asked for any privilege on account of his birth.' Philip was a 'born leader' who nevertheless needed 'the exacting demands of a great service to do justice to himself', although his virtues were 'marred at times by impatience and intolerance'.

By the summer of 1939, Philip was a cadet at the Royal Naval College at Dartmouth. A strikingly handsome figure, he was being groomed to become an exemplary young officer. When the King and Queen arrived at the college for a visit with their two daughters, Mountbatten arranged for Philip to have lunch with them. This was one of those meetings of destiny that tend to get inflated in recollection once the destiny is decided. Several such accounts suggest that Princess Elizabeth was smitten at first sight. Given that royal marriages were orchestrated within a carefully ordained gene pool, it is true that Philip was probably beyond eligible – he was a prime candidate.

Later, in 1943, the King, aware that Elizabeth was taking an interest in Philip, allowed that he was 'intelligent, has a good sense of humour and thinks about things in the right way'. But compared to Philip, who by then was worldly in every sense of the word, Elizabeth had led a sheltered life and was far from ready to take the plunge.

* * *

In 1952, with Mountbatten's plan to change the family name rebuffed, Kurt Hahn's words about Philip's character being marred by impatience and intolerance were borne out in his mood. He was as furious as Mountbatten, and this was just the beginning of the feud. It would simmer for another decade, until they found a Prime Minister willing to compromise. Philip's fury distressed the Queen for a long while. Added to all the challenges of her apprenticeship as monarch, it was suffered in private. There was no sign of a rift in public. The Queen's burden had been lightened at the start of her reign by the rapport she built with Churchill. When she came to the throne, Churchill told Colville, 'She is only a child.' But he used his magic with her: courtiers excluded from their meetings, standing and listening on the other side of a door, frequently heard mutual laughter. And she needed some of that spirit now.

CHAPTER 5

'THE MONARCHY WILL NOT SURVIVE...'

Someone was missing from every story written about the Queen: the Queen.

Fleet Street editors in the late 1950s treated coverage of the monarchy as both a daily obligation and, usually, a chore. With Princess Margaret slipping into the background (for the moment), the coverage was usually left to the small core of reporters accredited to the palace. Few reporters wanted the job. Few who had the job had any curiosity beyond the platitudes fed to them. They did get some exotic travel opportunities, though – particularly when the Queen toured the countries of her Commonwealth. The world empire was in the process of being subsumed into this very different arrangement. The newly independent nations were encouraged – but not obliged – to retain a familial feeling towards the 'mother' country, and, of course, towards the Queen. Moving from subjection to association (with benefits) was achieved partly because the Queen took the task seriously and because she had absolutely no whiff about her of Victorian racial superiority. She was, it seemed, naturally anodyne. In a tour that lasted for more than five months she gave 102 speeches without causing offence. She had a script, and she read it.

But that quality of inoffensiveness had its drawbacks. At home, without the exotic backdrops, the Queen had fallen into a robotic style of speaking. There was no sense of spontaneity or natural affinity for any setting other than the one place where she really seemed to be engaged with her surroundings: the racetrack. The Queen became more openly excited about horses than she did about people.

In the summer of 1957, I moved from the *Daily Sketch* to the *Daily Express* as deputy features editor. Geographically, it was a move of less than a quarter of a mile, to a 1930s architectural classic in black glass fronting Fleet Street itself. Professionally, it was the difference between night and day. Lord Beaverbrook encouraged a profligate newsroom that had permanent correspondents in every major world capital. The paper pioneered popular criticism of the arts. It had the sharpest social eye in the cartoonist Osbert Lancaster, and the best sports writers. But it also had to suffer the daily interventions of its owner, who steered every word of the political coverage and retained an attachment to the idea of the British Empire that was as entertaining as it was nuts. Because of that, the paper saw the monarch in an abstract way, respecting her as the disembodied figurehead of the imperial system, just as she was ensconced on the coinage and postage stamps. Behind her was the medieval figure that Beaverbrook designed as the paper's icon – a Crusader knight with shield and sword, steadfast in dominating the alien peoples.

Soon after I joined the *Express* in the summer of 1957, the newsroom responded to a tip and sent out for a copy of the latest issue of a quarterly magazine that no editor had ever heard of – *The National and English Review*. It was the Friday of a bank holiday weekend, and the office was lightly staffed and somnolent. The magazine's lead article changed all that, and would also seriously rattle the monarchy. Among its points was that:

The monarchy will not survive, let alone thrive, unless its leading figures exert themselves to the full … When she has lost the bloom of her youth, the Queen's reputation will depend, far more than it does now, upon her personality ... Unfortunately the relatively classless character of George V is not reproduced in his granddaughters ... The Queen and Princess Margaret still bear the debutante stamp ... The Queen's style of speaking is a pain in the neck ... She comes across in her speeches as a priggish schoolgirl ... Like her mother, she appears to be unable to string even a few sentences together without a written text...

The author of the article was 33-year-old John Grigg, 2nd Baron Altrincham, an Old Etonian with a habit of attacking his own class. He campaigned for reform of the House of Lords, correctly pointing out that many hereditary peers were 'not necessarily fitted to serve'. At the *Express*, we realised that Altrincham expressed a feeling that had been growing since the coronation, that the Queen increasingly lived in and represented a world that seemed insulated from reality. There was no way of knowing how general this feeling was. But it had never been articulated in such a blunt and personal way before.

The *Express* – like other papers, not ready to be complicit in the attack – decided to have it both ways. In the news pages, Altrincham's words were quoted in detail and treated as a sensational personal assault on the Queen. But the editorial page condemned Altrincham as 'destructive' and 'vulgar'. The *Sunday Times* went further, sounding preposterously like the membership committee of an Edwardian gentlemen's club, calling him 'a cad and a coward'. Following that lead, Altrincham was physically assaulted in the street by a bellicose member of the League of Empire Loyalists. The Archbishop of Canterbury called him 'a very silly man'.

One of Altrincham's observations that got less attention was that the Queen had had 'woefully inadequate training' to prepare her to be the monarch. This was cleverly shifting the problem from the Queen herself to unnamed people, most obviously the courtiers, of whom Lascelles would be the most culpable. But the problem was really larger than one person: the Queen that we saw and heard, the Queen that we reported on, was the product of a formal framework in which the whole appearance, tone and style thought fit for a monarch was imposed on her from an early age. Had she passively surrendered to this system without resistance? Or was it possible that she had been advised against asserting a tone and identity of her own? If so, who *was* she when allowed to be herself?

That fundamental question could not be answered, because all of the commentary, whether supporting Altrincham or the Queen, was directed at somebody that nobody really knew. For that matter, it could be argued that the newspapers had colluded in creating the version of the Queen that Altrincham was so harsh about because in many respects we (and the BBC) controlled the monarchy's public image as much as the palace did, based on a similar concept of its tone. No reporter and certainly no BBC producer had ever dared to say that the Queen's speaking style was a pain in the neck – although it was. That really made us seem as clueless about how a modern monarch should appear as Lascelles and the others who had nurtured Elizabeth over the years, and this could explain why, on the whole, the newspapers reacted so pompously and peevishly to the criticism. Fleet Street and the palace were locked in a mutually reinforcing delusion of what was right, and the Queen was taking the heat for it.

As it turned out, Altrincham soon heard that the Queen's first response to his attack was to say that he must be mad. Writing about his experience more than a decade later, Altrincham said that the Queen

had been treated, since her accession, to such a concentrated dose of flattery, not to say worship, that she must indeed have been surprised to find herself the butt of criticism. I was sorry to have hurt her feelings, but a continuation of the infallibility cult would in the long run have inflicted much graver hurt.

The Chief Metropolitan Magistrate who dealt with the man who had assaulted Altrincham, letting him off with a modest fine, said that 95 per cent of the public found Altrincham's critique offensive. That was not true. A public opinion poll showed that 35 per cent of those polled agreed with Altrincham, while 52 per cent disagreed. However, among those in the younger age group of sixteen to thirty-four the result was reversed: 47 per cent supported him and 39 per cent opposed him.

Who could provide a candid and objective view of the woman behind the mask as she then was? Even the most dutiful newspaper editor knew nobody equal to that task. At the *Express*, with all its expansive newsroom resources, there was not even the wish to try, nor did any other paper apparently feel the absence of an honest contemporary view of the woman at the centre of the royal narratives. In fact, it would take more than sixty years for such a flashback view to surface, and when it did it was hard to imagine a sketch of the Queen written with more lapidary skill – surely the equal in words of Goya's portrait of Charles IV of Spain and his family, one of the most subtly seditious royal portraits ever.

The difference is that, unlike Goya's 1800 masterpiece, this was a portrait of the Queen that was never intended to see the light of day. It was written by James Pope-Hennessy as he was gathering material for his biography of Queen Mary and surfaced in Hugo Vickers's 2018 book *The Quest for Queen Mary*. In this book, Vickers serves as one royal biographer exposing the technique of another, Pope-Hennessy, by revealing all the notes made by Pope-Hennessy as he worked his way through interviews with every still-living stem of Queen Mary's extensive European family tree. The published biography, though deftly written, omitted all the choicest of Pope-Hennessy's notes about these encounters and it is thanks entirely to Vickers that we now have them in possibly the funniest book about the royal family ever written.

Three weeks after Altrincham's tirade, Pope-Hennessy visited Balmoral while the royal family were at their regular summer retreat. It was his first visit there. He was a very sensitive architectural critic (he gives a devastating assessment of Sandringham, making it sound like a decaying grand hotel in some deserted Alpine resort) but found Balmoral 'far lighter, whiter, prettier and more spacious than I had imagined'.

His introduction to the Queen was disconcerting. After shaking hands, and a banal exchange about where Pope-Hennessy was staying, there was 'a three-minute silence, during which she looked at the lowering sky out of the window. I thought she hadn't heard; but as it seemed like a new technique of conversation I remained silent too.' After a description of the Queen's clothes – 'tartan skirt, a little olive-green tweed jacket and a complicated raspberry-coloured blouse' – he delivers his more personal portrait. I am quoting it at length because there is no equal to it in any contemporary account:

> By no stretch of the imagination can this Queen be called an historical figure. About the lower part of the face, which juts out more than one expects, she has a slight look of Queen Mary and Queen Charlotte, but that is all. She looks a little careworn, with lines from nose to mouth, and could easily arouse one's compassion were it not for some element which is hard to define – smugness would be too crude and unkind a word – it is rather that she clearly does not *feel* inadequate. She is not shy, but she is clearly living at great tension, and does not give an impression of happiness. Her hands are thin and worried-looking. She is extremely animated, gesticulates when telling anecdotes, makes comic or pathetic faces, and simply cannot remain still. One feels that the spring is wound up very tight. She is

THE MONARCHY WILL NOT SURVIVE...'

brisk, jerky and a little ungraceful ... She is kind and business-like and somewhat impersonal; her mother is far more feminine and knows how to simulate an interest in whoever she is talking to, whereas the Queen just talks, and sometimes is too busy trying to listen in to what her mother is saying across the table to catch on ... On the whole it is clockwork conversation, not at all difficult on either side, but not, on the other hand, memorable, interesting, or worth the paper it could be typed upon.

Pope-Hennessy makes no mention of the Altrincham effect, but it surely must have been an influence at the time, like a noxious mist clinging to the Balmoral carpets and tartan rugs. More crucially, it is worth parsing this description for clues to the behaviour of both the past and future monarch: 'she is living at great tension' and 'does not give an impression of happiness' are, for example, blunt and confident assessments that raise many questions.

Elizabeth was thirty-one years old and had been Queen for five years. Her apprenticeship covered a period that would have been seriously challenging for a far more seasoned monarch. Churchill, her first mentor in affairs of state, had finally stepped down in 1955, replaced by his long-time understudy, Anthony Eden. Eden then led the country into the disastrous military adventure that would turn out to be the terminal spasm of imperial power. General Gamal Abdel Nasser, the new Prime Minister of Egypt, announced that he was going to take over control of the Suez Canal, then jointly owned by France and Britain. The canal was seen as the inviolate property of the two European powers and Britain's crucial umbilical link to Middle Eastern oil. Eden told colleagues, 'Nasser must not have his hand on our windpipe.' The two governments then secretly colluded with Israel: the Israelis would invade the Sinai, and Britain and France would intervene on the pretext of stopping a war.

The plot was concealed from the public and a wartime level of censorship was imposed on the press and on the BBC. Among the military planners there was at least one dissident: the First Sea Lord, Mountbatten. Mountbatten went to the Queen to complain. It was an extraordinary act for a military commander to go directly to the monarch behind the back of a Prime Minister, but Mountbatten, as we have seen, had extraordinary access and influence at the palace. At Mountbatten's suggestion, the Queen asked Eden if before committing the country to intervening at Suez he would consult Hugh Gaitskell, the leader of the Labour opposition. Eden refused.

Soon after it began, the invasion was halted. America opposed it as a misbegotten relapse into gunboat diplomacy. Eden's premiership was destroyed. Nevertheless, a large part of the country thought Nasser should have been eliminated. What is forgotten now about the Suez crisis is that it divided the country in the same way and along many of the same inherent fault lines as Brexit. The issue became a crude litmus test of patriotism: opposing Eden was to betray Britain's world mission. Only two newspapers, the *Manchester Guardian* (as it then was) and *The Observer*, opposed the adventure from the start, and both were publicly reviled for it – even *The Observer*'s relatively liberal readership was divided, according to letters sent to the editor, with 866 supporting Eden and 302 against. As a result of its stand, *The Observer* suffered a boycott by major advertisers that lasted for years and helped the rise of the rival *Sunday Times*, which had supported the invasion. But in the wider world it was obvious that Suez was a humiliating debacle for Britain.

If she had any acuity at all, the Queen must have been shaken to witness such a serious rupture in the composure of her nation and one wonders what lessons she took away from the experience. It would prove to be one of the most damaging political crises of her reign – the country was nearly bankrupted by it. In this instance,

Mountbatten had been a realist while all those around him had been swept up in hubris. One thing she is likely to have resented is Eden's refusal to consult the Leader of the Opposition. Later, as she grew more assured in her audiences with Prime Ministers, she would surely not have let such a thing pass so readily. By that time the occupants of Downing Street realised that she was always well briefed on their political opponents and their policies and that she preferred consensus to deep divisions. Certainly, Suez had found her too conditioned by a phalanx of courtiers who were mostly lifelong jingoists. Eden was gone by January 1957, replaced by Harold Macmillan, a much more skilled politician whose outward appearance of an Edwardian grandee concealed an astute ability to gauge the public mood – a gift that neither the Queen nor those around her showed any sign of acquiring, even after the impertinence of Altrincham's critique. Pope-Hennessy's observation, 'One feels that the spring is wound up very tight', could have many causes, both within the family, as in the row about the family name, and in the nation itself.

Altrincham's assertion that the monarchy might not survive unless the Queen was transformed in voice and attitude rested, in turn, on a basic assertion that the monarchy was 'out of touch'. It was a charge that would recur for decades, culminating in the way the Queen and the palace reacted to the death of Princess Diana in 1997. But what did 'out of touch' actually mean – or, rather, what would it take for them to become 'in touch'? Was such a transformation ever going to be compatible with sustaining the legend of the monarchy? At this moment in 1957 it could truly be said that to her subjects and the world, the young woman on the throne was an enigma clothed in the garments of a legend, and the legend was dominant.

CHAPTER 6

ENTER TONY STAGE LEFT

Late in 1958, Lord Beaverbrook decided that I needed a broader world experience in order to be promoted to features editor. He sent me on a sabbatical stint to the New York bureau of the *Express*. It turned out to be a magical journey from a country still restricted in its pleasures to an unbelievably affluent dreamland. The paper's office was in Rockefeller Center, in one of the skyscrapers built during the Great Depression as a bold gesture of confidence in America's resilience. My desk overlooked the ice rink, which, in the bright and cold November evenings, came alive with skaters watched at eye level from an adjacent bar by martini-nursing suits. I was allotted a hotel room near Times Square, close to a place that as an aficionado of jazz was to me a cultural shrine, Birdland, where bands as great as those of Count Basie and Duke Ellington could amazingly be heard up close in the intimacy of a nightclub rather than the more restrained atmosphere of a concert hall. The glamour of all of this was lost on my office colleagues. All of them had been in America long enough for their way of life to seem routine. They commuted to wives and families in the suburbs, where, unlike in Britain, refrigerators, dishwashers and washing machines were standard and frozen TV dinners were being hailed as another step forward in America's gift for making life easier. I was invited home by a reporter who was sampling one of the meals for a story; we agreed that it was a marvel of the laboratory rather than the kitchen.

Looking for some stationery, I opened a filing cabinet and found a stack of cans of Campbell's tomato soup. They were there, I was told, because when Lord Beaverbrook was in New York, staying in his usual suite at the Waldorf Astoria, he was apt to skip room service and ask for the soup. As for the stationery, he preferred to recycle envelopes rather than use new ones so the staff gently soiled new ones before sending them to his secretary. Like some other self-made rich men, Beaverbrook saw no contradiction in practising parsimony while living in regal premises. The editorial staff were also expected to provide Beaverbrook with his own concierge service, arranging movie and theatre tickets for him, buying books and taking his medical prescriptions to the pharmacy.

Christmas was coming and all along Fifth Avenue the windows of the department stores displayed the cornucopia of gifts available. Outside each store, men in Santa Claus costumes rang bells and urged people inside, put there particularly to engage children. Where did these men come from, I wondered? It turned out that most of them were provided by a Salvation Army hostel in the Bowery, then still Manhattan's Skid Row. I proposed a story on this and the London newsroom decided it was appealing enough to need a photographer assigned to it. That is how I came to arrive before dawn at a midtown mansion to collect someone I had never heard of and to whom London had given preference over any of the many staff photographers. He was clearly well connected because, instead of staying at a hotel, he was the guest of a distinguished Democratic Party power broker, William vanden Heuvel, then counsel to the Governor of New York, Averell Harriman.

The mansion had a homely, non-stuffy feeling. Children were running loose. A slim young man appeared with a camera and a small bag of equipment. 'Tony,' he announced, with a handshake, and was ready to go. I had corrected my ignorance of his stature with some research before meeting Antony Armstrong-Jones. A year earlier he had taken an official portrait of the Queen, Prince Philip, Princess Anne and Prince Charles on Charles's eighth birthday. He had held a successful exhibition of his portraits, including those of Marlene Dietrich, Alec Guinness and Dame Edith Evans. Lord Beaverbrook had instructed the *Express* to hire him, although there was nothing in his work so far to suggest that he was suitable for an assignment like this, outside the studio and in a particularly rough setting like the Bowery on a cold winter morning. He was disarmingly aware of this, and as we went downtown in a limousine provided by the office he said he might need some help from me in setting up shots in the hostel.

In the event, he needed no help. He had a natural news photographer's gift of making himself invisible to his subjects. As I talked to some of the men about how they came to be so down on their luck that they had ended up in the care of the Salvation Army, Tony slipped away into a canteen where they were having breakfast and then into the room where they were transformed from hard-luck cases into jovial hucksters in Santa costumes. For someone whose posh and clipped Etonian accent could have made him as alien to these men as a man from Mars, Tony quickly got them laughing and at ease. His photographs were so evocative that instead of writing a story I simply wrote extended captions to the photographs. I didn't see him again during my New York sabbatical, but we agreed to meet when I got back to London.

* * *

Tony's London was not one I was familiar with. He lived in Pimlico in a studio he had converted from an ironmonger's shop. Soon after

I returned from New York he showed me around. His work and his social life were cleverly accommodated in a relatively compact space: darkroom and secretary's office on the ground floor and a spectacular basement and patio below, with a draped parachute serving to soften natural lighting for portraits.

Sometimes a street or a locality begins to acquire a style of its own that becomes the harbinger of a social shift. The disappearance of an ironmonger in Pimlico and its replacement by a photographer's studio was part of such a shift. Nearby appeared a shop selling Spanish tiles; several small bistros followed. Pimlico, Sloane Square and the King's Road were all part of territory being colonised by new ideas of urban style. In 1955, two of Tony's friends, Mary Quant and Alexander Plunket Greene, bought the freehold of a corner shop in the King's Road and began stocking it with what they called a 'bouillabaisse' of European clothes and fashion accessories and named it Bazaar. By 1959, Mary Quant was designing her own clothes and was the nucleus of a revolution in fashion. Old barriers were breaking down. 'Snobbery has gone out of fashion,' said Quant, 'and in our shops you will find duchesses jostling with typists to buy the same dress.' The idea of clothes as a leveller was exaggerated, but Tony himself well understood the social turbulence going on around him and the opportunities it presented to him – some of them libidinous. The *Express* invited its youngest women readers to submit photos of themselves with the promise that the three judged most attractive would get auditions for fashion modelling. The winner would get a portrait by Tony. The winner was one of those 'typists' Mary Quant invoked as upwardly mobile. When Tony came to my office with the prints, he had worked a Pygmalion magic. The girl glowed.

'You had her!' I said. He grinned.

The *Express* had helped Tony make his name beyond the privileged set he grew up among. Photography had at first been a hobby, but after going to Cambridge to study architecture he dropped out to try to make a living as a photographer. Before the *Express* there were friends to advance his career with low-paid but highly visible work – like Jocelyn Stevens, a contemporary at Eton, who bought a moribund society magazine, *Queen*, and transformed it into a glossy chronicle for and about the spinning nuclei of the new London culture. In his assignments for the *Express*, Tony was notable for the agility of his photojournalism that I had seen working with him in New York. He declared his attitude in an introduction to a collection of photographs of London that he published in 1958:

> I believe that photographs should be simple technically and easy to look at ... Their point is to make ordinary people react ... I use a very small camera, little apparatus, and no artificial lighting. Photographs have to be taken fast. It's no good saying 'hold it' like trying to hold your breath, you find you've lost it.

There are some clues to Tony's character in those few lines. First, the unconscious snobbery of 'ordinary people'. Tony was never ordinary people. Second, he was quite deliberately setting out to undermine the sacred rituals of traditional portrait and fashion photography. And there was no better place to do that in a way that would command attention than the royal family. Although there was no officially appointed royal photographer, Cecil Beaton had become virtually the house portraitist for the previous two decades. Beaton treated the subject in the same way he designed the costumes and stage sets for shows like *My Fair Lady*: as theatre of the most opulent kind. Arranged by Beaton, the Queen, her mother and her sister wore ballgowns and priceless jewels and Prince Philip wore uniforms layered in medals. These portraits took many hours to set up, with elaborate lighting and many wardrobe and make-up assistants. There was nothing natural about it, but it met people's expectations of how grand and exquisitely costumed the family should be.

The first indication that Tony would not play by these rules came with his family portrait for Charles's eighth birthday. First, it was shot outdoors, with natural light. The Queen and Prince Philip stood on a small ornamental bridge over a brook in the gardens of Buckingham Palace while Anne and Charles sat on a ledge beneath. Anne was leafing through a picture book. Charles looked coyly into the camera – he and his father were the only ones looking directly at the camera. It was artfully staged to suggest a bucolic and private idyll for a family seen, for once, in casual clothes looking relaxed.

The Queen had, apparently, liked the portrait and in the summer of 1959 it was announced that on her twenty-ninth birthday Princess Margaret's portrait would be taken by Tony. The result was quite striking: the photograph was closely cropped to Margaret's face and bare shoulders. She looked straight into the camera. Her hair was cut short in a contemporary way. The only adornment was a slender necklace of small diamonds. Margaret's twenty-first birthday portrait had been taken by Beaton. He drained her of life, reducing her to a piece of furniture in an over-decorated salon. This new Margaret was full of life, with a suggestion of impish spirit. In one stroke, the thwarted, broken-hearted lover of the Townsend saga was eradicated.

The *Express*, like all the popular dailies, ran the portrait large; there were comments about the daring suggestion of nudity in the bare shoulders, but the candour of the close-up was widely praised and Margaret was seen as a truly natural beauty when released from the trappings of a Beaton production. Tony had used the same technique in developing and controlling the prints in his darkroom, of bleaching out all background and setting up a strong black and white contrast, as he had for his portrait of the winner of our aspiring fashion model contest. At the time it never occurred to me that there could have been a similar liaison between portraitist and subject.

Indeed, that idea still didn't register when the paper's editor said to me, 'Something is going on with Tony. He's dropping a lot of the old crowd. He seems to have dumped Jacqui. See what you can get out of him.' Jacqui was Jacqui Chan, a gorgeous dancer from Trinidad who had performed in two West End musicals, where Tony had first encountered her as he took publicity shots of the cast. On visits to the studio in Pimlico I had seen her several times and she was open and relaxed about her presence there as a frequent overnight companion. Other similarly exotic beauties came and went in the racy entourage that Tony gathered around him. One of Tony's darkroom assistants, a young woman from a less worldly background than Tony's usual set, was so shocked to find on a roll of film a sequence of pornographic poses by one of Tony's models that she immediately quit. That was an unusual display of virginal innocence for the time and the place. Pimlico and the King's Road had become public catwalks for newly 'liberated' womanhood, often parading in the short skirts and boots that Mary Quant pioneered, and being reported around the world as the racy new look of a generation cutting loose.

Tony admitted that Jacqui had moved on. There had not been any tears. The relationship had never been very deep and had never restricted the sexual freedom of either of them. As for the new royal portrait, he said, it had worked wonders for his career. He talked about the recent ending of the Queen's hosting of Queen Charlotte's Ball, the annual ritual in which 400 debutantes were dressed up to be presented to the Queen and, with one curtsy, thereby entered 'society'. Most of them were introduced by their mothers, but there were several blue-blooded women who sold their services as grooming agents to make sure young aspirants made the list each year.

Altrincham's attack on the palace had included a blast at this ritual, which, he said, should have ended in 1945 if there had been any serious effort at creating a 'truly classless court'. It was said that the Queen was reluctant to concede this defeat to Altrincham, but after hesitating for a year, the palace's role was finally abandoned in 1958. Tony quoted Margaret as saying, 'We had to put a stop to it. Every tart in London was getting in.' (This still did not alert me to any new familiarity between Tony and Margaret.) Now, he said, mothers who wanted their daughters to be noticed called him to request a portrait. He rarely consented, but his status as a portrait photographer was now such that no person of distinction in politics, the arts or the sciences would turn him down if editors gave him assignments. He asked me to make that point to the editor of the *Express*, and that was it. No mystery to be uncovered.

Tony was a libertine by nature and by background. He was known as a sexual swordsman whose sword was formidable and was enjoyed by both sexes. These details were reliably reported to me by several of his friends who served as regular tipsters to the *Express*'s William Hickey gossip column, knowing that they could never pass into print. At Eton he had contracted polio and the infection had left him with a left leg that was an inch shorter than the right, but he had specially made boots that prevented a limp. He was slim and moved with the lightness of a dancer. At Cambridge, his light weight – less than nine stone – and his competitiveness had made him an ideal cox for the Oxford and Cambridge boat race in 1950. He led Cambridge to a three-and-a-half-length victory, at a critical stage intimidating the Oxford cox by calling out, 'Why don't you fucking move over!' When he wanted something badly – like an assignment from the *Express* – his eyes would turn on the charm while his voice became clipped and assertive. He was very used to getting what he wanted, but not in a petulant, entitled way: he knew the worth of his own talent and despised others who thought an Eton accent should be enough to get them work.

On 26 February 1960, Buckingham Palace issued this statement: 'It is with the greatest pleasure that Queen Elizabeth the Queen Mother announces the betrothal of her beloved daughter The Princess Margaret to Mr. Antony Charles Robert Armstrong-Jones, son of Mr. R.O.C. Armstrong-Jones, QC, and the Countess of Rosse, to which union the Queen has gladly given her consent.'

I was gobsmacked. And, of course, my credibility at the *Express* as a reliable source on Tony collapsed. Only a small handful of people had known of the event in advance. One of them was Tony's father, who spent months urging Tony to change his mind, warning that there was no way his life would remain normal once he entered into the embrace of the royal family – that they were, by definition, a family that was unable to live normally. Tony ignored that advice – and similar warnings from others. But, as the announcement said, the Queen had gladly given her consent, indicating that – at the very least – she was confident that Tony could successfully find a new normal for himself and his wife.

CHAPTER 7

THE SHOCK OF CHANGE

Tony and Margaret were married in Westminster Abbey on 6 May 1960. After a reception at Buckingham Palace they were driven down the Mall and then through the crowded streets of the City of London to the Embankment, by the Tower of London, where they boarded the royal yacht *Britannia*, which the Queen made available to them for a six-week honeymoon in the Caribbean. The best man at the wedding was Roger Gilliatt, a neurologist and son of the surgeon-gynaecologist to the Queen. He took on the role after two others proposed by Tony had been rejected by the palace: his close friend Jeremy Fry, heir to a chocolate fortune, and Jeremy Thorpe, a rising star of the Liberal Party – both because vetting by Scotland Yard revealed that they were bisexual and, in Fry's case, he had a conviction for homosexual soliciting. Three weeks into the honeymoon, back in England, Jeremy Fry's wife Camilla gave birth to a daughter, Polly. In 2004, a DNA test requested by Polly Fry confirmed that her father was, in fact, Tony – the result of a sexual triangle that all parties had reluctantly terminated just before the royal marriage.

Few if any people in Tony's set would have been shocked to have known that while Tony was already on course to marry Princess Margaret he had sired an illegitimate child. It could be viewed as a final, fond fling in a way of life he knew he was leaving behind. He had managed to keep two separate worlds separate – the courtship of

Margaret was conducted at a Thames-side hideaway in Rotherhithe, in London's Docklands, while his work and life in Pimlico gave cover to that stunning development. These arrangements were devious and risky, but he carried them off with aplomb. He also enjoyed how he was being cast in the media as a welcome agent of change in the royal family. For the first time, a member of that family had married somebody who had to work for a living. Tony and Margaret found themselves being presented as the promising new face of a modern monarchy in a manner that the Queen, still trapped in the grip of old men resisting new ways, could not herself duplicate.

In a way, the looser culture of west London had attached itself to the royal couple. They were 'trendy' – a new term for the fevered new metropolitan modishness that was getting a lot of attention. It was a term that the *Express*'s editor hated, and he banned its use. But from my first visit to Tony's studio I realised that a significant cultural gulf was opening up within a relatively short geographical distance – between Fleet Street and the worlds of Pimlico and Chelsea. Long before the editor sent me to find out what was changing in Tony's life, the sense of that gulf grew; alas, nothing that we reported in the pages of the *Express* reflected it.

On 20 July 1957, at an open-air rally in Bedford, Harold Macmillan, in his first year as Prime Minister, was reviewing the country's economy. 'Let's be frank about it,' he said. 'Most of our people have never had it so good.' It was a very modern piece of syntax from the mouth of a man who usually played the droll patrician overseeing a government of much younger men. But Macmillan had a knack for catchphrases and 'you've never had it so good' caught on, often repeated with ribald implications. It never became an official election slogan, but it caught the nation's spirit and even, perhaps, its aspirational lusts. At a basic materialistic level, Macmillan promised the kind of widespread domestic prosperity that I saw in America a year later – what the Canadian academic John Kenneth Galbraith had called The Affluent Society. At a more fundamental level, Macmillan was acknowledging that the rigid class divisions of pre-war Britain could not be sustained, and nor could the shape of a modern state continue to be influenced by those divisions.

Until the late 1950s, the Queen had reigned over a country that was not too bothered that the monarchy was an exalted edifice of the class system. Altrincham had rattled the chandeliers at the palace, but under the obdurate hand of men like Tommy Lascelles little had really changed in the way the royal machine worked, and the Queen herself was happy to go along with a few cosmetic changes – for example, she had some help from the BBC in changing the pitch of her voice and sounding more the author of what she said in speeches. Questions were raised in Parliament about the fact that the taxpayers were footing a bill of £10,000 a week for Margaret and Tony's honeymoon cruise, but generally the public loved the glamour that the pair provided.

And yet when the Queen's reign is viewed as a whole it is clear that these years were only hinting at what was to come. The Britain that she would reign over for the rest of her life would be transformed to a degree that no previous monarch had known. The monarchy would play no direct part in bringing about this transformation. At the least, the Queen might be carried along willingly with the current without the Crown losing relevance. Or she might be caught unawares and founder.

Macmillan was the first of the Queen's Prime Ministers to grasp this point. In the Netflix series *The Crown*, his is one of the few roles to be misrepresented and miscast. For the sake of drama too much is made of the fact that he was a cuckold. It is true that his wife, Lady Dorothy Macmillan, had a long-running affair with Robert Boothby, one of the first politicians to create a second career for himself as a television pundit. Boothby was also a heavy drinker and a flagrant pursuer of rent boys, although that was yet to be exposed.

Macmillan hardened himself to this indignity. He was well regarded on the world stage and managed to act as an effective intermediary
between President John F. Kennedy and the Soviet Union's bellicose
leader, Nikita Khrushchev. With another of his catchphrases he insisted that 'jaw-jaw is better than war-war' (adapted from an earlier
Churchill version) and helped negotiate a treaty limiting nuclear
tests. More consequential to the Queen's future role was a speech
that Macmillan made early in 1960 in South Africa after spending
a month touring Britain's African colonies. 'The wind of change is
blowing through this continent,' he said. 'Whether we like it or not,
this growth of national consciousness is a political fact.' These words
stunned the white rulers of South Africa and other white regimes,
particularly in Rhodesia. But they were a prescient admission of the
inevitable: the British Empire was no longer sustainable and the world
was being remade.

The wind of change was palpable at home, too. The government
struggled to understand how deeply the pressures for change ran,
particularly in the way the law still attempted to regulate private behaviour and popular culture. Official censorship of films, theatre and
literature stoutly upheld Victorian ideas of such concepts as 'public decency' and permissible practices between the sexes. (In fact, the word
'permissive' was frequently used as a pejorative by the self-appointed
moral critics of the day.) Macmillan had to deal with a cultural time
bomb that been ticking away since 1954, the Wolfenden Committee
on Homosexual Offences and Prostitution. For three years the committee struggled to recommend how to reform the laws that defined
homosexual offences and governed the treatment of convicted homosexuals and the laws that guided police in dealing with prostitution.
In 1958, prostitution was dealt with in a Bill that came down hard on
pimps and procurers but accepted that prostitution away from the
streets and in private was permissible. No action was taken to allow a

similar freedom for homosexuality in private. That failure perpetuated a pernicious double standard in the policing of sexual behaviour – a double standard of which the royal family had long enjoyed the benefits. Tony was only the latest member to freely switch partners between the sexes without fear of police action, while at less privileged and protected levels of society homosexuality was a criminal offence and severely punished as such, as was abortion.

At the same time as these repressions were left in place, the censorship of public culture faced its first decisive challenge. In 1960, as Tony and Margaret returned from their cruise through the Caribbean, a jury of nine men and three women was convened at the Old Bailey to hear a case brought by the Crown against a book publisher, Regina versus Penguin Books Limited. Of course, the Queen was not herself actually bringing this case to court; her law officers had taken it upon themselves to do so in her name. When the jurors were sworn in they had to read aloud the words 'I swear by Almighty God that I will well and truly try the several issues joined between our Sovereign Lady the Queen and the prisoner at the Bar…' If part of the mystique of the monarchy was still to act as the protector of public morals then somebody had decided that this should include preventing the publication of an unexpurgated edition of D. H. Lawrence's *Lady Chatterley's Lover*, an author whom the Queen had certainly never read.

The Crown's case collapsed in a trial that produced moments of high comedy, the jewel being when the leading prosecutor for the Crown, Mr Mervyn Griffith-Jones, asked the jury, 'Is it a book that you would even wish your wife or your servants to read?' The prosecution was particularly bothered that readers would discover that her ladyship had been sodomised by her gamekeeper, apparently an offence of rank as well as of lewdness. The answer was resounding: the jury cleared the way for publication and all 200,000 copies sold out within a day of the verdict. Three million more were sold in the next three months.

Launching the prosecution had been a collective misjudgement of the public's sophistication in both sexual freedom and literature. It left a sense that at the heights of authority – the Home Office, the office of the Director of Public Prosecutions, Scotland Yard, the Lord Chief Justice – there remained a belief that public taste in matters both public and private still had to be policed to protect the innocent from corruption: one of the Crown's assertions was that Lawrence's story 'put promiscuity on a pedestal'. Witnesses for the defence were asked at what age they became aware of four-letter words. It seemed to many people involved in covering the trial, including me, that the biggest shock to the frustrated morality police was the discovery that the general population was keen to enjoy the same sexual licence as their rulers did, and indeed many were – they took 'You've never had it so good' as a far more broadly liberating slogan than Macmillan had intended.

Incredibly, even after his defeat with *Lady Chatterley's Lover*, the Director of Public Prosecutions had not given up on trying to protect the public from books that – under the existing law – might 'harm public morality'. In 1964, the bawdy eighteenth-century novel *Fanny Hill, or Memoirs of a Woman of Pleasure* was the subject of another trial and this time the Crown won (an uncensored edition was finally published in 1970).

There was no indication that anyone inside Buckingham Palace comprehended the implications for the monarchy of this cultural tsunami. When Philip was being vetted before his engagement to Elizabeth, Tommy Lascelles had warned in a confidential note that he was unlikely to be faithful. This was digested with the equanimity of a household that had a long-established tolerance of royal philandering – it came with the weather. Of course, it was one thing to be broad-minded about what went on among one's own caste, and Lascelles was certainly sophisticated about that, but it was an altogether more challenging idea that the Queen's subjects might be enjoying the same laxity. Shifts in key social attitudes do not usually fit discretely into a single decade, but 1960 was the threshold of a decade in Britain in which many sacred temples would lose their foundational security – including the monarchy. In 1960, divorced men were not allowed to read the news on the BBC. Five years later the word 'fuck' was uttered on BBC Television for the first time – by Kenneth Tynan, theatre critic and cultural grenade thrower (and a friend of Tony and Margaret). The social repressions of a century were about to be swept aside.

The *Daily Express*, like all the popular dailies, had milked the Lady Chatterley trial for all it was worth in stimulating the public's prurience. But, like the original edition of the book, the papers were expurgated of intimate details, and that made their coverage somewhat mystifying. Two national newspapers, the *Manchester Guardian* and *The Observer*, did a far better job of describing the seriousness of the combat between the would-be state censors and Lawrence's power in showing the injury that class could do to deeply felt personal relationships. In *The Observer*, Kenneth Tynan explained that Lawrence wanted to reinstate the simple power of the four-letter words as they had originally been in healthy current use rather than as offensive expletives and, taking the most useful of them, he wrote, 'One fucks.' It was the first time the word had appeared in a Sunday newspaper, but there was no outrage.

This difference between the fluency of the 'posh' papers and what was possible on a popular daily had been eating away at me for a while. As I had seen from my trips between Pimlico and Fleet Street, the cultural insurrection taking place elsewhere had not really touched anything at the *Express*. So-called popular journalism was the last to get the message, and I wanted out. As the youngest features editor the paper had ever had, the next step up would have been as a deputy editor. That was a dangerous level to reach. Beaverbrook had a habit of summoning rising talents and asking them their opinions of how the paper might improve and then passing on that information to the editors, knowing that it would spread discord. While the Chatterley trial was going on, Beaverbrook summoned me to his flat in Arlington House on the edge of Green Park. The editor warned me in advance, 'Whatever you do, don't tell him how to make the paper better.' Of course, I did just that. Beaverbrook was eighty-one years old and had shrunk into a compact gnome, although the large head was still in itself a commanding presence with a broad skull, piercing eyes and a wide mouth from which curt Canadian-accented questions came like bullets. He sat in semi-darkness while he placed me near a lamp. It was unnerving because I couldn't judge the impact of what I said. As a result, my diagnosis was halting and I could see that most of it meant nothing to him – he had a fixed view of the world as it had been when he last liked it, around 1936, and nothing would shake it.

By the time I got back to the office, the editor had received the old man's call and berated me for failing to heed his advice. Nevertheless, it seemed that I had passed some kind of test and was safe in my job for the moment. It turned out that Beaverbrook had liked the way I had handled a series of pieces appearing under the name of the Duke of Windsor in which the Duke (or, more accurately, his ghost-writer) offered his advice on men's wardrobes. From his youth the Duke had been a natty dresser, setting a style of his own in woollen suits with a plaid design that became known as Prince of Wales check and with a double-knotted tie that was dubbed the Windsor knot. The copy for the series, written by a feature writer from notes provided by the Duke, lacked a convincing voice. It seemed to me very sad that apparently the Duke, living somewhat grandly in Paris, had complained to Beaverbrook of being hard up and the whole idea had been cooked up to provide him with some funds. Few if any *Express* readers would have found his tips useful since they depended on the skills of some of the most expensive tailors in the world.

The Duke was the only member of the royal family that Beaverbrook liked. He had taken his side during the abdication crisis and felt that had he been able to remain on the throne he would never have permitted the outrage (to Beaverbrook) of granting independence to India. The fact that the Duke had played pawn to Hitler didn't seem to count. Restricting his influence to dispensing fashion advice was about right, in my view.

While the *Express* supported the monarchy in the abstract, it tended to be cool towards the royal family as people. Before the Queen's coronation, Elizabeth and Philip had toured Canada, including the state of New Brunswick, where Beaverbrook was a favourite son and regarded almost as a local monarch himself. When asked if he wanted to meet the royal couple, he snapped back, 'Don't you know that Presbyterians are not monarchists?' His view of the Queen was later coloured by a perceived snub when, after a mix-up by palace staff, he was offered what he considered to be an inferior seat in Westminster Abbey for the coronation and refused it. In a later royal tour of Canada there was more confusion over an invitation to meet the Queen and no meeting took place.

Beaverbrook had an undisguised aversion to another member of the royal family, Earl Mountbatten, against whom the Beaverbrook papers had openly waged a vendetta for years. The reasons for it have varied according to sources. Mountbatten's part in the catastrophic Dieppe raid was sometimes cited and his role in speeding India's independence was more convincing as a reason, but, according to a veteran editorial writer at the paper who knew many of Beaverbrook's inner secrets, which he occasionally shared with me, the real offence was that in 1945 Beaverbrook discovered that one of his mistresses had, at the same time, been the mistress of Mountbatten. Whatever the truth, Beaverbrook's vendetta was unstinting and deeply personal.

All this was tantalising gossip, but it certainly did not lead to the *Express* openly siding with republicans or even criticising the Queen personally, as the Altrincham episode had shown.

I had learned a lot about rapid-response journalism at the *Express*, where my pages were often remade several times a night, but there was no depth to any of the reporting, and no appetite for introducing it. One night I decided to run a main feature that was 1,300 words long. Beaverbrook stipulated that nothing in the paper should be more than 750 words. But this piece, a powerfully visceral stream-of-consciousness first-person account by the motor racing ace Stirling Moss of what it was like pushing a car to the edge, would have made no sense if cut. Beaverbrook was in Canada and I gambled that I could get away with it. Twenty-four hours later, he called me at home from New Brunswick: 'Did you think I wouldn't notice?' After that it was clear that as long as I stayed within the constraints of the Beaverbrook formula, I had a future at the paper. If I did not...

Two months later, I handed in my notice. I had called David Astor, the editor of *The Observer*, out of the blue, and said I admired his newspaper immensely but it could benefit from being a little livelier. After lunch with him at the Waldorf Hotel – owned by a branch of the Astor family – I was offered a job but with a substantial pay cut. I took it.

For several years afterwards, I received notes from Beaverbrook, never more than 150 words, typed on quarto sheets, sometimes with comments in his own hand beneath the signature like 'With fond regards and wishes for your success'. The envelopes were always new.

CHAPTER 8

A RIVAL CALLED CAMELOT

It was Harold Macmillan who finally put to rest the long-running sore between the Queen and Philip about the royal family's name. Early in 1960, when she was heavily pregnant with her third child, Prince Andrew, Macmillan visited her at Sandringham. He was unaware of the deep feelings involved. 'The Queen only wishes (properly enough) to do something to please her husband – with whom she is desperately in love,' he wrote in his diary. 'What upsets me', he continued, '… is the Prince's brutal attitude to the Queen over all this. I shall never forget what she said to me that Sunday night at Sandringham.' He did not elaborate, but Macmillan promised to address the issue and then flew off for the African tour that led to his 'wind of change' speech. Arranging the details was left to the Home Secretary, Rab Butler, who personally experienced a similarly pressing request from the Queen, who, he said, had been in tears as she sought to placate her husband. A compromise was reached that Philip finally accepted. The title of The House and Family of Windsor would remain in place, but, with the arrival of any grandchildren whose position in the line of succession was low enough not to entitle them to be called 'Royal Highness', their surname would be registered as Mountbatten-Windsor. Thus it was that when Meghan Markle, the Duchess of Sussex, gave birth to a son in 2019, his name was promulgated as Archie Harrison Mountbatten-Windsor, which so flummoxed a lot of people that the whole history had to be explained. However, the compromise agreement had been flouted much earlier when Princess Anne married Captain Mark Phillips in 1973 and she signed the register as Mountbatten-Windsor. She had, apparently, willingly yielded to pressure to do this from Uncle Dickie and his well-trained accomplice Prince Charles.

The Observer's policy towards the royal family was basically to ignore them. Instead, David Astor wanted the paper to be alert to where the real power in a nation lay, in Britain and in the world. He had hired a writer, Anthony Sampson, who set out to make a fresh assessment of who really ran Britain and his reporting produced a classic book, *Anatomy of Britain*. In a later memoir, Sampson described *The Observer* as it was at the time I arrived: 'Its sixteen pages every Sunday seemed to be the centre of all debates, discussed at dinner parties and setting agendas for politicians. It was original and unpredictable.' In his writing, Sampson conveyed an almost voyeuristic excitement at discovering how powerful people lived and worked. This tone came dangerously close to self-parody when Sampson and the paper went overboard for a new generation who took command of the most powerful nation in the world. They were not alone. The 'New Frontier' of the Kennedy administration was not just a galvanising concept that promised refreshing youth and vigour applied to world leadership but, trumpeted as a cultural renaissance bearing the label of 'Camelot', it was headed by a President and First Lady who were show-stopping superstars.

The contrast between the first family in Washington and the royal family in Britain was immediately apparent. Sampson described the Kennedy Cabinet as stacked with 'diamond-hard minds'. This was no more hyperbolic than the language used by Kennedy himself, who had pledged to recruit 'the best and the brightest'. (The phrase was also a warning of hubris: the 'diamond-hard minds' led the nation into the quagmire of the Vietnam War.) Complementing the vision of virile governance, Jackie Kennedy introduced a level of sophistication and glamour to the White House that made the House of Windsor seem suddenly stuffy and paralysed by ritual, ossified in the glories of the past.

The difference in style of the two families was manifest when they met in June 1961. The Kennedys arrived in London after visiting Paris, where they had been feted as no American President and First Lady had ever been. Part of this was an instinctive reflex of pride in the French that France had set the pattern for the American rejection of monarchs and French support had been invaluable to the American Revolution. But part of it was also that the Kennedys, and particularly Jackie, were chic and sexy and pointedly modern. Behind them they had a press corps that had uncritically imbibed the Kennedy propaganda machine, which operated as much on the methods of the Hollywood publicity machine as it did on traditional political messaging. In fact, it married the two and in this compelling picture it was Jackie who most caught the people's attention. Jack Kennedy himself noted somewhat ruefully that 'I'm the guy who accompanied Jackie Kennedy to Paris'.

The Queen was not used to being overshadowed by another woman. During the frequent visits to London of other heads of state, the wives were always in the background, often barely glimpsed. A year earlier, President Charles de Gaulle had been treated to a three-day state visit that included staying at Buckingham Palace and being treated like a monarch himself, a role that he was comfortable with. Madame de Gaulle disappeared into the wallpaper. De Gaulle was unusually complimentary about the Queen: 'Her judgements on people and events were as clear-cut as they were thoughtful.'

Without any apparent effort, Jackie Kennedy drew all the attention. The Queen was not amused. What happened was indiscreetly retold with characteristic relish by the novelist and waspish raconteur Gore Vidal, who was a member of the cultural salon that Jackie attracted to the White House. 'I think the Queen resented me,' Jackie told Vidal. 'Philip was nice, but nervous. One felt absolutely no relationship between them.' Jackie was equally candid with Cecil Beaton, this time about the details of style that Beaton was very familiar with. She was unimpressed by the décor in the palace, by the furnishings and even by the flower arrangements. More personal was her critique of the Queen's dress and her 'flat' hair style.

The Queen could hardly be held responsible for the aesthetic failings of Buckingham Palace. It was not like the White House, a much smaller edifice that had managed to keep its original architectural coherence as a late eighteenth-century renaissance mansion (designed by James Hoban, an Irish-American) despite frequent and extensive renovations – and being burned down by the Brits in 1812. The palace, on the other hand, was an agglomeration of various architectural periods and styles, beginning with George III, some elegant and some hideous, that had been stuffed with furnishings collected according to the whims of its occupants, ranging from oriental treasures to second-rate antiques and bibelots. There were 775 rooms, fifty-two bedrooms and ninety-two offices. There was no chance of it ever having the kind of manageable scale and publicly accessible charm of the White House, where Jackie had instantly become a well-informed and sensitive curator of its historical qualities. Nonetheless, Jackie had been gratuitously insulting and indiscreet. But no lasting damage was done; a year later the Queen gave a lunch for Jackie and her sister Lee Radziwill and they found common ground for an ice-breaking conversation: Jackie was an accomplished horsewoman and the President of Pakistan had just given her a gelding as a present.

By then Jackie was established as the most cosmopolitan First Lady the White House had seen in a long time. She was fluent in French and had a degree in French literature from George Washington University. Her cultural range was broad. International artists of the calibre of the great cellist Pablo Casals were invited to give recitals and American arts flourished with her support – she created a series of concerts for young people featuring some the nation's most talented young musicians. Jackie felt that the White House had always been intended to be seen as 'the people's house' and called in experts to lead a renovation that honoured the 'museum character' of the building. It was not all high-brow. The Kennedy circle included stars like Frank Sinatra and Marilyn Monroe, the latter (notoriously) appearing at a gala event to sing 'Happy birthday, Mr President' in a glittering dress that concealed nothing of her bodily allure.

Without any intention of doing so, Jackie's appearances at Buckingham Palace were making an uncomfortable point. The royal family were philistines. Neither the Queen nor Philip had shown any engagement with the arts beyond obligatory visits to royal command performances at the opera, theatre and cinema. If there was one national event that did light up the Queen's interest, it was the annual Royal Ascot horse races. The palace had gathered a formidable art collection over two centuries, but British monarchs were not known as patrons of national artists in the way that other royal houses in Europe had once been. As far as the Queen was concerned, the art collection was just another piece of inherited treasure. Unlike Jackie Kennedy's, the Queen's education, limited to what was thought to be the basic essentials of history and the amorphous constitution, had not included anything to stimulate a lively interest in the arts, and she had not felt the lack of it.

Given what was happening in the arts in Britain at that moment, the absence of any royal participation might seem extraordinary – but the truth was that, on the basis of long experience, none was expected of them. The British political class was just as philistine. French Presidents were committed champions of French culture and there was a whole generously funded ministry devoted to it – this was, understandably, partly a highly motivated mission to defend the French language against the ineluctable onslaught of English on world culture, but it was also part of a tradition that the state appreciated and understood the value to society of a vibrant national culture. British Prime Ministers were usually all business and little drawn to the broad range of the creative arts. Churchill, a literary giant in his own field of political and military history, as well as an amateur painter of talent, never saw patronage of the arts as a political virtue. Macmillan, the head of an accomplished publishing house, showed no personal interest in culture beyond literature.

The royal family had a forebear who was very different. Prince Albert, Victoria's German consort, was a true polymath and daring in his advocacy of intellectual progress and change. He was president of the Society of Arts but used this platform for a wider mission: to urge the inclusion of science in the cause of making the nation modern as he insisted it needed to be. He arranged a knighthood for Charles Lyell, one of the most distinguished scholars at Cambridge, who outlined the basic mechanics of natural evolution a decade before Darwin did. He urged Cambridge University to modernise the way it taught science so that the Queen's empire should be in the vanguard of industrial innovations. His most lasting and spectacular achievement was the exhibition of the 'Industry of All Nations' that he started to plan in 1849, resulting in the Great Exhibition of 1851 in Hyde Park. The architecture of the exhibition building itself was as astonishing and modern as the exhibits within – the vast and shining Crystal Palace framed from cast-iron and glass. Queen Victoria exulted in the sight of it: '…astonishing, a fairy scene'. The historian Thomas Macaulay lost his usual restraint. It was 'a most gorgeous sight; vast; graceful; beyond the dreams of the Arabian romances'.

Because of Albert, the monarchy began to be seen differently by the public – as a catalyst of change. The Queen ordered a great ball to be held at the Guildhall in the City of London – the heart of mercantile Britain – to celebrate the exhibition's success and, according to Albert, a million Londoners turned out to welcome them, and remained in the streets until dawn. Victoria was openly enamoured of Albert and his ability to overcome the more conservative of her ministers. Privately, the couple were as industrious in producing children as Albert wanted the nation to be in producing the goods of the future; their first of nine children was born nine months after their marriage. But Albert's early death in 1861 turned Victoria into an inconsolable widow and completely drained the monarchy of its new energy. Thereafter nobody turned to Buckingham Palace for innovative ideas or deep artistic engagement. Kensington Palace, however, was a different story.

Tony Armstrong-Jones had been present at the creation of a major insurrection in the tone of British theatre. On 8 May 1956, John Osborne's *Look Back in Anger* opened at the Royal Court Theatre in Sloane Square. The lead character, Jimmy Porter, was not a nice chap and today would doubtless be condemned by the #MeToo movement. He was slowly burning with a kind of rage that many young men across the country shared: he had risen from the working class, had a university education but then found that a good education did not change his class status. In Osborne's writing (and particularly in Richard Burton's performance in the 1959 film version), Jimmy becomes a cruel misogynist venting his bile on upper-class young women. Tony took many of the publicity photographs for this and other Royal Court productions. The work gave him an early and useful introduction to the authors and actors of the new wave, as well as to Kenneth Tynan, the brilliantly polemical theatre critic of *The Observer*, who championed Osborne's work and damned the safe, bourgeois 'drawing room' dramas that then filled most of the London stage. The paper's film critic, Penelope Gilliatt (married to Roger Gilliatt, the best man at Tony's wedding), was equally influential as British film discovered the same unsettling realities of class repression with *Room at the Top*, *Saturday Night and Sunday Morning*, *The Loneliness of the Long Distance Runner* and, later, *Sunday Bloody Sunday*, for which Gilliatt wrote the screenplay.

If Jackie Kennedy had seen a new blooming of talent as potent as this, its authors would have been swiftly invited to the White House and their work celebrated as part of a national renaissance. But in London there was no chance of either royal or political patronage – in fact, both the palace and the political class thought the new plays and films were unseemly intimations of a new coarseness in the arts. It was not polite to mention that the royal family's most direct involvement in the London theatre had been the generations of princes who joined the line of stage-door johnnies. They assumed a *droit de seigneur* to enter the dressing rooms of any actresses they fancied, and several long-lasting liaisons began that way. Managements tolerated it because it brought them publicity, but today it would look like a sex-trafficking ring.

And so, while the Queen appeared above and indifferent to the fermenting artistic renaissance, Tony and Margaret were in the middle of it. From an early age Margaret had shown musical talent; she was a confident pianist and gave pleasure to her father by leading improvised family sing-alongs of popular tunes. She danced with natural skill, sang with gusto and as an adult her high soprano voice enabled her to hit F above high C. The palace allowed a manufacturer of upright pianos to market a special model in her honour, imprinted with the name Princess Margaret Rose (I own one that was originally owned by the editor of the *New Musical Express*). She developed an interest in jazz and built a collection of jazz records, first within the limits of 75 rpm recordings and then more comprehensively with LPs. When Count Basie appeared at the Royal Festival Hall, she went to two performances in one day – this was a hunger for the real thing that I knew myself because no British big band ever came close to the competence of the American maestros. When Louis Armstrong played in London – his repertoire by then was aimed more at mass audiences than jazz aficionados – she met him afterwards and he was astonished to hear that she had read the work of Alan Lomax, a signal historian of jazz and blues, and wanted to talk about the roots of Armstrong's music in New Orleans. 'Your Princess Margaret is one hip chick,' Armstrong told reporters.

Tony's appreciation of music was stunted by the fact that he was tone deaf. But he brought to the marriage an entourage of friends from the theatre, film, television, journalism and the visual arts who were challenging all the assumptions of what was permissible as judged by Her Majesty's deeply rattled censors. Thus Margaret found herself simultaneously inhabiting two worlds that were in tension with each other. She was in a state of what could be called social schizophrenia that, by virtue of her royal blood, was unique to her: obliged to uphold her royal rank while enjoying the wit of people who had no time for any kind of privilege. But it was even more tricky for her than that. Both of those worlds looked at her and her behaviour through the specific lens of their own prejudices.

This situation did not bring out the best in either side. As she got to know Tony's crowd, they went through several stages of adjustment to the experience of spending time with her. They weren't like the old 'Margaret set' of the pre- and post-Townsend period, who were well drilled in the etiquette of when to genuflect and how to obey the hierarchy of table settings and details like the fact that they should remain seated until she got up and left. (George Harrison of the Beatles once had to point out to her that the rest of the party wanted to go home but they couldn't until she left – she apologised for not noticing and left.) Nonetheless, most of the new crowd were gobsmacked by the frisson of royalty that she carried with her. Tony was a careful host.

He put Margaret at ease with some very clever people who would have been intellectually intimidating in other circumstances. And Margaret was, in return, obviously drawn to people who were far more worth listening to than the chinless wonders of the old days.

But certain characteristics were ingrained on both sides. The 'luvvies' of stage and screen had big, sensitive egos. In their company you knew that the effusive compliments to your face would often be followed by bitchy accounts to others afterwards – or bitchy notes in their diaries. Some of them were gifted mimics and retold conversations in Margaret's posh 'jolly hockey sticks' style. For her part, Margaret (no mean mimic herself) often complained to Tony that these people were too familiar with her. One thing about Margaret that some people had a lot of trouble accepting was that she had strong views of her own about the arts and no hesitation in expressing them. For example, when she declared that she didn't like the music of Stephen Sondheim it was resented as though she had no right to an opinion and was just speaking as a royal know-nothing. In fact, as with anyone else, her views were formed on her own terms and within the bounds of her own taste, which was catholic but sometimes conservative. One of the few people who saw the unfairness of this was Gore Vidal, who said that Margaret was too intelligent for her station in life – and that comment spoke volumes not just about Margaret but about the philistines in the palace.

Cecil Beaton was appallingly insulting in his diaries. He described Margaret as 'a poor midgety brute', a 'wealthy seaside landlady' and 'a little pocket monster'. But that had as much to do with Tony as it did with Margaret. Beaton could never overcome his bitterness at seeing Tony gradually acknowledged as a rising photographic talent and one who had rendered Beaton's work – once considered groundbreaking – old hat. But Tony was finding that his social ascent came with unaccustomed public attacks – some from people he thought were friends.

I got a direct sense of how hurtful this could be to Tony from one of his friends, Cedric Price, a young and acclaimed architect. Tony enlisted Price and Frank Newby, a structural engineer, to design a new aviary for the London Zoo in an open competition. Their design, a striking break from zoo conventions (and, as it turned out, a harbinger of radical changes in zoo design), was selected. Some of the popular dailies complained that the competition judges had somehow been swayed by Tony's privileged status. The aviary was dubbed 'Tony's birdcage' and he was called 'one of Britain's leading birdcage designers, not an overcrowded profession'. Nobody seemed to recall Prince Albert's Crystal Palace, a similarly visionary and predictive departure in public architecture, albeit on a grander scale, or the way that Albert's innovations were warmly welcomed by the public. (After Tony's death, the aviary, on its fiftieth anniversary, was officially granted listed status as an architectural landmark.) This stream of petty prejudice erupted again when Tony was invited to join the Council for Industrial Design as an adviser. Tony had a personal cause to pursue. He wanted industrial designers to take into account the special needs of disabled people – his own experience in a wheelchair when recovering from polio had left him with a certainty that wheelchairs and many impediments met by people with disabilities should be attacked with a fresh eye. His work for the Council was unpaid and he occupied a small office there, but once more Fleet Street lashed out. What were his qualifications? Who thought he had anything to offer to British industry that they did not already have? He was 'just a photographer with a royal wife'. The job had been cooked up as a 'sinecure' for an otherwise underemployed person. In these rantings, the papers were displaying an odd prejudice, not understanding that egalitarianism sometimes moves sideways, not up or down, and that Tony was in a new position that he wanted to use creatively.

Tony stuck with it. He had one sympathetic supporter in the palace,

Prince Philip. While in no way being a Prince Albert himself, Philip had heard complaints during numerous trips abroad that British goods exported to the former colonies, where because of traditional ties they faced little competition, were frequently shoddy and poorly designed. In other places beyond the Commonwealth, people had complained that British products always came packaged with labels and operating instructions exclusively in English, whatever the language of their destination. Philip made several speeches about this and was, as a result, lampooned for being agitated about packing cases.

*   *   *

To those who saw them frequently, Tony and Margaret were highly compatible in one department. 'They couldn't keep their hands off each other, even with other people present,' said one friend. Tony was able to act with a practised insouciance when it came to encounters with old lovers in Margaret's presence. In 1961, after a Christmas dutifully spent with the royal family, they went to Ireland to stay with Tony's mother, Anne, Countess of Rosse, and her second husband, Michael Parsons, the wealthy Earl of Rosse, at Birr Castle. Snootier members of society regarded Anne as a climber and called her Tugboat Annie because she 'drifted from peer to peer'. Old flames were among the house party: Billy Wallace, the most persistent of Margaret's old tribe of chinless wonders, and his wife – and Jeremy Fry and his wife Camilla. Whether or not Tony knew then that Camilla's new daughter Polly had sprung from his own loins, we will never know, but the *ménage à trois* that he had enjoyed with the Frys was certainly unknown to Margaret. She was too much in love to notice anything being concealed at the house party.

In any examination of the personalities of the two daughters of George VI, Margaret's verve and musical acumen and her suddenly expanded experience and enjoyment of Britain's cultural pacemakers is a strong distinguishing feature; the young Elizabeth, regardless of the shadow of her future life of duty, certainly never displayed any verve or any sign of the rebellious effervescence of her sister, which was probably just as well. Now resolutely locked into performing the role of monarch but without any inkling of what it might take to become not just a monarch but a truly modern one, Elizabeth was as safely conservative and stolid as her sister was volatile and unpredictable. The salon at Kensington Palace was freewheeling and fun. In contrast, when people were invited to dine with the Queen at Windsor, the ritual was choreographed to the last detail. As James Pope-Hennessy had noted, the Queen was not a natural conversationalist at dinner. She didn't permit general or three-way conversations. People had to wait until she addressed them directly. She prepared carefully but avoided anything reflective: talk had to bubble along on the surface and each subject had its allotted span. The outside world was less and less predictable, but at this table the world was as carefully ordered as the napkins and place settings: knowing one's place was the thing.

CHAPTER 9

MOCKING THEIR BRITANNIC MAJESTIES

The King's vast naked ballooning buttocks thrust out into the street, almost filling the gates of St James's Palace, the royal residence at the edge of St James's. Robert Walpole, the first politician skilful enough in handling a monarch to create the office we know as Prime Minister, has mounted a pillar in order to plant an adoring kiss on the King's arse. This cartoon from 1740 by an anonymous artist was for sale in one of the many print shops that fed the public's appetite for a powerful new form of social commentary. It was titled *Idol-Worship or The Way to Preferment*. Walpole's skill in containing the powers of King George II aroused a healthy scepticism in the public, who suspected that in his transactions with the monarch the Prime Minister had shown too much sycophancy. Nobody – apart possibly from the King himself – saw anything outrageous in the crude symbolism of the cartoon. Grotesquely inflated bums and breasts were a familiar part of the cartoonist's vocabulary, applied to all stations of the capital's life and power networks. Farting was openly drawn as salvoes fired off between political combatants. Better that than knives.

The Hanoverian royals – some of whose physical features still pop up today from the royal DNA – endured a level of public mockery that had become unthinkable by the first half of the twentieth century. They offered rich material. In 1787, James Gillray, the most celebrated and savage of the cartoonists, portrayed George III, Queen Charlotte and the Prince of Wales seated at dinner outside the gates of the Treasury. They are gorging like gluttons on the public purse. Parliament had just agreed to pay off the prince's debts, which in today's money were around £35 million, an astonishing level of profligacy but typical of the debauched heir to the throne. His grand new London residence, Carlton House, was also funded by the Treasury. Gillray regularly drew him as a potbellied voluptuary mindless of all disapproval. But Gillray's acknowledged masterpiece, etched in 1792, depicts – with unusual restraint and precision – a royal coupling. The Duke of York, George III's second (and favourite) son married Princess Frederica of Prussia in 1791. The princess was petite, with dainty feet and a taste for opulent clothing. Gillray portrayed the intimacy of the wedding night with delicate obscenity: a close-up of two slender ankles and diamond-encrusted slippers parted as her loins invite the embrace and, moving atop her feet, a pair of the prince's heavy buckled shoes. The title was: *Fashionable Contrasts; or the Duchess's Little Shoe Yielding to the Magnitude of the Duke's Foot.*

How did this level of lusty commentary cease to be respectable? For much of the eighteenth century the daily lives of the royals were intermingled with those of the people of London in a way that was lost once Queen Victoria and her family moved into Buckingham Palace. The rude in-their-face scrutiny provided by the Georgian cartoonists reflected the rude social familiarity of the classes with each other as the capital city grew with exceptional speed. By the mid-eighteenth century, one in ten people in England lived in London. The capital grew from a population of around 675,000 people in 1700 to nearing a million by 1801, on the way to becoming the first world city. No other European city could keep pace with it. At the core of it were three secular centres of power: St James's Palace, the Westminster Parliament and, a mile or so to the east, the financial and mercantile titans of the City.

Part of the reason Walpole had been able to establish the new rules for a semblance, at least, of a nascent constitutional monarchy was that the makers of new wealth, riding on the industrial revolution and the rapid expansion of international trade, wanted their say in running the country on more modern lines. The new money, represented in London by around 1,000 families, mingled with the old money, around 4,000 families composed of aristocrats and landed gentry.

Among all these densely housed groups there was a healthy appetite for gossip and entertainment – a lot of it at the expense of the monarchy. Gillray's favourite, the Prince of Wales, provided plenty of gossip and entertainment, particularly in his long-running affair with a twice-widowed Catholic called Mrs Fitzherbert. (Bearing in mind what was to follow, there would seem to be ample material for a Freudian analysis of why Princes of Wales have successively yearned for the caress of older women.) The laxity that allowed the lampooning of the royal family was possible because, as Henry Fielding wrote, it was London 'where the nobleman and his taylor [*sic*], the lady of quality and her tirewoman, meet together and form one common assembly'. London, said another observer, was 'one universal masquerade … in which all distinction of rank is lost'. Nightly revellers in Vauxhall Gardens, dancing to Handel's lighter works, or besotted by his rapturous arias, wore masks that removed all the inhibitions of class from some brief but passionate encounters. But there were less attractive sides to this great crush of bodies and lusts. Elegant clothes often adorned unwashed bodies – bathing was scant even among the upper orders. Perfumes and rouge and powder were more than soap. They countered stench and infirmity.

In the early 1960s, the only members of the royal family who really lived like Londoners were Tony and Margaret, and they did so with eighteenth-century familiarity and energy. To the consternation of Margaret's security staff, they would zoom off for their nightly engagements on Tony's motorbike, with Margaret riding pillion. Crash helmets, like masks, provided anonymity. They were frequently mingling with a growing crowd whose talents were devoted to restoring those eighteenth-century metropolitan riffs of insolence and satire directed at figures of authority, but this time they were enhanced by the mischief of theatre, television and journalism.

Deference was the habit that now had to die. It's not easy to pin down exactly when and how the British shed an instinctive deference towards the full cast of authority figures who had come to expect it of them, ranging from High Court judges to the Archbishop of Canterbury. Of these, it was the Queen who enjoyed the longest immunity from mockery. As late as the mid-1960s, according to a public opinion poll, almost a third of the population believed that the Queen was chosen by God. Deification of that kind presented satirists with the risk of being seen as blasphemers – or worse. As we have seen in the case of Altrincham, a well-reasoned critique from a respectable public figure provoked a violent response.

There was, however, someone who deserved acclaim as the spiritual father of this new generation of satirists waiting to strike. Malcolm Muggeridge had dared to make an astonishing attack on the royal family before Altrincham. A brilliant controversialist, Muggeridge became one of the first people in Britain to become famous by earning the title of a 'television personality'. He had been a wartime spy, a gadfly journalist of the left and, in middle age, turned out to be a television natural, but his attack on the monarchy was too much for the BBC, who barred him from the air (excommunication might be a more apt term since the row generated an almost religious fervour). In 1955, he wrote a piece for the *New Statesman* in which he said, 'The royal family ought to be properly advised on how to prevent themselves and their lives from becoming a sort of royal soap opera.' It was the first time that that association was made, but, unlike Altrincham, Muggeridge had targeted the institution, and not the Queen or any other member of the family personally. The piece passed mostly without notice until it was revised and expanded for the mass-circulation American weekly the *Saturday Evening Post* two years later under the title 'Does England Really Need a Queen?' As well as being ejected by the BBC, Muggeridge was blackballed by his club, the Garrick, and the historian Sir George Clark said he should be horsewhipped in public. Muggeridge allowed that he may have made a mistake by treating the monarchy as essentially comical. In view of the fact that it enjoyed such fanatical support, he said, it should be taken more seriously.

Muggeridge became a hero to the cast of a four-man show called *Beyond the Fringe* that opened in the West End in the summer of 1960. In a provincial run before reaching London, the show had received mixed reviews. But in *The Observer*, Tynan praised it as a breakthrough in creating contemporary satire, and the four players, Alan Bennett, Peter Cook, Jonathan Miller and Dudley Moore, became instant stars. Their sketches worked like accelerants poured on a combustible pyre of social unrest. Nonetheless, they were not arsonists of a class war or radical firebrands. Cook, who wrote most of the material, came from a family of colonial civil servants and went to Cambridge to read French and German. Moore came from the Essex working class and was a musical prodigy who won an organ scholarship to Oxford. Miller came from a north London Jewish family; his father was a paediatric psychologist and his mother a novelist, and Miller himself studied medicine at Cambridge and qualified as a doctor. Bennett's father was a butcher in Leeds. He had a first in history from Exeter College, Oxford, and for a while taught medieval history.

And so this is what the defiance of deference and the coming of egalitarianism looks like in 1960 – at least, this is how it surfaced within a specific cohort. In itself, *Beyond the Fringe* is not the final triumph of egalitarianism over privilege, a mission that has never been

completed in Britain. We're looking at a particular movement of attitudes at a particular time in a metropolitan setting. It has a selective
but influential impact. The four players had no political agenda. They
were natural performers but gifted in ways that distinguished each
from the other. Cook was instinctively able to write caricatures that
were devastatingly recognisable – his impersonation of Harold Macmillan shocked audiences who had never seen a politician so mercilessly treated. Moore fell easily into partnering Cook as they invented
surrealistic conversations between an idiot savant and his acolyte,
as Pete and Dud – a cruel cut at working-class pretensions. Miller
had fun as a performer, particularly spearing intellectual pretension,
but was too much the polymath to remain in satire. Bennett had an
unnervingly accurate ear for British class differences as they were expressed in language, as well as an ability to see through the language
to the torments hidden beneath, and thus became one of the most
enduring playwrights of his generation.

Cook's treatment of Macmillan ranked with the attacks on the
monarchy by Muggeridge and Altrincham as a warning that no figure
of authority would any longer be safe from satire, and at first it had
the same shock effects. Politicians, like the monarchy, had grown used
to living safely above ridicule, although in the mid-nineteenth century it was the political class that replaced the monarchy as targets.
One reason for this is that the royals no longer 'put themselves about'
among London society as the Georgians did; once they retreated into
the vast halls of Buckingham Palace, they had a protective bubble
around them. Muggeridge had posted his own advance warning of a
shift of attention back to the royal family: 'To put them above laughter, above criticism, above the workaday world, is, ultimately, to de-
humanise them and risk the monarchy dying of acute anaemia.' (This
poses the question of what a royal needed to do to become 'human'
– something that nobody was clear about.)

Harold Macmillan was so intrigued by talk of how he was being lampooned by Cook that, urged on by Lady Dorothy, he went to see the show for himself. Spotting the Prime Minister from the stage, Cook began to ad lib, making the caricature even more cutting. Macmillan didn't like it; he wasn't that kind of sport. Neither he nor Cook saw the irony of this: the Macmillan that Cook mocked was actually the Prime Minister's own well-rehearsed public version of himself as the droopy-eyed, languid Edwardian – whereas in truth Macmillan was a ruthless political in-fighter who used the mask to conceal how progressive he really was. Another attempt to mock Macmillan backfired. Vicky, the *Evening Standard*'s veteran cartoonist, introduced him as a caped comic book hero called Supermac. In this role, Supermac was the world-girding statesman who could instantly solve any crisis that called for his intervention. But Macmillan lived up to the part, enjoying a run of success mediating between Kennedy and Khrushchev. Instead of accepting the cartoon's view that Macmillan pursued delusional British world influence, many people thought he was unusually effective.

And it fell to the Queen herself to give a considerable boost to Supermac's performance on the high wire. This involved her returning to Africa to try to solve a diplomatic crisis that Macmillan suggested needed all her emollient skills. In 1957, Kwame Nkrumah, a charismatic revolutionary, had led the former colony of the Gold Coast to independence and became the first Prime Minister of the new state of Ghana. He became President when Ghana became a republic in 1960. In his youth, Nkrumah had spent a fruitful ten years in America, earning masters' degrees in arts and science, and while there he resolved that the African colonies could gain freedom only by acting together as a pan-African revolutionary movement. This background gave him an astute feel for how to exploit the Cold War rivalry of the west and Soviet Russia. He saw how Nasser in Egypt had persuaded the Russians to finance a dam on the Nile and he wanted to build a dam on the Volta. He made a trip to Moscow and it looked like Ghana might go the way of Egypt – pulling out of the Commonwealth and becoming a Soviet client state. President Kennedy was alarmed and shared his concerns with Macmillan – both leaders feared that Nkrumah was turning into a despot, but he was gambling that by playing off the west against the Russians he could get a more congenial deal on financing the dam.

A complex Cold War game was under way and it was not something that the Queen would normally have been called upon to resolve. But she had had to postpone a previously planned royal visit to Ghana when she became pregnant with Andrew, and now she wanted to press ahead, even though Ghana was thought to be a dangerous place. Two bombs had gone off in the capital, Accra, as political factions erupted. Macmillan sent Duncan Sandys, the Secretary of State for Commonwealth Relations, to Accra to assess whether the Queen should go. Churchill, her old mentor, wrote to Macmillan of 'widespread uneasiness' over her safety and the risk of seeming to endorse 'a thoroughly authoritarian' regime. Sandys reported that he felt it was safe for her to go. The Queen agreed. She told Macmillan, 'How silly I should look if I was scared to visit Ghana and then Khrushchev went and had a good reception.'

As it turned out, the royal magic apparently remained potent in the former colony. The centrepiece of the visit was a state ball, staged with all the glamour of an imperial appearance by the Sovereign. The Queen took to the dance floor with Nkrumah and the photos were published around the world: in Moscow, if he saw the astonishing scene, Khrushchev would have understood the meaning of this calculated gavotte. And it was calculated by both dance partners. The BBC's reporter had gushed that the people of Ghana 'went out of their minds' for the Queen. When the two heads of state drove through

Accra in an open car, 'she didn't bat an eyelid', The Queen was 'very poised – not smiling too much – just right'. But Nkrumah had silenced his opposition by the simple manoeuvre of appropriating his people's adulation of the Queen.

That did not matter to Macmillan – Nkrumah and Ghana were back on side with Britain. All Macmillan had to do was to make sure that Kennedy now came through with the money to build the Volta Dam. He called Kennedy and without any subtlety revealed just how well he had understood the gambit: 'I have risked my Queen. You must risk your money.' The money was duly produced.

The Queen had shown great courage and determination in sticking to her plan to visit Ghana. She had been in the job long enough, and was so personally engaged in the future of Africa, that she carried a sureness of touch about the ability of Africans to distinguish between the ephemeral interests of their politicians and their vestigial feelings towards her – after all, she had been in Africa when suddenly fate made her the Queen. She had also taken the measure of Nkrumah as she sat regally alongside him. He was, she wrote to a friend afterwards, 'muddled' in his world view and 'vainglorious' in his ambitions for himself and his country. Nkrumah was deposed in a military coup in 1966 and never returned to Ghana, living most of the rest of his life in exile in Guinea. A series of military rulers followed. In spite of this, Ghana, the second largest source of gold after South Africa, has had one of the world's fastest-growing economies. It remains a member of the Commonwealth.

Macmillan recognised his debt to the Queen. 'She loves her duty and means to be Queen and not a puppet,' he wrote. None of her Prime Ministers had ever seen her as a puppet. But until now none had ever thought it necessary to defer to her in any degree, as Eden had shown at the time of Suez. Macmillan knew better how to use the monarch.

However, as the Queen demonstrated great skill in handling the speed of change in Africa, Buckingham Palace still moved at the speed of a horse-drawn vehicle. Britain had developed the world's first jet airliner, the Comet, which in one stroke doubled the speed at which people could fly. But the business of the nation as it flowed on paper to the monarch and back to her ministers in the red boxes marked for her eyes only moved by the same means and at the same speed as it had for Queen Victoria. Every weekday morning at 10 a.m. a horse-drawn brougham pulled up at the Privy Purse entrance to Buckingham Palace. The Queen's messenger loaded the boxes containing the papers she had read in the previous twenty-four hours and the brougham set off through the London traffic for Whitehall, St James's and Victoria. The liveried coachman was impervious to the din around him. Taxis and buses yielded to this apparition – the impatient present deferring to the stubborn past, a diagram of a people learning to be British in a new way while tolerating an institution that was serenely ossified.

The Prime Minister managed this dichotomy with composure. The label Fleet Street had coined for him was 'unflappable', and it stuck. But from his experience in settling the feud about the family name Macmillan had gained an unsettling insight into the way Philip behaved towards the Queen, and at the same time he had his own marital torments to live with. In a decade that was becoming more impertinently curious about public figures, the Prime Minister and the monarch both wanted and needed to preserve some private space for private matters. Did they, perhaps, recognise that need in each other?

CHAPTER 10

THE TROUBLE WITH PHILIP

Late in 1960, Prince Philip received a request to sit for a portrait by an artist whose name he didn't recognise. But since the portrait was commissioned by the *Illustrated London News*, a weekly magazine popular with the English gentry and a staple of dentists' waiting rooms, Philip agreed. When the artist arrived at the palace, Philip recognised him: 'By Jove, you're the osteopath. I never connected you with this appointment.' Philip had forgotten the name but remembered the face and the voice, one of many in a blur of faces from his past. It was the past of a man about town, of parties that mixed blue bloods and showgirls, millionaires and bohemians, a full life that was curtailed by marriage. The artist and the osteopath was Stephen Ward.

Philip had known Ward a long time. On New Year's Eve 1946, Philip and Ward were both guests at a party in Knightsbridge when Ward had to intervene to prevent an argument. A stand-up comedian appeared on a small improvised stage and spotted Philip, who was in naval uniform. 'We're honoured to have a naval officer with us tonight,' said the comedian, 'so I had better keep my jokes dirty, otherwise the Navy will get a good name.' Philip began to barrack him. The host was about to restrain him when Ward whispered to him, 'You can't do that. That's Prince Philip of Greece.' Philip's companion at the party was a Canadian fashion model, Maxie Taylor. Six months after that party, Philip's engagement to Princess Elizabeth was announced. Early in 1947, Ward moved into a spacious set of rooms in Cavendish Square and gave a house-warming party. Philip was a guest. It was an address he remembered immediately when Ward arrived at Buckingham Palace to draw his portrait. As Ward recalled, 'We discussed the old days, polo and the fact that he had a rare condition called "rider's bone" in the thigh.'

Drawing portraits had begun as a hobby for Ward. Quite often his subjects were his patients. One of these was an art dealer and gallery owner, Hugh Leggatt, and when Ward made a portrait of him, Leggatt was impressed enough to offer Ward a show in his West End gallery if he could persuade enough illustrious people to sit for him. Ward kept a little black book of contacts and they became useful in lining up sitters, who now included Harold Macmillan, J. Paul Getty, the richest man in the world, and Sophia Loren, while she was filming *The Millionairess* at Elstree Studios. It was the success of the show at Leggatt's gallery that brought Ward the magazine assignment. His portrait of Philip so impressed the editor that it appeared on the cover of the issue dated 24 June 1961. Philip stared straight from the page, with the appearance and confidence of a matinee idol. The caption read: 'Prince Philip's many activities and interests are so well known to our readers that it is unnecessary to give the brief summary of them, which is all that is possible in this space.'

Behind Philip's life of 'many activities and interests', there were persisting frustrations. The argument over the family name was settled, but in a compromise that Philip was unhappy with. Ward had mentioned seeing him play polo. People who watched him were struck by the merciless way he treated his ponies: 'He drives it, and he wants a machine out in front of him so when he steps on the throttle it goes, when he brakes, it stops, and it goes fast left or right,' said one player. Another noted that he 'needed to play polo to get rid of all of his pent-up frustrations ... but after a few games he would be a different man – the frustration gone'.

One of his sources of frustration was Charles. The Queen had ceded to Philip all decisions on the education that her children should receive, believing this to be the natural order of family responsibilities. In one respect Philip did not follow the customary choice of the upper-class and the most socially ambitious parents by sending his son to Eton. Philip believed that his own education, Cheam followed by Gordonstoun, would produce the best outcome – which was, apparently, a replica of himself, or what could be called the Mountbatten model of manliness. Charles, however, did not fit happily into that model. In Philip's own words, this meant that 'school is expected to be a Spartan and disciplined experience in the process of developing into self-controlled, considerate and independent adults'. Judging by how this doctrine had turned out in Philip himself, the 'considerate' element was fungible. He wasn't at all prepared to consider that the heir to the throne might not be suited to join the Spartans; Charles was, to anyone who took the trouble to notice, far more Athenian in character. In the five years that he spent at Cheam, Charles had shown a deep aversion to participating in group activities, whether on the playing field or in the classroom. As he recalled later, he was a loner: 'I always preferred my own company, or just a one to one.' The Queen understood this and saw how tortured Charles was, but Philip had no patience with him. In April 1962, he was sent north to the rigorous climate of Gordonstoun.

A second and more opaque area of Philip's frustrations concerned his libido. During the first decade of the Queen's reign, the news-papers tap-danced around the subject, full of curiosity but afraid to strike. They faced long-established conventions about how hard to press stories about the sex lives of the royal family. Edward VII was the most recent monarch with the record of a rampant libido, and the Edwardian newspapers were muzzled about that. Edward VIII's infatuation with and surrender to Wallis Simpson had led to far more public scrutiny, but the carnal qualities of the relationship had remained off-limits. George VI was never suspected of a roving eye and was a model of fidelity. But Philip was a far more vulnerable case. For a start, there was Lascelles's warning about his likely philandering. And now there was a new generation of tabloid journalism finding its ground and looking for scandal.

There were two parts to understanding Philip's behaviour. The first was his record before marriage. It would have been a very unworldly person who imagined that Philip, with his leading-man looks, his obvious physical energy and his place in a transparently decadent demi-monde of displaced European princes, had led a monastic life before marrying Elizabeth. However, the issue was not so much how much of a royal rake he had been as how easy it would have been for him to terminate the role upon his marriage. The greater the variety and spice of that life, the greater the challenge of saying goodbye to it. And then there was the added burden, unique to Philip's situation, of the Queen's own feelings, her massive popularity, and the question of how the public would feel were Philip to be seen to have strayed. None of this can properly be judged without getting a picture of the environment in which Philip the rake had thrived.

The first time Fleet Street picked up what they believed to be the scent of a serious fling by Philip was in 1957, when he returned from a four-month trip on the royal yacht *Britannia* during which he circumnavigated more or less the entire British Commonwealth, from the Antarctic to Kenya, from Papua New Guinea to the Seychelles. The trip meant that he was away from London during the Suez crisis (and Mountbatten's intervention with the Queen) and his ninth wedding anniversary, as well as missing the family Christmas at Sandringham. It did not take much of an effort by the tabloids to paint a suggestive picture of marital neglect – abetted by a randy crew of sailors aboard *Britannia* and Philip's long-time soulmate, his private secretary Mike

Parker. It was Parker who unwillingly provided the opening for the newspapers to pounce. Late in the trip he suddenly had to leave for London when his wife filed for divorce, citing adultery by him (although she failed to prove it). There was no doubt that over some years Philip and Parker had happily behaved as a buddy act in the way that was common in Philip's milieu. In fact, Mrs Parker felt that her real rival was not any one dalliance but the absolute devotion her husband had to his job and to whatever demands Philip made of him at any hour of the day or night. The *Britannia* cruise, dubbed 'Philip's Folly' by the papers, was the last straw for her.

The assumption that Philip enjoyed the sexual hunting licence of an alpha male was a natural one for a Fleet Street editor to make at the time. Long before the rest of the country felt the sexual freedom brought to the 1960s by the contraceptive pill and the beat of the Rolling Stones, London was a honeypot for men of means and power. For Philip there was a place where the joys of this privilege could be shared discreetly with like-minded others, a kind of social switchboard set up exclusively for lascivious male amusement. The instigator was Sterling Henry Nahum, a photographer who went by the professional name of Baron. In post-war London, 'portrait by Baron' became a sought-after mark of status for a wide swathe of ambitious people from business, the arts and high society. Baron was so successful that his Mayfair studio worked like a factory to deliver at least five portraits a day at a fee of at least thirty guineas a session – a price that at the time could secure a suite in a luxury hotel. When Tony Armstrong-Jones flunked out of Cambridge and needed to learn the rudiments of professional photography, his barrister father paid Baron to take him on as an apprentice. He made good use of the opportunity by mastering how to manipulate prints in the darkroom for flattering results and, in August 1951, left after a year to set up his own fledgling business in Soho.

Long before Tony jump-started his career in this way, Baron

founded a weekly lunchtime gathering in a private room at Wheeler's, a well-regarded English seafood restaurant in Soho. It was called the Thursday Club. Mrs Parker talked of the Thursday Club in the same disparaging way she talked of Buckingham Palace, as a place where her husband seemed far happier than when he was with her. She said that the Queen herself referred to members of the club as 'Philip's funny friends'. If so, this was a rather naïve view of what 'funny' meant. Baron, in a posthumously published memoir, set out the purpose of the club:

> I suggested forming a little club to lighten the gloom that surrounded us all, and that we should meet with friends once a week. No issues of importance would be allowed, no international questions would be solved. The club would be devoted to absolute Inconsequence. We would eat as well as we could, tell stories and swap reminiscences.

To the waiting staff at Wheeler's, the lunches often seemed like a posher version of a rugby club piss-up, with the same coarseness of language and sexual braggadocio (though not the songs). Philip and Parker were evidently spirited members of this company. So too was Stephen Ward, as well as another portrait artist – unlike Ward, a full-time professional with a striking modernist style of his own – who enjoyed an illustrious clientele in the arts and society, Feliks Topolski. There was a thread linking Baron, Ward and Topolski that, in part, explained their ability to mix so easily with the other members of the Thursday Club fraternity – politicians, actors, tycoons, aristocrats and royalty whose lives otherwise circulated in separate orbits. All kinds of glamorous young women, from debutantes to showgirls, sat for portraits and chatted about their lives and hopes to the photographer and the artists. Without quite realising it, some of them were being auditioned for an informal invitation to meet members of the Thursday Club and Philip's 'funny friends', whose idea of fun was very broad-minded.

One such introduction took place just a month after Ward's portrait of Philip was published, and it was engineered by Ward. In the political and cultural life of the country, the consequences would be cataclysmic. For Philip, it would suddenly render the Thursday Club and its associations radioactive. Saturday 8 July 1961 was the beginning of what turned out to be the hottest weekend of the year – ideal for an escape to the country for those able to make one. Ward had the use of a cottage on the estate at Cliveden, the family seat of the Astors (and a place notorious for its role in the 1930s as a nexus for high-placed appeasers). Both he and his landlord, Bill Astor, had planned weekend house parties and, since they were neighbours, the guests of both would at some point intermingle. One of Ward's guests was a lithesome nineteen-year-old cabaret dancer named Christine Keeler. One of Astor's guests was Macmillan's Secretary of State for War, John Profumo. On their first evening there, Keeler was cavorting topless in the Astor swimming pool when Profumo appeared and…

I was entirely ignorant of all of these events when they happened, but my journalistic career would soon converge with them. David Astor had accepted a lot of my ideas for improving the presentation of *The Observer*. I convinced him that the authority of a serious newspaper did not depend on it looking grey and dense, which was still the belief of some other papers, particularly *The Times*. Good writing and photography benefited from appearing in a more modern format. Improved sales followed, but our most direct competitor, the *Sunday Times* (not then linked to *The Times*), was undergoing a rapid transformation with the help of generous funding from its new owner, Roy Thomson. Following a custom that was common in his native Canada, Thomson announced that the *Sunday Times* would launch a magazine section printed in colour on high-quality paper. Thomson referred to it as a 'colour supplement' and this phrase was seized upon by critics who argued that its main purpose was to pull advertising away from magazines to the newspaper, not to add editorial quality. Astor swallowed this argument whole, but I did not. Denis Hamilton, the editor-in-chief of the *Sunday Times*, wanted top writers and photographers to see the magazine as a new and powerful outlet for their work. *The Observer* had no deep pockets to match Thomson's. Countering the *Sunday Times* with our own magazine was too much of a gamble for the management. (The *Sunday Times* magazine lost more than £1 million in its first year, which heartened Astor. His joy was misplaced. The financial losses were easily borne by Thomson, and the paper's circulation was boosted by 150,000.)

I proposed that instead of launching a magazine we changed the page size of the paper to tabloid, which would bring two advantages: it would nearly double the number of pages and make it far easier to divide it into sections that could each build a role of their own. I pointed to European quality papers like *Libération* in France that followed this model. But Astor choked on the word 'tabloid' and feared that *The Observer* would end up looking like a posher version of the *Daily Mirror*. Even though I was careful to use the term 'quality tabloid', he still would not yield. (The quality tabloid eventually arrived in Britain when *The Independent*, *The Times* and *The Guardian* adopted the idea.) Somebody told Denis Hamilton at the *Sunday Times* (it was not me) that I was frustrated by the rejection of my idea. Hamilton had been following the changes I made at *The Observer*. He called me and offered me the job of deputy editor of the new magazine and I accepted. Euphemisms about 'parting amicably' are often used in cases like this, but I was genuinely sorry to leave *The Observer* after a relatively short time there; David Astor was one of the great editors of the day and the paper was heavy with talent.

The cover of the first issue of the *Sunday Times* magazine (produced before I arrived) caught the zeitgeist of the cultural wave I had first picked up when calling on Tony at his Pimlico studio: there were multiple shots of Jean Shrimpton, the most exquisite model of the hour, wearing a dress by Mary Quant and photographed by David Bailey (who was also Shrimpton's lover) – three icons in one assignment. Mark Boxer, the magazine's editor, had had a central role in the new wave as editor of *Queen* magazine, where Tony had worked for him. Hamilton had told me that he wanted me to complement Boxer's brilliant visual instincts with a counterweight of serious journalism. It was an arrangement that suited both of us. As I settled in, I was impressed by the way Hamilton was carefully nurturing new talent and steering the paper away from the conservatism of its previous owner, Lord Kemsley.

Hamilton proved unusually tolerant of my restlessness. In the autumn of 1962, I left the paper to become editor of a new weekly news magazine, *Topic*. It lasted all of ten issues because the owners, one of whom was the future Tory star Michael Heseltine, ran out of cash. Talking to Hamilton before I left the *Sunday Times*, I foreshadowed an idea that became *Topic*'s mission: that a weekly newspaper should rise above the news cycles and selectively analyse significant stories at greater length. When *Topic* collapsed, Hamilton called. 'Come back and bring the two best people there with you. I want that kind of reporting in the paper.'

Three weeks before the three of us (the other two being Ron Hall and Jeremy Wallington) turned up at the *Sunday Times* building in Gray's Inn Road, at about one o'clock on the afternoon of 14 December 1962, shots were fired at the door of 17 Wimpole Mews, Marylebone, the home of Stephen Ward. Ward was not home but two young women were: Christine Keeler and another cabaret dancer, Mandy Rice-Davies. The shots were fired by a Jamaican lover of Keeler's whom she had recently dumped, John Edgecombe. Nobody was hurt, but Edgecombe was arrested later in the day. The *Daily Telegraph* reported, 'Miss Keeler, twenty, a free-lance model, was visiting Miss Marilyn Davies, eighteen, an actress, at Dr Ward's home…'

Tick tock, tick tock….

Our first work at the *Sunday Times* was not notable. We delivered scattershot analysis of the past week's news, but it had no significance. The section was called Insight, with the rubric 'the news in a new dimension'. Some people joked that it should have been called Hindsight. I knew that we needed a breakthrough story, one large enough to demand an original investigation that could be told as a long and lucid narrative. It finally arrived in the form of a tip I had from an old friend I had known from my time at the *Daily Express*, Robin Douglas-Home. He was a dashing man about town, a freelance writer and also a part-time nightclub pianist with looks that combined those of David Niven and Leslie Howard. He called me on the phone and said, 'Look up the stories on a girl called Keeler' – being unusually cryptic. 'Wimpole Mews. As a government minister leaves by the front door, a Russian agent enters by the back door.' I asked if it was a joke or a riddle. 'Find out,' he said, with a laugh.

That was the beginning of a prolonged game of cat-and-mouse, lasting until late in March 1963, in which we developed a story that was founded only on widespread rumours, told in fragments by various newspapers and bedevilled throughout by the threat of a punitive libel action. One paper, the *Daily Express*, devised a way of sailing closer to the wind than anyone: on the front page they printed a picture of Keeler, with a story recalling the shooting, and, separated from it by only one column, a story about John Profumo, saying he had offered Macmillan his resignation because of an impending reorganisation of the Ministry of Defence. Inside there was a larger story on Keeler in provocative poses, including one in which she was draped only in a towel. The *Express* had 13 million readers. No more than a few hundred, mostly in Westminster, understood the coded message as you would understand a wink: the *Express* had a lot more on Keeler and Profumo but could not risk printing it. The pressure on the Macmillan government and Profumo reached such a point that on 22 March Profumo made a personal statement to Parliament, saying, 'There was no impropriety whatsoever in my acquaintanceship with Miss Keeler.' He said that he met a Soviet naval attaché named Ivanov only once (Keeler was rumoured to have been sleeping with Ivanov at the same time). The linking of the two men was the basis for the most explosive allegation, that in some way via pillow talk there had been a serious security breach. (Given Keeler's lack of sophistication, we had already decided that this idea was risible.) To make plain to the newspapers that we were under threat, he added, 'I shall not hesitate to issue writs for libel and slander if scandalous allegations are made or repeated outside the House.'

The *Sunday Times* lawyer, James Evans, went through all of our notes and was engrossed. 'Wonderful work,' he said, 'but you can't print a word of it.' But Profumo was lying. It was one of the most barefaced lies ever told to Parliament. And it did not hold. On 5 July, Profumo resigned, admitting the affair – but not any security breach. By then we had researched the whole timeline of the scandal and on the following Sunday, with the skilful support of James Evans, we published the first of several long investigations, headlined 'THE THREE PHASES OF THE AFFAIR'. To us, one figure had emerged as central to the story, like a face developing slowly on a print in a photographer's darkroom: Stephen Ward.

Within weeks our reporting led to us being commissioned to write a book. This gave us the scope to go deeper into the political and cultural background of the scandal, although we had only three months in which to complete the manuscript. Against that deadline we were, in a real sense, writing a first draft of history; at the very least, we were aware that we were catching the unique fever of the moment in a way that anyone coming later could never recover because it would not be evident from any of the newspaper coverage. For example, almost immediately we stumbled into a segment of the story that triggered a very raw nerve: Prince Philip's links to Stephen Ward.

We knew nothing of Ward when we began. We quickly saw that his supple hands as an osteopath had been the making of both a very successful business and a steady social ascent. We discovered that among his early clients was Winston Churchill, who at the time was complaining of back trouble. Ward had twelve sessions with Churchill at his home in Hyde Park Gate. Ward told friends that each one was a battle of wills. Churchill wanted to have the purpose of each stage of the treatment explained to him before he consented to it. It was evidently successful, because when Ward said that he was an amateur portraitist, Churchill told him to take up painting 'because it lasts for ever'. Other patients were Elizabeth Taylor, Ava Gardner, Mel Ferrer and King Peter of Yugoslavia. There was no mention yet of Philip. But it was evident that Ward was a connector of worlds that otherwise had few connections, and that he flaunted those connections to give himself status among the rich and famous. We didn't know that another similar connector was the Thursday Club – indeed, we never discovered the club's existence.

But we did talk to another club member, the professional portraitist Feliks Topolski, after hearing that he knew Ward. Topolski seemed to relish being swept up in our net and, without any prompting, said, 'I'll talk about anything – except Prince Philip.' We paused right there. It was the first time anyone had mentioned Philip. 'OK,' we said, still processing the moment. Then we pressed on: it turned out that Topolski was not only a useful source on Ward but he knew about the ménage in which Mandy Rice-Davies and Christine Keeler shared the flat at Wimpole Mews, and about Ivanov's visits to Keeler. Afterwards we considered whether to follow up the lead on Philip but put it aside for the moment – the political strands of the story were leading us to Macmillan and why the Prime Minister had been gulled into accepting Profumo's lies for so long, and we had an interview the following day at Downing Street for an off-the-record briefing from Macmillan's press secretary.

Two days later, the *Sunday Times* switchboard put a call through to me saying that a man called Shaw wanted to speak to me 'in an official capacity'. Shaw said he was an official of the security services and would be obliged if I, together with my colleagues Hall and Wallington, would meet him the following morning at St Ermin's Hotel, close to St James's Park Tube station.

We went at the appointed time, directed to a room on the third floor. Shaw, a man I estimated to be in his mid-fifties, was flanked by two much younger and more sharply dressed men – I had a feeling that they did not normally work with Shaw and that, perhaps, they were the real instigators of the meeting. Shaw said he had been following our stories in the paper and said they had been 'illuminating'. He asked if we were writing a book, and I confirmed that we were. He was aware that we had been briefed at Downing Street. Then he handed over to one of the younger men. It was obvious that he knew about more or less every interview we had so far conducted, and he asked if anyone had mentioned Prince Philip. We looked at each other – once again, we were taken by surprise. I said that Topolski had mentioned him but that we had no interest in Philip. He was irrelevant to the story we were telling.

'*Irrelevant?*' piped up the other younger man in disbelief, as though almost offended by the thought. '*Really?*' Shaw also seemed surprised by my response. I explained that the gravity of the political crisis provoked by Profumo was the focus of our book, together with the forthcoming trial of Ward, who had been arrested and charged that he 'did knowingly live wholly or in part on the earnings of prostitutes'. That was more than enough to keep us busy. The two younger men did not seem persuaded, but Shaw said, 'So be it,' and the interview was over. There was no explicit warning. As we went into the street Wallington said, 'How the hell did they know about every bloody interview we have had?' That was truly unnerving, and we never had an answer, but the logical suspicion was that they had a source inside the paper. Discussing the whole thing much later with somebody familiar with the security services, and knowing by then that Ward himself had had a minder at MI5 because he had volunteered, some-what garrulously, to exploit his contacts with Ivanov to keep them informed of Soviet intentions in London, we determined that 'Shaw' was a pseudonym for an MI5 official and that the other two men were probably from Buckingham Palace's own security detail.

The case against Ward was an establishment stitch-up. He was no pimp, any more than Keeler and Rice-Davies were prostitutes. But his role as the great connector had made him suddenly vulnerable. From his flat in Wimpole Mews he had served at the centre of a kind of sexual bourse in which girls were introduced to powerful men and consensual affairs followed, sometimes ending in marriage, mostly not. Once he was charged, he became a pariah and his list of patients went from sixty to four in a week. He didn't wait to be sentenced. With the jury still deliberating, he took thirty-five grains of Nem-butal, enough to kill a horse, and died in hospital three days later. Some time afterwards, a later member of the Insight team, Phillip Knightley, reported on a conversation with a lawyer who told him that in the final days of the trial, the judge – Sir Archie Pellow Mar-shall, an unworldly and puritanical man nicknamed by colleagues 'the hen' – had received a phone call from 'a person very high up in the judiciary'. That person asked if Marshall was confident of getting a conviction and the judge had replied, 'Don't worry, I'll get him on the immoral earnings charge.'

Philip escaped attention. His associations with Ward were then known to very few people outside the circuit of the Thursday Club. At the time we did not even discover that Ward's portrait of him had been on the cover of the *Illustrated London News*.

Two days before Ward committed suicide, an elegantly suited man called at a Bloomsbury art gallery that was staging a show of Ward's drawings. He purchased every drawing of members of the royal family that was up for sale, including those of Philip, Princess Margaret, the Duchess of Gloucester and the Duke of Kent. Without revealing his name, he handed over a bank draft for £5,000 and took the portraits with him. They were never seen again. It was widely believed that the man was Sir Anthony Blunt, Surveyor of the Queen's Pictures, a man used to removing compromising evidence, and with his own enduring secrets he hoped to keep.

CHAPTER 11

MONEY TROUBLE

Tony came back into my professional life a year before the Profumo affair. Denis Hamilton hired him for the *Sunday Times* as a photographer to work primarily for the magazine, although his title was artistic adviser. The deal was that he would get £5,000 a year but work only a total of nine months, to allow for his royal duties. That sum caused some pain inside the paper because it was higher than the salaries of most of the senior editors, and it caused outbreaks of overheated horror from the usual critics of royal privileges. These included David Astor, who wrote in *The Observer*: 'It will inevitably seem unfair to rival newspapers and magazines that the Queen's close relative is used for the enlargement and enrichment of the Thomson empire.' I am sure Astor was sincere, but his outrage was partly personal – Hamilton had realised faster than other editors that Tony the photographer did not see why having moved into the gilded cage of royalty he should have to give up his true vocation. Mark Boxer, the editor of the magazine, knew this and it was he who told Hamilton, which led to Tony being hired.

It was not Antony Armstrong-Jones who joined the paper but Lord Snowdon. When Princess Margaret became pregnant, she and the royal family decided that Margaret's heirs should have titles, and this meant that one had to be found for Tony. I knew that Tony valued his family's Welsh background; like other Welshmen who became famous, he felt that in the constellation of British cultures Wales was the underdog. I didn't at first realise that Tony wanted to express this in a grandiose way; that didn't seem his style. But it was: his first choice was Earl of Carnarvon, but there was one of those already. So instead he took the name of a mountain, albeit a relatively small mountain. (Inevitably, some wit declared that he had made a mountain out of a molehill.) A month later, in November 1961, an heir was born, David, to become Viscount Linley.

At the magazine and then later at the newspaper, where I became managing editor in charge of the news, I worked closely with Tony and Mark Boxer to find him assignments that were worthy of his gifts. Part of the deal was that his credit would be no larger than that given to other photographers, both staff and freelance, and at first it was 'photographs by Lord Snowdon', until it was later shortened to the iconic simplicity of 'Snowdon'.

At first I felt an unaccustomed awkwardness in dealing with him – it wasn't his fault, it was mine. There was the issue of how to refer to his wife. On that point, Tony was always firm: it was Princess Margaret. Second, but equally exploratory, was gauging whether being Lord Snowdon had altered the candid self-knowledge he had always shown with me. From that first assignment on the Bowery in New York, it was one of the qualities I liked in him. He still didn't turn on the Eton posh with anyone; the accent was combined with the same quick and levelled wit he had deployed talking to those hard-luck cases as they donned their Santa gear.

But, of course, he wasn't really the same. He had become the sole subject of a daring social experiment: the first commoner to gain admission to the Windsor bloodline. Superficially, it seemed like a progressive idea: Tony and Margaret, the breakaway couple who would give a much-needed shot of excitement to an otherwise hidebound family. Neither of them was actually equipped to live up to this role

– because it *was* role-playing and it was not really natural to either of them in very different ways, shaped by their contrasting backgrounds. For official engagements in public, Tony adopted Prince Philip's tic of walking one step behind his partner with hands clasped behind his back and head pitched slightly forward to suggest an amiable interest in his surroundings while remaining the lesser figure of public interest. But he looked, and was, bored. Margaret was never anything like as dutiful as her sister in public engagements. If it was a cultural event – a film premiere, a night at the theatre or ballet – she was animated and happy and if, as usual, Tony was with her, they were convincing avatars of the Swinging Sixties. But if it was one of the obligatory visits beyond London to celebrate municipal achievers, she could barely conceal her haste to leave.

However, it was in his new level of domestic comforts that Tony's life had been changed in an inescapable way. It was here that his style of life was most clearly extracted from normality as most people know it: he had to accept what was normal for his wife and the family he had married into. Margaret's household was officially managed by the palace-appointed comptroller, Major the Honourable Francis Legh (illustrating the inbreeding of the palace network of officials, he was the nephew of Sir Piers 'Joey' Legh, previously glimpsed when, as equerry to George VI, he introduced the young princesses to Peter Townsend). Tony himself directed five of the household staff: the chef, the butler, the under-butler, the chauffeur and the footman. The housekeeper, the nanny, the nursemaid, the kitchen maid and Margaret's dresser were all handled separately by Margaret. Tony had never had any servants until he married. He ran a casual, bohemian style of bachelor ménage where he was self-sufficient and able to provide anything from a fried breakfast to a late-night glass of champagne and mend anything that broke from a light switch to a motorcycle. Throughout her whole life Margaret never lifted a finger to carry out any chore – she never even learned how to switch on an electric kettle. She embodied a sense of royal entitlement that the Romanovs would have shared and that Tony could never embrace. (The Queen lived in a similar cocoon of imperial splendour, but she had no choice; it came with the job. Margaret was under no obligation to sustain this style, but she did.)

All of this cost a lot of money. At the time Tony joined the *Sunday Times* we were at the start of an investigation into the costs to taxpayers of maintaining the royal family in the style to which they were accustomed. We never discussed this with Tony and I had no intention of doing so, nor would he have responded had I done so. Hamilton had told him that there would never be any discussions with him that were not related to his work. But we had already done enough reporting to know that in one respect, at least, Tony had been unfairly attacked for the way he had handled work carried out at his royal household, the twenty-room apartment known as 1A Kensington Palace. As was often the case with attacks on the royal family's expenses, this one was initiated by the gadfly republican Labour Member of Parliament for West Fife, Willie Hamilton. He had written more than 100 letters of complaint to the Ministry of Works, which was responsible for the maintenance of the palace and the grounds.

Unlike any of the other royal properties occupied by the family, Kensington Palace was architecturally a national treasure in every sense of the phrase. It began its life as a palace in 1689 under the direction of King William III and Queen Mary II, who were rare examples of monarchs with taste. They had it converted from a Jacobean mansion on the same site in what was then the village of Kensington. The conversion and enlargement were put into the hands of Sir Christopher Wren, Surveyor of the King's Works and the architect who bequeathed London more fine buildings than any before or since. It wasn't a *sui generis* Wren creation on the scale, for example, of his

Royal Naval Hospital at Greenwich. But the project was carried out with Wren's control of detail and his extraordinary ability to create majestic interiors without grandiose exteriors, as he notably did with his many churches. He also acted as patron to the best craftsmen in the land.

Of all the members of the Windsor family, Tony was the only one with any sense of how exquisite Kensington Palace was and he was appalled at the neglect it had suffered at the hands of the Ministry of Works. No. 1A had been hit by an incendiary bomb during the Blitz. The damage done by the fire, and by the fire brigade in fighting the fire, had never been more than patched over. It needed an extensive restoration, balancing the necessary modernisation of its plumbing, wiring and heating with work that honoured the quality of its original craftsmanship. Like Wren, Tony knew where to go for that quality, for example, finding black and white Welsh slate from a quarry owned by his godfather, Michael Duff, for the floor of the entrance hall. He called on his uncle, Oliver Messel, a distinguished designer, to provide a bookcase in keeping with the seventeenth-century carpentry. A new fireplace in the main drawing room was actually an old one, salvaged by Tony from a Victorian mansion that was being demolished. A large carpet made in Spain was donated by the aldermen of the City of London. A baby grand piano was a gift from Tony's mother and stepfather. Tony himself improvised to give the utilitarian Ministry of Works doors more heft by gluing mahogany panels to them. A beautiful embroidered bedspread for Margaret's bedroom was made by the School of Needlework.

The initial budget for this renovation was £70,000, but according to the official figures released at the time it ended up costing £85,000, an eye-watering sum to most people at a time when a new four-bedroom house in a fashionable London suburb could be bought for around £12,000. In reality, the work cost far more. An accounting released decades later put the sum at £300,000, more than £5 million in today's money. At the time, the admitted overrun of £15,000 was enough to make Willie Hamilton and fellow watchdogs apoplectic.

Had this been truly a case of a royal couple carelessly spraying public money on a vanity project to satisfy their own sense of luxurious entitlement, it would have been lamentable. But it wasn't. It was the real price of restoring a treasured national heritage property to an expected standard. The larger role of Kensington Palace was to serve as a royal compound for the younger members of the family who were bringing up their children in the capital. Tony had set the standard for how the rest of the complex should be upgraded – and put No. 1A on a foundation that others would later honour and continue to improve. In 1981, Prince Charles and Princess Diana moved into Apartment 8, a short walk from 1A. In 2017, Prince William and Kate Middleton, the Duke and Duchess of Cambridge, moved into 1A after another refurbishment that cost £12 million. Prince Harry and Meghan Markle later moved (briefly) into Nottingham Cottage, a charming two-bedroom annexe of the palace.

The Queen herself was not directly in the line of fire over the Kensington Palace expenditures. As was often the case, Margaret provided a convenient lightning rod to attract complaints of extravagance. This began to annoy Margaret and Tony with its unfairness, but they could not make a public response. Nonetheless, the Queen had cause to take notice of the perceptible groundswell of protest about why the public purse still had to pay for a royal cavalcade that had more in common with past imperial grandeur than it did with a diminished modern role: millions of the Queen's subjects were existing on less than £10 a week, and at least half a million children lived in conditions of deep poverty. In 1959, Geoffrey Bocca, one of Lord Beaverbrook's favourite feature writers, had written of a 'Cheshire cat monarchy, consisting of a bright smile surrounded by nothing, a frightened, timorous monarchy, hoping not to be noticed so that the death sentence may be delayed'. But things had changed since then. They *were* being noticed. For example, there was a studied reluctance in the palace to accept that survival might mean demonstrating a readiness to cut back on opulent trappings that had no place any longer in either the nation's role or the Queen's.

The civil list, through which Parliament controls the royal purse, dates from the seventeenth century and was initially designed to stop kings spending money on mistresses. By the mid-twentieth century it was funding the most luxurious family lifestyle in the world, including the two small airliners of the Queen's Flight, maintained by the Royal Air Force; the special string of carriages forming the Royal Train; and what had become the most conspicuous target for scrutiny, *Britannia*. The very term 'royal yacht' had the ring of a past age, but the fact was that *Britannia* was by far the grandest ever built. Her eighty-two predecessors, beginning with one built for Charles II, were basically sporting yachts that never ventured outside British waters. *Britannia* was the first to be a truly ocean-going vessel. The mystery is how such an extravagance was possible when *Britannia* was conceived in 1951, a time of continuing post-war austerity. Two gestures were offered to mollify critics, both disingenuous: she was designed to be adapted as a hospital ship in time of war, and in the event of a nuclear Armageddon she would cruise off the north-west coast of Scotland with the royal family aboard with her hatches battened down until the nuclear fallout dissipated. Firstly, she was never to be needed as a hospital ship because they were an idea whose time ended with the Crimean War and the age of gunboat diplomacy. Secondly, with only a four-minute warning likely before a nuclear strike, there would hardly be time for the family to pack their life jackets never mind reach *Britannia*'s berth.

Britannia's maiden voyage was in April 1954, when she called at

Malta to collect Prince Charles and Princess Anne and then sailed the short distance to Tobruk, Libya, to pick up the Queen and Philip at the end of a tour of the Commonwealth. *Britannia* was far from being an example of the latest ideas in naval architecture. She did not have the sleek lines of an ocean liner but rather the tubby, broad-beamed look of a Clyde ferry boat – perhaps not surprising since she was built at Clydebank in the John Brown shipyard. Because of this, she had a tendency to roll in high seas, which meant that anyone without sea legs was prone to suffer acutely from seasickness in even a heavy swell.

At the Queen's direction, the interiors were designed by Sir Hugh Casson to replicate, as far as feasible, the private quarters of Buckingham Palace, with chintz-covered armchairs and matching carpets and curtains. There was a similarly decorated state dining room that seated fifty-six people. (During Tony and Margaret's honeymoon she had insisted on wearing full evening dress at dinner; the pair of them must have seemed strangely feudal at a table that was largely empty.) Even the ship's telephones were replicas of those used at the palace, not those used by the Royal Navy. The strangest feature was the wheelhouse. Instead of being on a bridge above deck it was below deck with no view of water at all – the man at the wheel was blind, depending on voice tubes linked to the bridge. And she was the last Royal Navy vessel in which the crew slept in hammocks.

Tony and Margaret's Caribbean honeymoon aboard the royal yacht had inevitably renewed the accounting instincts in Willie Hamilton. He requested, and received, information from the Ministry of Defence on the costs of running *Britannia*. This revealed that in five years she had been used for just 337 days and that a large part of that time was spent for purposes of leisure, including voyages around the beautiful islands of north-west Scotland when the Queen was at Balmoral, and to Cowes and the Isle of Wight when she was at Osborne, the Isle of Wight retreat built for Queen Victoria. *Britannia* cost £2.25 million, the equivalent of more than £40 million now, to build and fit out. In 1962 she had a refit at a cost of more than £60,500. In defence of the royal expenditures, Lord Cobbold, the Lord Chamberlain, said that the Queen's duties were so arduous that she could never take 'a complete holiday'. As we reported this in the *Sunday Times*, we noted that the Queen actually spent a third of the year at her various rural estates.

Willie Hamilton's objective was to portray the monarchy as 'a dying industry'. He dismissed the idea that it could be preserved by reforms: 'It is difficult to believe that in a century in which old institutions based on heredity, ancient rituals and meaningless pomp are being challenged as irrelevant and even dangerous appendages to the body politic, the monarchy, however tarted up, can survive beyond the end of the present reign.'

But Hamilton could not sink *Britannia*. Macmillan's government knew that for the moment most people thought that Hamilton's parsimony was out of place, the nit-picking of a latter-day Scrooge. The royal yacht would continue for another forty years, maintained as a symbol of regal status appropriate to a seafaring nation. There were to be further honeymoons aboard her for the royal family: Princess Anne and Captain Mark Phillips; Prince Charles and Princess Diana; Prince Andrew and Sarah Ferguson – proving that a honeymoon on *Britannia* was no assurance of continued marital bliss. Indeed, it might be seen as a curse. All the marriages launched aboard her ended in divorce, including that of Tony and Margaret.

In all fairness, *Britannia* should not be remembered as a floating palace of pleasure so much as a floating version of Buckingham Palace with the same peculiar upper bourgeois tastes in furnishings. She was not in any way comparable to the billionaire-owned superyachts, with their own helicopters and submarines, favoured today by Russian oligarchs and the titans of Silicon Valley. The forerunners of these vessels were really created by two Greek shipping magnates, Stavros

Niarchos and Aristotle Onassis. In the 1950s and 1960s, their luxury yachts were fixtures of the Mediterranean summer playgrounds of the rich and famous; both Niarchos and Onassis sought status by inviting illustrious guests to cruise with them. Winston Churchill was a frequent guest of Onassis, while Niarchos invited Margaret and Tony to his private island, Spetsopoula, and the yacht took them on a tour of some of the historic sites of ancient Greece. Margaret and Tony knew full well that they had now joined an elite list of highly desirable guests and they were happy to go along for the ride. The young Aga Khan, who had succeeded his playboy father in 1957, had gambled on building an £80 million resort on Sardinia, then a backward and relatively unglamorous island, and he pulled off a much-needed publicity coup by inviting the royal couple to stay, as well as giving them a cruise on his yacht.

And so yes, this was the new Tony who was also a working photographer with us at the *Sunday Times* with the credit of Lord Snowdon. While the terms of his contract ruled out any royal portraits, his elevation to a previously undreamed-of level of celebrity was of great professional use to him – and us. There were few people who would turn down a request to have their portrait taken by him, an ease of access that the editors of other papers seethed about but were powerless to curb.

However, this seeming advantage also had a downside. Tony became typecast in a way that he had not been before. Instead of continuing as a photojournalist, he was working in a narrower range, mostly with portraits. This was a time when photojournalism was entering a golden age in Britain. There were several reasons, the main one being that other newspapers were forced to follow the *Sunday Times* and introduce magazines, which provided both the space and print quality that had been lacking. For security reasons, Tony, as a member of the royal family, could never be allowed to put himself at risk in situations where the best photojournalists made their most impact – for example, in war zones or in places where his personal protection could not be guaranteed. Among the talented new generation of photographers who competed with Tony were two with outstanding gifts: Don McCullin and David Bailey. McCullin was discovered by *The Observer* when they saw a portfolio of his work covering a local gang of his contemporaries in a working-class area of north London. He was to become legendary as a war photographer, particularly in Vietnam. Bailey – he was always known simply as Bailey – also from a poor East End background, had a very different but equally individual eye... for the libidinous icons of Swinging London, of whom he became the most enduring chronicler. It was said that he made love to women through the lens of his camera and that they responded in kind.

Mark Boxer's choice of Bailey to shoot the cover of the *Sunday Times* magazine's first issue was astute. Bailey's ability to identify the cultural stars of the time was, if anything, sharper even than Tony's. Bailey had come up from the streets in a way that was alien to Tony and his sensibilities, and now Tony, as well as being posh, was royal. Bailey cleverly decided to show how he embraced both low and high life in a portfolio of portraits of celebrities as varied as the Beatles, Cecil Beaton and the East End mobsters the Kray twins – and Tony. He packaged this work in a new format, a box of poster-sized high-quality prints. Tony blew a gasket when he discovered that he was included in the same evaluation of fame as the psychopathic Krays and prevented the publication of an American edition by withholding his signed permission. (The hairdresser Vidal Sassoon did the same thing because he felt that Bailey had made him resemble a gangster.) Tony's response was widely seen as a mean move against a fellow photographer who was excelling him in the impact of his work. It was also a marker of Tony's new level of influence as a royal with a title – the American publishers were more susceptible to pressure from him than any London publisher would have been.

As we worked together at the *Sunday Times*, I noticed a strange quirk in Tony's behaviour. He was being paid far more than the staff photographers, some of whom were at least his equal in talent. But he was always agitated about money, wanting the paper to cover all of his expenses on an assignment even if some were dubious. The more time he spent in the company of the very rich, the more he seemed to worry that he had to be seen as living up to their level. Other people outside the paper noticed it too – Len Deighton, the breakthrough novelist of the hour with *The Ipcress File* (I met him when we worked together at *The Observer* to create his novel cooking guide, the cook-strip), asked me, 'Why does Tony always act as though he's skint?' I had no answer. Perhaps living with a royal with all of Margaret's entitlements and moving among a family who never carried money had created this unsettling complex. For whatever reason, it remained with him for the rest of his life.

CHAPTER 12

BEWARE THE KINGMAKERS

In October 1963, the Queen was drawn into a political crisis that, at the time, appeared to have compromised her. The impression was left that the monarch's tradition of neutrality when a new Prime Minister was being selected had been breached. This was, in fact, unfair, but such high passions were aroused that the suggestion of a royal misstep lingered for years afterwards. I was closely involved in reporting the crisis at first hand and saw it very differently.

The drama really began in July, during the high summer fever of the Profumo affair. At the *Sunday Times* Insight team, we were drawing together the first detailed timeline of the political course of the crisis and it was damning of the way in which the Prime Minister had handled it. The ultimate mystery was why Macmillan had not personally interviewed Profumo as the first rumours of the scandal circulated. Before he finally confessed, Profumo had been interrogated four times by ministers and officials and he held steadfastly to the line he took in his statement of innocence to the House of Commons; had he faced the Prime Minister, he might well have cracked. We discovered that the security services had taken 123 days to give Downing Street a dossier on Ward, Keeler and Ivanov. In other words, there were plenty of other people who looked derelict. But once Profumo confessed, the raging dogs of Fleet Street and Westminster fell upon the Prime

Minister. The *Daily Mail* headline was 'MAC: THE END'. The *Mirror* declared, 'His future, short of a miracle, will be brief.'

As the spooks who called us to the meeting to warn us off Philip knew, two of us, Jeremy Wallington and me, had gone to Downing Street to discuss Macmillan's failure to act. This was not a normal off-the-record briefing. We were not members of the Westminster lobby system, in which accredited political correspondents are briefed on condition that their sources are not revealed. We never accepted those terms. But the paper's veteran Westminster correspondent, James Margach, had become an early supporter of our work and frequently fed us tips that he could not act on himself. When we showed Margach the damning timeline, he phoned Macmillan's press secretary, Harold Evans, and persuaded him to see us.

Evans was an unruffled, taciturn veteran who had developed a subtle style in spinning the Prime Minister's side of a story. It helped that he had Macmillan's total confidence and that he revered the Prime Minister for his unflappable command of the office. Wallington handed him a pasted-up assembly of our timeline. He considered it silently for a minute or so and then said, 'I think I can help you.' Indeed he did: he filled out gaps in our knowledge of who had known what and when, and he told us who had been present at the interrogations of Profumo. And then I asked him the obvious big question: why had Macmillan not interrogated Profumo himself?

His explanation was astonishing – but credible. Margach had told us that the huge unspoken-of shadow over Macmillan's life was Lady Dorothy's long affair with Robert Boothby. Many people in Westminster knew about it, but it was never reported. Evans now brought it up. Macmillan, he explained, never wanted to know of any of the sexual adventures that the rest of Westminster found engrossing. He was above such squalid gossip. He had believed Profumo's denial and could never believe that any Member of Parliament, let alone any of his own ministers, could so brazenly lie in a public statement. Members of Macmillan's clubs didn't lie, he said. It therefore came as a jarring shock to the Prime Minister and his own expectations of decency when Profumo's perfidy was exposed. Moreover, there were far more important issues – like negotiating a nuclear test ban treaty – that needed his time. Another worry was the case of Kim Philby.

We could understand Macmillan's workload as well as Evans: as if Profumo were not enough of a scandal, on 1 July the government had revealed that Philby, a Middle East correspondent for *The Observer* and *The Economist* who had disappeared from Beirut six months earlier, was in fact the long-sought Third Man in the ring of Soviet moles who had penetrated and undermined British intelligence for decades. This was another awkward part of Macmillan's past, because he was the Foreign Secretary in 1955 when Philby – with as much bravura as Profumo – had glibly denied any wrongdoing and been believed. (The full, astonishing Philby story would be a part of Insight's own workload for several years to come.)

What to make of Evans's defence of Macmillan? We were restricted in retelling it because what we called 'the cuckold defence' could never be put into print for fear of libel charges. Moreover, it seemed to me like a convenient piece of pop psychology that would need a more clinical assessment than we were able to provide. We did use a direct quote, unattributed, from Evans about how Macmillan saw his own state of mind at the time: 'My spirit is not broken, but my zest has gone.' Our published rationalisation of Macmillan's behaviour was that he had suffered from a 'wilful amnesia' – but we did not explain its causes.

In fact, through the rest of the summer the embattled Prime Minister seemed able to hang on to power until the next real test of his leadership, the Conservative Party conference in Blackpool in October.

As it turned out, Macmillan never made it to Blackpool. As the delegates began arriving, he was in the King Edward VII Hospital for Officers in Marylebone facing an operation for an enlarged prostate, not yet knowing whether the problem was malign or benign. (Macmillan's life had been saved in the same hospital during the First World War when he was sent there, seriously wounded, from the Battle of the Somme.)

The Blackpool conference was an annual assembly and display of the Conservative Party's unique culture and grassroots following: 4,000 delegates from 547 English and Welsh constituencies. Here was a piece of England (and Wales) showing up as one of the most enduring and restless political tribes in Europe, if not the world. Successful Tory Prime Ministers had to know how to manage, soothe and generally schmooze all the factions within the tribe, which always spanned a full gamut from progressives to reactionaries. In this art Macmillan had, indeed, always been Supermac. It was also a constituency that – it was reasonable to believe without any evidence – the Queen would be comfortable among; they were certainly solid monarchists to the last person.

At around 5 p.m. on the first day of the conference, the dapper, skeletal figure of the Foreign Secretary, the Earl of Home, arrived on stage to make a short speech, assumed to be one of emollient greeting. Instead, he said he had been asked to read a message to them from the Prime Minister. The punchline was buried in the second paragraph: '…it will not be possible for me to carry the physical burden of leading the party at the next general election … In these circumstances I hope that it will soon be possible for the customary processes of consultation to be carried on within the party about its future leadership.'

And so it was that the country – and, critically, the Queen – suddenly faced the prospect of choosing a new Prime Minister who would take power without having been elected by a full national vote. It was only the fourth time in history that a monarch had been put in the position of approving the appointment of a Prime Minister who had not run for office in a general election. Since the mid-1800s, the norm had been that elections offered a simple binary choice between one party and another and the leader of the winning party automatically became Prime Minister. That did not guarantee that the monarch was happy with the result. In 1866, Queen Victoria privately described the then-elected Prime Minister, William Gladstone, as 'this half-crazy and in many ways ridiculous old man'. But Victoria had to accept the people's choice. Elizabeth II may well have formed similar opinions of some of the Prime Ministers she has officially blessed, but we will probably never know. In 1963, the choice of the new leader of the Tory Party, and therefore the new Prime Minister, was left to a mechanism over which the Queen had no say and which was concocted as the party was thrown into ferocious internal combat. In fact, there were no 'customary processes of consultation'. But Macmillan, as infirm as he was, had his own strong idea of what should happen and he made it happen, without any recourse to Buckingham Palace.

This was a compelling political saga, and Denis Hamilton decided that Insight should be the team to tell it as a chronological narrative in the same way we had tracked the Profumo affair. He gave me carte blanche to direct the coverage and to dive into it myself as I chose. The front page of the Weekly Review section was cleared for us for two successive weeks. The paper had never before attempted such an ambitious political coverage and I relished it. My first two decisions were fundamental to how it turned out. The first was to work alongside James Margach, who was our main reporter in Blackpool. I told him to file everything he could gather in raw form and that the rest of the team would supplement his reporting, while I would pull the whole thing together. But it was my second decision that unlocked the real secrets behind the public noise.

Winston Churchill's son Randolph was regarded as the wild man of the family, disarmingly conscious of how impossible it was to live up to the legend of his father, ferociously loyal to that legend, and belligerent against anyone disrespectful of it. As the assigned custodian of all of his father's papers, he was in control of how they were being reviewed and catalogued in preparation for the massive official biography. Randolph read the Insight book on Profumo, *Scandal 63*, and summoned me to his country seat at East Bergholt in Suffolk, where he was presiding over a team of researchers led by a young Martin Gilbert (later the renowned historian Sir Martin Gilbert). His purpose was, he said, to give me some background on Profumo that he thought would be useful as future guidance. What had been proposed as an afternoon visit was extended to an overnight stay, including a gloriously bibulous dinner followed by long nocturnal speculation about the future of the Tory Party.

I had been warned in advance that Randolph was widely reviled among his contemporaries, that he was boorish and near impossible to work with. That was not my experience on first contact. Martin Gilbert and his research staff were in awe of his memory of political events and his clear judgements on their significance. As I found out, this extended to his being able to deliver verbal reconstructions of whole scenes involving his father with verbatim accuracy. He had lived acutely at the confluence of great men as they steered Britain through a ravaging war and its aftermath, and he understood how much of a privilege it was. He was very honest about how hard it was to make a mark of his own in the presence of such a commanding father. I raised this with him in a long interview I did with him later for the *Sunday Times*. He said:

> Much as I revered and reverence him, I wasn't prepared just to be an
> aide-de-camp and go along, I wanted to have a show of my own. So,
> struggling to establish my own individuality and personality I often

said and wrote rather reckless things … I was looking to establish an individual position, and it's very hard to do so, obviously, when you're living in the shadow of the great oak tree – the small sapling, so close to the parent tree, doesn't perhaps receive enough sunshine. I became sort of bloody-minded, I suppose, and wanted to strike out on my own and adopted possibly rather an arrogant attitude towards people and institutions at a time when I didn't really have the ammunition or skill to hit the target. But I hold neither guilty feelings nor reproaches about that.

Randolph had had a lifelong love–hate relationship with Evelyn Waugh, including some wartime service together. At the time I arrived in East Bergholt they were conducting a civil exchange in correspondence about the one subject they agreed on: horticulture. Waugh was giving advice on the cultivation of tulip trees. But Randolph always provoked the bile in Waugh and when Randolph's doctors removed a tumour from one of his lungs and announced that it was benign, Waugh said it was 'a triumph of modern medicine to locate the one thing in Randolph that is benign'.

I never felt that way: as improbable as it had at first seemed to me, we hit it off and Randolph immediately became a close friend and for a long while the best inside source on British politics that Insight ever had. So my second decision was to return to East Bergholt and find out what he knew.

There were three viable candidates to succeed Macmillan. Each was idiosyncratic rather than ideological. The party's progressives favoured Rab Butler, a wealthy and patrician figure with a long track record of being effective in the Cabinet. The party's base in the more conservative shires wanted Lord Hailsham, a fiery orator who sometimes seemed on the brink of lunacy. Hovering timorously in the background, declaring that he really didn't want the job at all, was the Foreign Secretary, the 14th Earl of Home. If the Queen had any preference at all, it would have been for Home, a prototypical Scottish laird whom she knew well, and given the polarising effects of the other two candidates, he seemed a good and calming compromise. (At Eton he had been tutored by Sir Henry Marten, who had been the young Elizabeth's history tutor when she was being prepared for the throne.) There was also something perversely attractive in the idea of a man who protested at a moment of vicious party in-fighting that he had no taste for power, though there were concerns that he might be two sandwiches short of a picnic: much fun had been had at his expense when, on being appointed Foreign Secretary, he said it helped him to count by lining up matches on the table.

When I arrived at East Bergholt, a domestic crisis had overtaken the political one. Randolph's cook, having endured one too many of his tantrums, had fled in the night and deliberately turned off the refrigerator in reprisal, ruining a batch of his favourite dessert, home-made blackberry ice cream, and jeopardising dinner arrangements. Fortunately, Randolph's mistress, the wife of a complaisant neighbour, had moved in and recruited help to prepare and serve an ample meal, minus dessert. It soon became clear to me that Randolph had set up his own nerve centre to monitor the cabals that had gathered around Butler and Hailsham – Home had no cabal and was still behaving like a man who was above the squalor of a political horse race.

What followed after dinner landed me directly in the centre of the fight to decide the Tory leadership and, therefore, the next Prime Minister. During the course of the night, Randolph attempted to tele-phone the three candidates themselves as well as some of their lieuten-ants. He made sure that I was in earshot. Hailsham snorted grumpily that he thought he had had a deal with Home not to oppose him – a deal made, he said, while they sat in the back of a taxi – but he had heard that Home was coming off the fence. Butler was not taking any calls. Home picked up the phone himself, so amazing Randolph that he cupped his hand over the mouthpiece and said to me, 'He answers the phone himself, they live like bloody coolies these days.' He then said, 'Alec, I hear that you are the Prime Minister's own choice as the man to heal the wounds of division.' Home replied, 'Well, Randolph, I don't know about that, any such speculation would be premature.' Randolph replied firmly, 'Alec, steady on parade, steady on parade, that's what the party needs.' Home politely bid him goodnight. It was around one-thirty in the morning. There was one more call to make, to another Cabinet member, a Butler-backer and a hero to the progressives, Iain Macleod. He picked up the phone, too, but snapped, 'Fuck off, Randolph.'

Before we went to bed, Randolph reviewed the field. He had no time for Butler, whom he regarded as too flaccid and unequal to the challenge of facing the Labour Party's leader, Harold Wilson, in a general election. Hailsham had the balls to tear into Wilson but was too intemperate to unite the party. Home also lacked the appetite for the savagery of an election but had proved himself a safe pair of hands as Foreign Secretary and a natural unifier. Randolph liked Home, possibly because unlike Macleod and other Cabinet ministers he always took Randolph's calls. Home also knew that Randolph had his own direct line to President Kennedy and was a useful backchannel in the so-called special relationship with Washington. (I had once been present when Randolph made a 'hello, Jack' call to Kennedy.)

There was little time left to make the choice. The ritual required that the Queen would 'send for' the new Prime Minister as soon as the party – and Macmillan – had decided who that was to be. That meant that before she could send for anybody the Queen would have to see Macmillan in hospital to receive his advice and recommendation. It was a highly unusual situation because nobody, including the Queen, was clear about the ground rules. And, in fact, the party itself was still feuding about those rules. Barely two months earlier neither Hailsham nor Home, as peers of the realm, would have been eligible candidates. But at the end of July a Bill had been passed allowing hereditary peers to renounce their peerages, and Hailsham had already declared his intention to do so.

I returned to the office from East Bergholt on Thursday 17 October and it was apparent that Macmillan would have to hand over by Friday. Just as I was sharing the story of my night with Randolph with the Insight team, I had a call from Harold Evans in Downing Street. He wanted another meeting with me and Jerry Wallington to explain the Prime Minister's role. As it turned out, Evans outdid himself in the art of elliptical briefing. He explained that Macmillan had ordered that four groups should be consulted for their opinions on the successor: the Cabinet, the 350 Tory Members of Parliament, the Tories in the House of Lords and the heads of each constituency of the party across the country. This last 'sounding' was far less precise than the others and its opacity became an issue later. But Evans's key line, dropped without pause or comment, was '…when the Queen sends for Alec…' We understood the rules – no further question was to be asked; we had been given the scoop.

Of course, it was useless as a scoop because it was Thursday and we didn't publish until Sunday. But this briefing had consequences. As soon as we returned to the office, I went straight to see the paper's deputy editor, William Rees-Mogg (now far less well known than his eccentric son Jacob). William (never a Bill) wrote the paper's editorials (in longhand) at a time when Hamilton had steered it away from its old blind allegiance to the old Tory Party and towards progressive conservatism. He had been a helpful supporter of Insight from the start, when it was being attacked by other editors as a turn towards journalistic impertinence. When I delivered the word that Macmillan's choice was Home, the blood drained from William's face. 'It must not be. *It has to be stopped*,' he blurted with a passion I had never seen before.

He left in a hurry. At midnight, there was a meeting at 33 South Eaton Place in Belgravia, the home of Enoch Powell, the Minister of Health. It had been called by Iain Macleod as an urgent summons to all supporters of Rab Butler, although it was William Rees-Mogg who alerted Macleod and who joined a small band of ministers as they decided to try to stop Home. The meeting broke up at 2 a.m. and at some point around dawn a message was sent from them to Sir Michael Adeane, the Queen's private secretary, that there was a majority in the party for Butler – which was absolutely not true by that point. They asked for a delay of several days, believing that given more time Butler's strength could be confirmed. They seemed happy to forget that on Tuesday the Cabinet to which they belonged had voted unanimously to endorse the procedure that had eventually produced Home. In fact, a majority of the Cabinet now supported Home, who also had a narrow lead among junior ministers and backbenchers. The Tory peers, predictably, were overwhelmingly for Home. In any case, the Butler cabal's message was ignored by the palace and at 9.15 a.m. on Friday 18 October, Harold Macmillan's principal private secretary, Timothy Bligh, set off for Buckingham Palace to deliver the Prime Minister's official letter of resignation to Adeane, who then told Bligh that the Queen was ready to go to the hospital in Marylebone to receive the Prime Minister's proposal for who should succeed him. She was there by 11.15 a.m.

There had never been a meeting like this between an outgoing Prime Minister and the monarch. A week earlier, Macmillan's prostate gland had been removed in an operation that lasted an hour; there was no trace of cancer. Now, with the Queen on her way, he was wheeled out of his room in his bed, complete with attached tubes, and taken by lift to the matron's room on the ground floor. Adeane sat in an adjoining room, leaving the Queen seated beside Macmillan, the two of them alone. There is no record of what was actually said, but it was clearly an emotional moment for both of them. Macmillan had been an avuncular guide to the Queen and was well aware of the private as well as public strains of her life. On 8 October, President Kennedy had sent a personal letter to Macmillan, addressed 'Dear Friend,' after signing the nuclear test ban treaty, writing, 'History will eventually record your indispensable role in bringing about the limitation of nuclear testing; but I cannot let this moment pass without expressing to you my own keen appreciation of your signal contribution to world peace.' The Queen had seen behind Macmillan's 'unflappable' mask as he kept her informed of his frequently raw encounters with Nikita Khrushchev, proving to be the statesman the world needed. Now he told her that he felt too weak to speak spontaneously. Instead, he read a memorandum explaining how the 'soundings' taken of the party had come out in support of Home. He gave her a copy of the memorandum. More must have been said because the Queen spent half an hour by Macmillan's bedside before heading back to the palace. Just before 1 p.m. it was announced that she had sent for Home.

The following Sunday, the long Insight story, headlined 'HOW HOME WON', gave the *Sunday Times* the edge in explaining how thick with backroom intrigue the selection process had been, and particularly how the path for Home to win had been opened up by the bitter loathing of the Hailsham and Butler camps for each other. Some of the more dramatic details were from Randolph. Rees-Mogg had given us the outlines of the midnight cabal meeting at Powell's house. The Butler camp were sore losers and Iain Macleod decided to write a long piece for *The Spectator*, headlined 'THE MAGIC CIRCLE', claiming that a clique of Macmillan-led old-guard Tory elitists had stolen the premiership, implying that Macmillan himself had improperly steamrollered the Queen into accepting his choice. From my viewpoint, as someone without any political axe to grind and with all the deep In-sight reporting to go on, this charge was absurd. Powell, Macleod and Butler were themselves a symptom of the problem, not the solution: like the other factions, they were partisan networkers in a situation where the normal process could not work. Macmillan had improvised as decent a remedy as he could for the exigencies of the moment; the Queen had no power to do anything other than follow his guidance. Later, as Prime Minister, Home put through reforms that followed Labour Party practice: in future the Tory leadership would be decided by the parliamentary party.

There was, nonetheless, an undeclared force that had worked against Rab Butler. From my experiences with Randolph it became clear that the Churchill family, and many others in the Conservative Party with knowledge of how precarious Winston Churchill's position had been when he first came to power in 1940, would never forgive Butler for his behaviour in the country's darkest hour.

The key date was 17 June 1940. Churchill had been Prime Minis-ter since 10 May. On that day in June there was a chance encounter in St James's Park between Butler, who was under-secretary to Lord Halifax, the Foreign Secretary, and Björn Prytz, Sweden's ambassador in London. Halifax and Butler were among many, inside and out-side the government, who still held out a hope that total war with Hitler could be avoided by making 'peace' with him. Butler invited Prytz back to the nearby Foreign Office and relayed a message from Halifax that 'common sense and not bravado' would dictate the Brit-ish government's policy. In case that was too nuanced, Butler added that if and when peace negotiations began, Halifax might replace Churchill. When Prytz relayed this conversation back to Stockholm, it was intercepted by British intelligence and passed to Churchill. When Churchill confronted Halifax with the transcript, Halifax claimed it misrepresented his and Butler's words. That was clearly a lie because Prytz was fluent in English and had sent the message in English.

Halifax and Butler were at the edge of treason. But Churchill knew all too well that his future and the nation's were far from secure and that Halifax could not at that moment be sacked. But by the end of the year, with the nation behind him, he was confident enough to shunt Halifax off to Washington as British ambassador, neutering his influence in London and basically ending his political career. Churchill was kinder to Butler – and kinder than in the same circumstances others might have been. Butler was far younger than Halifax and an able administrator. Churchill chose him to design a sweeping reform of British education, which was successfully carried out in 1944. But the taint of appeasement clung to Butler and you could say that the Tory leadership contest in 1963 was actually decided in 1940.

Whether the Queen felt the same way about Butler is unknown. He had the manner of a natural mandarin, a class that the Queen was never comfortable with; they were too intellectual for her. That could never be said of Home, who, after kissing hands with the Queen, renounced his peerage and became Sir Alec Douglas-Home. She seemed pleased to have him in Downing Street. So, for different reasons, was the Leader of Her Majesty's Opposition, Harold Wilson. In a speech on the day that Sir Alec was anointed, he said:

> The message that has been sent out to the world is that in 1963 the government party in Britain selects its leader and the country's Prime Minister through the machinery of an aristocratic cabal. In this ruthlessly competitive, scientific, technical-industrial age, a week of intrigues has produced a result based on family and hereditary connections. The leader has emerged – an elegant anachronism.

In those two sentences, Wilson had not only defined an adversary; he had defined the theme of his own party's claim to power, and defined the Tory Party as the antithesis of himself. Wilson would be – in a phrase he later used – the apostle of change driven by and made necessary by 'the white-hot heat of technology'. The Tory Prime Minister, counting with the help of his matchsticks, was of another age. Wilson had also implied that the Queen had, whether willingly or not, been a party to an establishment stitch-up. Within a year the Tories would be gone. The Queen's hand would be kissed by a man bent on radical change – a force that the Queen would have to accommodate as best she was able.

CHAPTER 13

THE SLUMBER
OF CENTURIES

In 1849, Prince Albert, the one-man whirlwind of change in Buckingham Palace, spelled out his personal mission to the nation in a speech:

> No human pursuits make any material progress until science is brought to bear on them. Some cultures slumber for centuries but from the moment science has touched them with her magic wand, they have sprung forward ... Look at the transformation which has gone on around us since the laws of gravitation, electricity, magnetism, and the expansive power of heat have become known to us. It has altered the whole state of existence ... We owe this to science, and science alone; and she has other treasures in store for us, if we will but call her to our assistance.

Albert had a galvanic effect on British industrialists. They were open to innovation as a path to fortune and went forth into Victoria's empire and beyond to change the whole world – for example, with railways that instantly multiplied the speed of people and trade over land. Albert was less successful with his own family. Bertie, the Prince of Wales and future King, was seven years old and proving a stubborn and temperamental student, a trial to his tutors. Seeking improvement,

Albert imposed a regime of Teutonic rigour, with lessons from eight in the morning to six in the evening, six days a week. It didn't work. As prince and then as King Edward VII, Bertie was shaped by sloth and lust. He had no head for science. Albert's hope of establishing a lasting union between the monarchy and progress – private enterprise and private capital would prosper, he said, when connected with the authority of the Crown and the person of the Sovereign – never came to pass. He was the first and last renaissance man in Buckingham Palace.

And it would take well over a century before a like-minded Prime Minister crossed the palace threshold, in the person of Harold Wilson. The Queen, it is fair to say, had never encountered a Prime Minister like Wilson.

He did not instantly resemble a fiery agent of change. I first met him when, as Leader of the Opposition, he was deftly orchestrating the response to Profumo's lying statement to Parliament, already scenting Macmillan's blood in the water. Surrounded by hotter heads, he favoured patience and stealth rather than a frontal assault. On first encounter I felt like I was being assessed by a bank manager sizing me up to decide on the prudence of an overdraft, sucking on a pipe and gimlet-eyed. Wilson was the most academically distinguished politician to lead his party, having been appointed an Oxford don at the age of twenty-one. This governed his approach to every problem. He liked to amass information, sift it for significance and then find a consensus for action. Some other members of his Cabinet were equally donnish – nine of them had been to Oxford – but none was as politically astute. I don't know how well briefed on him the Queen was before he kissed hands, but he was about as far from his predecessor, the languid Scottish laird, as it was possible to be.

On 16 October, when Wilson set out for the palace, he wore the expected striped trousers of a morning suit but a normal suit jacket. It was as though he was describing his own feelings about the monarchy:

respect for protocol up to a point, but also intimation of change. With him, he took his wife Mary, their two sons, his father and the woman who had long been his office gatekeeper and conduit to the Labour Party, Marcia Williams. No Tory Prime Minister had turned up with such an entourage. There was a message here too: Wilson was proud of his father, an industrial chemist who had inspired his son to be an achiever. Wilson had won a scholarship to secondary school, been captain of the school and had a first-class degree from Oxford. This was a meritocratic family and at the age of forty-eight Wilson was an example of how far and how fast talent could rise without the boost of privilege. The family and Williams remained in a side room while Wilson was with the Queen.

Various accounts of the meeting were circulated afterwards. The palace's own spin was that the Queen surprised Wilson, and unsettled him, by immediately raising the issue of the future exchange rate for the pound, which was under pressure on the international currency markets. This story was nonsense and condescending. It wasn't until Wilson and his ministers were shown the Treasury's books that they realised that the Tories had bequeathed a huge deficit in the balance of payments. Wilson set up a new Department of Economic Affairs to bring clarity and design to economic policy and a new Ministry of Technology to promote science-based industries – an idea that had languished since Prince Albert had proposed it. At the recent Labour Party conference, Wilson had previewed his intention: 'The Britain that is going to be forged in the white heat of this revolution will be no place for restrictive practices or for outdated methods on either side of industry.'

Buckingham Palace itself would not have come out well from an audit of its own outdated methods or domestic arrangements. Like the country, the royals were living beyond their means. Since the Queen's accession, the costs of running the royal households, met by the state, had risen by 280 per cent. Some of the costs seemed Tudor-like in their lavishness and antiquity: Clarence House, the Queen Mother's residence, had a staff that included two peers, seven army officers, a Mistress of the Robes, two Ladies of the Bedchamber, three extra Ladies of the Bedchamber, four Women of the Bedchamber and six extra Women of the Bedchamber – a lot seemed to be necessary to sustain that bedchamber. It was said that the Queen Mother found Wilson uncomfortable to talk to. Perhaps she detected a hint of his Yorkshire Baptist austerity. But the tumbrils were not rolling down the Mall; there was no immediate threat to the comforts of the palaces.

Nonetheless, the peasants were restless. Neither the monarchy nor the government could escape the far more openly insubordinate spirit of the age. Denis Hamilton's *Sunday Times* was demonstrating that when a serious newspaper brought its authority to a deeper scrutiny of the news, it had a powerful effect. And the resurgence of social and political satire that began with *Beyond the Fringe* had gone national through television.

Of all the national institutions that over the years had been woven into the complex tapestry of British cultural life, probably the least likely to cause offence until now had been the BBC. Nominally independent, most vitally in its news coverage, the corporation was actually open to coercive policing from two directions. Internally, there was a board of governors who appointed the director general and who were supposed to make sure there were no transgressions of taste or political bias. Externally, there was the fact that the government decided the BBC's financial budget by setting the licence fee that every owner of a TV set paid as a kind of tax. And yet it was the BBC that now applied accelerant to the satire revival, lifting it from a relatively small metropolitan audience to one of many millions almost overnight.

At 10.50 p.m. on Saturday 24 November 1962, the BBC launched *That Was the Week That Was* – or, as it was more popularly known,

TW3. In the mind of one BBC executive who had a role in launching the programme, Donald Baverstock, the word 'satire' was poison: 'The word "satire" will not appear in the programme and will not be used in connection with it in our publicity.' It didn't matter what they called it. From almost the first minute, the programme shattered all the conventions of British political and social humour. The lampooning of Harold Macmillan begun by *Beyond the Fringe* became a weekly highlight as performed by Willie Rushton as a kind of benign, out-of-touch old buffer. There was a brilliantly heretical sketch in which the world's major religions were subjected to review by the criteria of consumer values; another on homosexuality in which one judge asks another, 'What do you give these homosexual johnnies?' and the other replies, 'Half a crown and an apple, generally.'

As one sacred cow after another was targeted, the royal family seemed off-limits. It was not until towards the end of the first series, in March 1963, that the taboo was broken. David Frost, the show's anchor, performed a monologue called 'The Royal Barge'. It had been written originally for *Beyond the Fringe* but was banned from public performance by the theatre censor, the Lord Chamberlain, on the grounds that it ridiculed the royal family. (The author was a young Cambridge graduate, Ian Lang, who later rose to become a Tory minister in Margaret Thatcher's government.) Frost had acquired the sketch and often performed it when he did stand-up comedy in clubs – it was part of a regular repertoire he called his 'Bumper Fun Book'. It had nothing like the bite of other *TW3* material, but because it featured the Queen it was considered risky for the BBC – even more so because it was as much mocking the BBC as the monarchy. Frost delivered it in the same fawning tones as the BBC's senior current affairs commentator, Richard Dimbleby:

The Royal Barge is, as it were, sinking. The sleek, royal-blue hull of the Barge is sliding gracefully, almost regally, beneath the waters of the Pool of London ... perhaps the lip readers amongst you will know what Prince Philip, Duke of Edinburgh, has just said to the captain of the Barge ... And now the Queen, smiling radiantly, is swimming for her life. Her Majesty is wearing a silk ensemble in canary yellow...

It seems so innocuous now. And it's doubtful if the Queen would have found any offence in it then; she might well have laughed, along with the 12 million of her subjects who were now watching *TW3* every Saturday. The whole problem with this kind of censorship was that a few assumed power in deciding what the many should enjoy, and that the few were inevitably trying to uphold the values of another age. That system was being undermined but was not yet finished, as the fate of *TW3* showed. The show's second season was in full force in October 1963 when Macmillan was replaced by Home, who provided the writers with an irresistible new target. Frost appeared as Benjamin Disraeli, as though sending in Disraeli's eloquent but barbed style a greeting to Home as his successor:

> Your bleak, deathly smile is the smile today not of a victor – but of a victim. You are the dupe and unwitting tool of a conspiracy ... of a tiny band of desperate men who have seen in you their last, slippery chance of keeping the levers of power and influence within their privileged circle...

Largely on the basis of this one sketch, the director general, Hugh Greene, decided that *TW3*'s second season should end prematurely at the end of 1963 and never return. Greene had been warned that the Tory government held in its hand the future of the BBC: the charter under which the corporation was allowed to exist and which determined its funding was up for a long-term renewal. Killing off the satirists was the price of making sure that the charter was renewed.

The programme was dead, but in its brief existence it, together with *Beyond the Fringe*, coalesced a potent band of talents who would go on to violate many shibboleths and be part of lasting changes to the way the British viewed any form of authority. Some of them were already friends and frequent guests of the one couple in the royal family who were as impatient with conformity as they were: Margaret and Tony.

The apartment at Kensington Palace developed into the same kind of social salon that the Duke and Duchess of Kent had established in Belgravia in the 1930s – indeed, one member of that set, Noël Coward, joined this one. At the piano, Margaret played and sang Coward songs and he swooned. 'She has an impeccable ear,' he noted in his diary, '… and her method of singing is really very funny.' In some ways the guest list seemed odd: in this supposedly more egalitarian age, a number of leading insurrectionists enthusiastically enlisted in what was really a form of royal patronage. Nobody better represented this contradiction than Kenneth Tynan. He was a self-declared republican, he championed the most anti-establishment playwrights and filmmakers, and he was openly louche – he announced that 'sex means spank and beauty means bottoms and always will' (he liked walloping bottoms with a hairbrush). But Tynan was happy to serve as a kind of informal impresario to the Margaret and Tony set, introducing them to a stream of show-business celebrities.

In fact, the definition of celebrity was changing as categories of fame changed. During the run of *TW3*, David Frost was declared 'the most famous man in Britain' – much to his delight and the chagrin of his fellow performers. Margaret and Tony's salon elevated and changed their own kind of celebrity by association with the eclectic fame of their guests. And their own gilded celebrity made the royal family itself seem more modish than perhaps they either wanted or deserved to be. Tony understood and enjoyed his fame and sometimes pushed it upwards in ways that must have had courtiers at the palace choking over their morning tea. For instance, one night as he and Margaret were dressing to go out to a formal dinner, he went with a camera into Margaret's bathroom as she was bathing. Her hair was already coiffed as she lay soaking and relaxing – something she often did. Tony took the tiara that she had chosen to wear that night and put it on her head and, stepping back to frame a shot that discreetly concealed her nakedness, he took his most impudent and yet beautiful portrait of her, using just natural light, in which she smiles luminously into his lens. Tony's legs are visible in a mirror near the bath. Not even David Bailey could have seduced as natural and intimate a look from a subject as this. The portrait appeared only after Margaret's death, when Tony included it an exhibit of his portraits. It conveys more of the quality of the bond between them when the marriage was working than anyone else was able to see at the time.

But association with this wing of the royal family could bend brains. Those not invited to Kensington Palace got snarky with those who were. John Wells, a comedian, character actor and contributor to the satirical weekly *Private Eye* who became a *TW3* regular, was an early victim of such a feud. He was the son of a rural vicar and a lethal mimic of middle-class sanctimony, and for some reason this persona greatly amused Princess Margaret, who called up *Private Eye* asking for 'Jawn'. His colleagues at the *Eye* scorned what they considered his social climbing and continuous name dropping. Tynan, too, was attacked for what also became a common charge against some members of the Wilson government – that he had turned into a 'champagne socialist'. Tynan, though, had discovered that it was a lot more fun to be a champagne socialist than a hair-shirt socialist of the kind who reviled him and the monarchy. Later, the great American social observer Tom Wolfe gave his own term to the phenomenon of radicals seen to be too happy to fraternise with high society: radical chic. Margaret and Tony really pioneered that movement.

But of all the cast of talents drawn to Margaret and Tony, the most unexpected and the strangest was Peter Sellers. This relationship began when Tony was assigned to shoot a group portrait of the creators and lead performers of *The Goon Show*, the great 1950s catalyst of British surrealistic comedy on BBC Radio – Sellers, Spike Milligan and Harry Secombe. In her twenties, Margaret was addicted to the Goons and even, some said, actually infected by them in the form of a Secombe-like high-pitched giggle that she developed. Tony told Sellers of his wife's addiction and Sellers agreed to join a party at Kensington Palace. In Margaret's eyes, Sellers was instantly a trophy celebrity. And Sellers reciprocated, which amazed many who knew him. For Sellers was a tortured soul with very few real friends and an instinctive aversion to social engagement. The film director John Boulting, who conjured up one of Sellers's finest performances in *I'm All Right Jack*, as the spiritually desolate Marxist trade union official Fred Kite, said of him, 'He is a human being who has need of friendship but whose great tragedy is that he is incapable of the real sacrifices that flow from deep friendships.' And yet Margaret and Sellers clicked from the moment they met. Tony also got along with Sellers, though David Bailey said that to him Sellers and Tony 'were like two old witches together, so nasty to everybody'. Boulting recalled that Sellers had frequently and openly mocked the monarchy. At a London film premiere he was presented to the Queen, who, in one of her rote questions, asked what he was doing. 'Standing here,' he said sullenly. But he had now totally succumbed to Margaret's spell.

While at Apartment 1A, Kensington Palace, the joy of partying stretched long into the night, Buckingham Palace was relatively joyless. Prince Charles and Princess Anne saw very little of Swinging London. Charles was incarcerated in the penitentiary-like regime of

Gordonstoun and Princess Anne was a boarder at Benenden in Kent, an academy that aimed to combine erudition with perfect breeding. Previously both had suffered at the hands of their principal nanny, Helen Lightbody, an unrelenting Victorian taskmaster to whom the Queen had left much of the early character development of her first two children. Nannies were often problematic at the palace. Elizabeth and Margaret's own nannie, Marion Crawford, known as 'Crawfie', had been popular with the two princesses, a stalwart throughout the war and regarded as almost a member of the family. But in 1949 she shocked them and disgraced herself in their eyes by writing her memoirs. It was an anodyne and adoring account, but it violated the sacred rule that nobody should cash in on their service with the family.

The choice of Lightbody was – unfortunately for Charles and Anne – a case of a severe reflex reaction in a direction opposite to the relaxed touch of Crawfie in the nursery. Belatedly, the Queen and Philip realised that there was no light touch with Lightbody. Philip was especially annoyed that she favoured Charles over Anne; Charles was submissive while Anne was rebellious. Philip's belief in gender stereotypes had placed a burden on Charles that he was never able to carry, but, seeing something of himself in Anne, Philip wanted to release his daughter from the tyrant of the nursery and the moment to do so apparently came when Lightbody barred Charles from enjoying a dessert that the Queen had requested for him. She departed, replaced by a much younger and more tolerant nanny, Mabel Anderson.

It was too late to undo some of Lightbody's work; the combined effects of her and Gordonstoun were indelible on Charles. A test of all parenthood is to allow children to develop their own natural characters, to be themselves, rather than expecting them to be someone they will never be. Philip never seemed to grasp that idea with Charles, but the Queen's next two sons, Andrew and then Edward, who was born in 1964, escaped that onerous regime, thanks partly to the arrival of Anderson and partly to the Queen herself, who, stung by criticism that she had been a remote mother and left too much to Philip (and the equally firm-minded Mountbatten), now made an effort to be more present in the lives of the younger princes. Harold Wilson noted that she was always eager, at the close of his Tuesday audiences with her, to move on to the nursery for the children's baths. On such mundane details rested the idea that the Queen had become a more relaxed mother. In any event, the Queen was about to confront one of the most lingering phantoms of her family.

CHAPTER 14

THE MAN WHO KNEW
FAR TOO MUCH

In the spring of 1964, Arthur Martin, an officer of MI5 whose job it was to interrogate people suspected of being undercover spies for Soviet Russia, called at a penthouse flat in Portman Square, a residence that was part of the Courtauld Institute. It was occupied by the distinguished art historian Anthony Blunt, the Surveyor of the Queen's Pictures. Blunt was expecting the visit; he had already been interviewed eleven times by MI5 and he realised that Martin now had enough evidence to identify him as the most sought-after traitor in Britain, the so-called Fourth Man in the cadre of spies that Soviet Russia had recruited in Cambridge in the 1930s; three others, Guy Burgess, Donald Maclean and Kim Philby, had escaped to Russia. The fifth and final member, John Cairncross, who was teaching at a university in Ohio, had confessed to Martin a few weeks earlier.

In John le Carré's signature novel of treachery and retribution, *Tinker, Tailor, Soldier, Spy* – published ten years after Martin's interrogation of Blunt – the Martin figure in the story, George Smiley, closes in on Moscow's mole inside British intelligence, Bill Haydon, and traps him in a carefully planned night operation. There was no such drama that night in Portman Square. The moment had something of the strained civility of a club member being accused of cheating at cards before being asked to resign. The whole closing of the net on

Cairncross and Blunt was conducted with remarkable decorum, as between gentlemen and not adversaries. (Philby, in terms of the damage he did and the deaths he caused, was the most lethal of the five. He had dissembled his way through several similarly civil interrogations without being nabbed.) Blunt poured himself a glass of gin and then, like a man suddenly shedding a burden, confessed and started to talk. Martin had eased the way by assuring Blunt that if he fully cooperated in the MI5 debriefings he would not be prosecuted. And, indeed, neither he nor Cairncross ever faced a trial.

But unlike the other four, Blunt was a walking depository of two kinds of secrets.

The first kind involved filling in what blanks remained of the deep penetration of the British and American intelligence services by the Soviets before, during and after the Second World War, including how key details of the Anglo-American development of the atomic bomb were passed to Moscow. It was probably fair to say that by the time Blunt confessed there was little left to be disclosed. Cairncross and Blunt had been rolled up by pure chance. Michael Straight, a former speechwriter for President Roosevelt and a left-wing journalist from a wealthy family, had been offered the job of chairman of the Advisory Council on the Arts by the Kennedy administration. Straight had been at Cambridge with Blunt and fell deeply under his influence. He was more of a communist fellow-traveller than a committed Soviet agent like the other five (and quit the party in disgust when Stalin signed a non-aggression treaty with Hitler in 1939), but he had known full well that Blunt and Burgess were active and treacherous agents. This knowledge had eaten at his conscience for years: between 1949 and 1951 he had gone to the British embassy in Washington three times intending to tell what he knew, and then changed his mind. (Had he done so, the Cambridge Five would have been shut down before their worst work was done.) But in 1963, facing vetting by the FBI for the new post, Straight finally cracked. In fifty hours of interviews, the whole Cambridge ring was described in detail. Once the American intelligence agencies digested Straight's account, they were appalled by MI5's failure to detect such a deep and enduring penetration of British security. Martin was called to Washington to debrief Straight. He had to admit to Straight that Blunt had so far successfully denied being the Fourth Man. But that was over now. Cairncross and Blunt were unmasked as the remaining moles.

The second category of secret, unique to Blunt, was far more sensitive.

This compartment of his life really began in the spring of 1945. Blunt and Sir Owen Morshead, the keeper of the royal archives at Windsor Castle, were driving in a military truck to a brooding nineteenth-century edifice, the Friedrichshof, one of a number of castles near Frankfurt owned by the Hesse relatives of the Queen – a branch of the royal family tree who were distant cousins of George VI and who, before the war, had become very close to the Duke of Windsor.

Everything that follows should be seen in the context of the role of German royalty and the German aristocracy under the Nazis. One of Hitler's shrewdest steps, taken early as he consolidated his power, was to make clear that, unlike Stalin and the communists, he was not setting out to butcher the upper classes of Germany. He co-opted their support on his own terms: as long as they were loyal to his interests, they would be left unmolested with their land and their money. In his masterly history of the Third Reich, Michael Burleigh points out that Heinrich Himmler's black-garbed SS appealed to aristocrats because of its embrace of equestrian events: 'The result was an SS membership reeking of the *Almanach de Gotha*.' This policy appealed to all the German royals who were related to the Windsors and it facilitated Hitler's courting of the Duke of Windsor, who was the ultimate prize to be recruited from the *Almanach de Gotha*.

Blunt and Morshead were following immediately in the wake of General George S. Patton's Third Army as it made its final headlong drive towards Berlin and as the Soviet Army raced there from the east. They found that the Friedrichshof had been taken over by the Americans as a rest camp for troops on leave from the battlefield. They were redirected to a townhouse three miles away, where they found the man they were seeking, Prince Wolfgang of Hesse.

Morshead presented Wolfgang with a letter signed by George VI requesting that he should hand over a cache of letters that had passed between the Hesses and members of the British royal family in the 1930s. But there was a problem of protocol, and the Germans were sticklers for that. The titular head of the family was Wolfgang's twin brother Philipp, the Landgrave of Hesse. But he had been detained by the Americans for interrogation because he had been a Nazi and a lieutenant general in a unit of storm troopers. (He fell out with Hitler in 1943 and survived both the Flossenbürg and Dachau concentration camps before being found by the Americans.) Wolfgang told Blunt and Morshead that he could not authorise handing over the papers – but his 72-year-old mother, Princess Margaret of Hesse, could. And, duly armed with a letter bearing her authority, they drove back to the castle, where, according to Wolfgang, the documents were stored in the attic in two packing cases.

However, the letter from the dowager princess did not impress Captain Kathleen Nash of the US Women's Army Corps, who was in charge of the rest camp. She said that any papers in the castle were now the property of the US Army and she lacked the authority to release them. This was a bizarre confrontation. In theory, Blunt outranked Nash; he wore the uniform of a British Army major. But neither he nor Morshead must have seemed like military types. They looked and spoke like British toffs. And Nash herself was a familiar counter-type, the adamantine military bureaucrat. But Blunt and Morshead were smarter. Blunt told Nash that she should telephone her superior officers in Frankfurt and, as he persisted until she did, Morshead slipped away, taking two British soldiers who were with them, and found the packing cases. When Nash finally appeared after making the phone call, Blunt, Morshead and their haul were already on the road. (There was an even more bizarre sequel: Nash and a US Army colonel discovered a cache of Hesse family jewels worth, in 1945 money, at least $3 million and managed to smuggle them back to the US, where they were hidden in a luggage locker at a railway station. The so-called Kronberg heist was a sensation when the two were arrested and later jailed.)

At this point it is important to remember that there are usually two points of origin for family (and official) documents, one being the sender and one the receiver who then replies. This is often overlooked in stories where the pursuit of missing documents is in progress, and it was crucially important in 1945 and 1946 when Britain and the US set in motion a widespread and urgent search for documents in the German archives. They already had timelines and origins for much of what they sought. In this case, Morshead would have been informed by knowledge of letters secreted in the royal archives at Windsor received by Edward both before and after the abdication, although probably not those received by his younger brother, the Duke of Kent, who lived outside the reach of the palace's archivists. And the contents of the letters in England had implications that were clearly taken very seriously not just by the royal family but by Winston Churchill, who had authorised Blunt's mission and made clear that it was urgent.

Blunt, fluent in German, was an officer serving in MI5 in Europe from September 1944, when he arrived in liberated Paris, until the end of the war. (Coincidentally, Malcolm Muggeridge was also in Paris, working for MI6.) His assignment was top secret. This was discovered when the Allied command in Paris set up a special unit of art experts to track down and recover irreplaceable artworks that had been looted by the Nazis during their occupation of Europe. Blunt, as a pre-eminent expert on European old masters, should have been an obligatory hire for this unit, and his recruitment was requested, but MI5 would not release him. As the credentials he produced to Captain Nash proved, Blunt was directly in the service of the King, as an intelligence officer, not an art historian.

Correspondence from the 1930s would not alone have filled two packing cases. Morshead's cover story was that he was looking for letters between Queen Victoria and her eldest daughter, also Victoria, who married Frederick III of Prussia and became the mother of Kaiser Wilhelm II. It was, of course, absurd that the recovery of correspondence from a century earlier merited a special and urgent mission to Europe while the war still raged. Before he fell out with Hitler, Prince Philipp, the Landgrave, whose wife was the sister of King Umberto II of Italy, had been used as an intermediary between Hitler and Mussolini. Since Hitler gave a misplaced importance to the British royal bloodline, it made sense for him to also use Philipp as a backchannel contact with the two British princes, Edward and George, who were avowed sympathisers with Germany. Another royal cousin, Charles Edward, Duke of Saxe-Coburg Gotha, had been educated at Eton and, also like Philipp, was an officer in the storm troopers. In the short time Edward was King, Charles Edward spent time with him, encouraging the use of the family's backchannels to Germany. Coburg played to Hitler's delusion that the monarch had decisive influence on the Baldwin government, and he reported that Edward had complained to him, 'Who is King here, Baldwin or I? I wish to talk to Hitler and will do so here or in Germany. Tell him that, please.'

No, Blunt and Morshead were on what was called a weeding expedition: this term was used to cover a decades-long programme to sift any documentation, official or private, recording contacts at any level between Britain and the Nazis throughout the 1930s and into the early 1940s. Whatever it was that Blunt and Morshead found has never seen the light of day. The importance of their mission was, however, obscured by a far more dramatic discovery in Germany months later, after the war was over. British and US intelligence combined forces in Operation GOLDCUP, the code name for a sweep through Germany to locate documents from the German Foreign Ministry that were dispersed in selected locations across the country – an operation complicated by the fact that some of these locations were in areas occupied by the Soviet Army.

All in all, 170 truckloads of documents – about 400 tons – were gathered and taken to Marburg Castle in Thuringia for examination, page by page. The British team, called the Foreign Office File Team, was led by Lieutenant Colonel Robert Currie Thomson. The examiners discovered that crucial periods were missing from the documents, including anything covering connections between the British royal family and German diplomats during the 1930s and early 1940s. However, by chance, the Americans had captured a German soldier, Karl von Loesch, who had worked at the Foreign Ministry translating English documents – it turned out that von Loesch had been at school in England with Churchill's son-in-law Duncan Sandys.

The Americans handed over von Loesch to Thomson. He had a highly consequential story to tell: as the Nazis saw impending defeat, he was ordered to destroy what were considered the most sensitive documents. These covered several phases of secret Anglo-German conversations, beginning not long after Hitler came to power and continuing to the outbreak of war in 1939. The basic theme of these contacts was that war between Britain and Germany could be avoided. Neville Chamberlain's 'peace in our time' capitulation to Hitler at Munich in 1938 was the public face of this belief. In private, among appeasers and including the two royal brothers Edward and George, the Duke of Kent, there was a deeper determination to placate Hitler. Von Loesch revealed that microfilm copies of some of the most secret documents had been made on the orders of von Ribbentrop – Wallis Simpson's frequent guest while he was ambassador in London – and these had survived.

Von Loesch had taken these copies to the grounds of an estate twenty miles from Marburg and buried them under tarpaulin in a ravine. This meant that they were in territory just taken over by the Russians, but Thomson and his team nonetheless crossed into the Russian zone with Loesch without being intercepted and recovered thirty rolls of microfilm. These included copies of a dossier titled Operation WILLI that set out in detail the Nazi effort to capture and suborn the Duke and Duchess of Windsor on the border of Portugal and Spain in 1940, with the idea of holding the Duke until, with the capitulation of Britain, he would be installed on the throne as Hitler's satrap. Thomson's team realised the stunning implications of their discovery. By this time, in the autumn of 1945, Churchill was out of power and Clement Attlee was Prime Minister. Thomson sent the files to the Foreign Office and they, in turn, sent copies to 10 Downing Street and Buckingham Palace. At the Foreign Office, the permanent under-secretary Sir Alexander Cadogan noted, 'King fussed about Duke of Windsor File & captured German documents.' Attlee passed the gist of the documents to Churchill, who replied, 'I earnestly trust it may be possible to destroy all traces of these German intrigues.'

The Operation WILLI files were released by the Americans in 1957, much to the annoyance of the Duke of Windsor. But Blunt and Morshead had made sure that far more damning documents never fell into American hands. This became a cause of concern again in 1964, when MI5's interrogation of Blunt threatened to renew interest in his role in Germany in 1945. And the risk increased when the interrogation changed hands. MI5 was awash with internal politics; defending themselves against American charges of dereliction, the MI5 leadership was worried that Martin was overzealous and too eager to satisfy American demands for more information. Martin was replaced by Peter Wright, from the Science Directorate. Wright was no less dismayed than Martin when he sought to corroborate Blunt's account of his relationship with Buckingham Palace – particularly in the period before he was given the position of Surveyor of the Queen's Pictures, when he was also, of course, in frequent touch with his Moscow handlers. Michael Adeane, the Queen's private secretary, assured Wright that the Queen 'has been fully informed about Sir Anthony, and is quite content for him to be dealt with in any way which gets at the truth'. This, however, came with a significant caveat. There was one matter that the Queen wanted kept out of the investigation – an assignment that Blunt undertook on behalf of the palace in 1945. 'Please do not pursue the matter,' Adeane insisted. 'Strictly speaking it is not relevant to considerations of national security.'

Recalling this later in his book *Spycatcher* (which made him a pariah to British intelligence), Wright said, 'I never did learn the secret of his mission at the end of the war.' The palace, he said, had become adept at the 'difficult art of scandal burying over several centuries', while MI5 'have only been in the business since 1909'.

While he was still under investigation by Martin, Blunt received a visit from an old friend from his days at Cambridge, a reunion that was electric with emotion. At Martin's suggestion, Michael Straight went to Portman Square, knowing that Blunt was aware that he had unmasked him to the American investigators. 'Anthony was standing at the entrance to his flat,' Straight recalled in his memoirs. 'He looked pale and skeletal, as he always had; he did not appear to be broken in spirit. I had assumed he would be directly hostile; I was surprised by his thin-lipped smile and the grip of his hand.' As they moved into the living room, hung with priceless paintings from the

Courtauld collection, Blunt claimed that the whole experience was cathartic: 'When they said that you had told them your story, it lifted a heavy burden from my shoulders. I was immensely relieved.'

They sat down and discussed their mutual enthusiasms in art. Straight was rich enough to collect masterpieces. He said he had bought a landscape by Gaspard Dughet, a pupil of Nicolas Poussin, and Blunt's reputation as an art historian rested largely on his deep passion for and understanding of Poussin. They were still discussing the meaning of paintings by Dughet and Poussin – like connoisseurs with nothing more troubling on their minds – when Martin walked in.

*　*　*

Blunt was appointed Surveyor of the King's Pictures by George VI immediately after he returned from Germany. He remained in royal service, secure from exposure, until he retired in 1972. He was, in a technical sense, truly part of the family. He was a third cousin of the Queen Mother, who was one of his fans at the palace, as was Queen Mary, who sometimes popped into the Courtauld to hear his lectures. There was probably no safer place than Buckingham Palace for a former Soviet mole to serve out his days after confessing his treachery. He was beyond question highly qualified for his post and moved among the connoisseurs of fine art as the equal of any. He talked and taught about art with a passion that was infectious. Indeed, his manner was naturally that of the kind of epicene academic pedant that Alan Bennett brilliantly mimicked. Bennett, drawing on his own history as a teacher of medieval history, provoked peals of laughter in theatre audiences by acting as such a classically British type. But behind his distinguished façade Blunt was fully aware of the coercive hold he had on the palace. He knew and they knew he knew. He knew as much as anyone had ever been able to know about the royal family's attitude towards Nazi Germany in the 1930s. The only people he had probably shared at least some of this knowledge with were the Russians, and they were not going to do anything to jeopardise his services for them – once Blunt's wartime treachery was complete, he was still regarded as a useful guide to British politics as viewed from the heights of the palace. How much of a hold over the palace did this give Blunt? Surely the full and damning magnitude of the royal secrets is self-evident from the extreme lengths that everyone involved went to in order to suppress any risk of their disclosure.

Churchill's attitude might seem puzzling from this distance. In 1940, he was a truly embattled Prime Minister. His government had been purged of the faint of heart, several of whom had actively hoped for rapprochement with Hitler. (Churchill had attempted a rapprochement with Mussolini to keep him out of the war and later went to some lengths to destroy any records of that.) The Duke of Windsor was out of sight in the Bahamas but still causing mischief. Why would Churchill have any remaining sympathy for him? But Churchill had an Edwardian's belief in the value of the monarchy as the bedrock of national identity – just as he had retained an anachronistic affection for India and the Victorian empire. Within this great and complex man it was possible to hold two positions that to others were incompatible – for example, that fascism was evil and had to be eradicated and that the monarchy's continued appearance of integrity was more important than exposing fascist sympathies in the royal family; they were an aberration that should be scrubbed from the records. He was also surely swayed by his deep regard for George VI, who, after his visible wobble of resolve in 1939, had become to the nation as firm a bulwark in war as Churchill himself. Churchill never altered his belief in the correctness of suppressing the truth about the Windsors and the Nazis. In August 1953, the subject of the captured German

Foreign Office files on the Duke of Windsor came up again for review and Commander Colville noted in his diary, 'The P.M. still set on suppression.'

And what about the Queen herself? She had readily consented to Blunt keeping his job until he reached the retirement age of sixty-five – eight years later. Sir Alec Douglas-Home, now the Prime Minister, was – incredibly – never informed of this deal. It was, in fact, agreed to by Henry Brooke, the Home Secretary, who decided not to consult Downing Street.

In 1965, Adeane made it clear to Wright that the German connection was firmly off-limits as far as the palace was concerned. This certainly indicates the Queen's determination that the disclosure of Blunt's treachery should not inadvertently reveal a piece of family history that she supposed was permanently purged from accessible records. We don't know just exactly how Blunt's inconvenient knowledge of that history became explicit in the discussions of what to do with him. Nobody would use such a vulgar term as blackmail. But Blunt surely knew he held an ace in his hands. In recognising that, the Queen and her advisers were more than ready to turn a blind eye to the damage he had done to the country on behalf of his handlers in Moscow – every bit as much as the reviled Burgess and Maclean, if not at the same level of infamy as Philby.

Of course, in a cover-up of this order, with a large number of dispersed documents to discover and suppress, there is always the possibility that the purge is incomplete. In this case the purge went beyond just locking stuff away for fifty years under the usual time-lapse rules governing sensitive official papers – it is highly likely that many documents had actually been destroyed. But there was one source of assiduous document collection and annotation safely beyond the reach of the Queen's archivists: America.

PART TWO

CHAPTER 15

A TITAN PASSES, A
TRAGEDY STRIKES

The Queen was now far from being the novice that her first Prime
Minister, Winston Churchill, had so patiently tutored. And she
knew that Churchill was entering his dotage. His last political speech
had been back in 1959, campaigning for Harold Macmillan, who defeated the Labour Party with a whacking majority of 100 seats. Since
then honours had been showered on him from all over the world;
the one he most valued was being made an honorary citizen of the
United States in 1963 when, because of his frailty, Randolph had read
his acceptance speech. In July 1964, the *Sunday Times* political correspondent told me that the great man was about to make his last visit
to Parliament, the cockpit that he had once so masterfully dominated.

There were no steps taken to turn this into a special occasion. It was
ineffably sad to see him sitting in his special place on the government
front bench mostly unaware of what was going on around him, a
silenced giant serving out his more than sixty years as a Member of
Parliament almost like a visitation from some distant and ever glorious age. I decided that we must do something significant to record the
moment and I commissioned our gifted young political cartoonist,
Gerald Scarfe, to go to the House of Commons and sketch a portrait
of him. What followed was very nearly a repetition of Churchill's bal-
listic response to the Graham Sutherland portrait presented to him as

an eightieth birthday present in 1955, which he said made him look like 'a down-and-out drunk who has been picked out of the gutter'. The painting was later secretly incinerated under the direction of Lady Churchill.

Scarfe, who had the gift of transforming certain physical features of a politician into a visual shorthand for their most egregious characteristics, did not take that course this time. Instead, he conveyed a sense that no camera could have caught of deeply touching pathos. Churchill's most forceful feature, his domed head, was tilted slightly down in the manner familiar from his most combative encounters. The eyes, though sightless, were similarly challenging. And the chin was sunk into a slumped, exhausted body. In a strange way it was as though, apprehending the significance of this captured moment, we should acknowledge that the great man had been exhausted not by efforts to make himself famous but by his efforts to save his people and his country, if not the whole civilised world.

My editor-in-chief, Denis Hamilton, was troubled by the portrait. He quite often deferred to me after allowing me to argue a case – he had backed me on some controversial investigative stories – but this time I could see that he thought people would be upset by seeing Churchill in such a declined state. A couple of the older editors agreed with him. The final blow came from Randolph. Hamilton called him and described the drawing. Randolph strongly objected to it. Then I called Randolph, but he wouldn't budge. The portrait was never published, although Scarfe has since published it himself and I have a framed copy of it above my desk now as I write. Six months later Churchill was dead. He suffered a massive stroke early in January 1965, remained unconscious for almost two weeks, and died early on 24 January, at the age of ninety.

Few events can ever really be said to suddenly sever one age from another. The outbreak of a war usually does. The death of one man rarely does. Even though the Queen's long reign saw many illustrious departures, Churchill's ranked for her above all others as truly the passing of an age – in terms of both the size of the man and the size of British influence and power that had once been suggested by his sheer presence and, during its decline, had been figuratively represented by her. The two of them had shared that loss together with a mutual sense of diminishment, knowing that it was irreversible. Without Churchill, even an enfeebled Churchill, there was nothing left of that age. Everything would feel that much smaller. The novelist V. S. Pritchett caught the feeling in one sentence: 'We were looking at a past utterly unrecoverable.'

The funeral had been planned years before. The Queen ordered that it should be 'on a scale befitting his position in history' and, breaking with the tradition that monarchs did not attend non-family funerals, announced that she would attend. Also breaking with tradition, the service would be at St Paul's Cathedral, not Westminster Abbey. St Paul's had seen the funerals of the two men who equalled Churchill as warlords – Nelson and Wellington. At the *Sunday Times* we had also anticipated the event and planned massive coverage of it. What made it a white-knuckle operation for us was that the funeral service fell on a Saturday, our press day. Weekends were normally a slow news time. In fact, as managing editor I had a policy of putting most of our news resources into a synoptic analysis of the past seven days, often led by investigative stories, allowing little space for breaking news. This time we had only a few hours to cover one of the most epochal events in British history.

The body had been lying in state for three days in a flag-draped coffin in Westminster Hall. At 9.45 a.m. on the Saturday, it left Westminster on a gun carriage pulled by 104 sailors from the Royal Navy and followed by men from eighteen units of the military, heading for Trafalgar Square, the Strand and then Fleet Street and Ludgate

Hill to the cathedral. The sky was grey. The air was sharply cold to the breath. Despite all the military colours, the overall tone was colourless, almost monochromatic – London has that power to suppress light and embalm in grey. We had placed some of the world's finest photographers, including Henri Cartier-Bresson, along the route, some in positions on the upper floors of buildings. We captured some fine panoramic images, but Cartier-Bresson, instead of being drawn to the pageant, turned his camera on the crowds for close-ups. In those few faces, tightly wrapped against the cold, he caught what the big picture missed – intimate moments of personal loss. Our biggest competitor was live television. More than 350 million people across the world watched the broadcast. But in a few frames from his Leica Cartier-Bresson delivered a unique miniature requiem.

The Queen's contemporary Prime Minister, Harold Wilson, had been governing with a majority in Parliament of only four, which left him unable to carry out the sweeping reforms he had promised. In March 1966, he rectified that. Labour won a majority of ninety-six seats in a snap election and Wilson made it clear to the Queen that there would be a huge cultural and social shift to reflect the widespread sense that the country was being held back by Victorian constraints on the freedom of ideas and personal behaviour. Government censorship of the arts would be ended, as would capital punishment and the criminalisation of homosexuality. Abortion and divorce laws would be liberalised. The number of universities would be nearly doubled with a new wave of the so-called red-brick colleges to finally counter the dominance of Oxbridge, and the BBC would provide university-standard home-tutoring with broadcasts from the Open University. What this meant, in effect, was that many of the nation's institutions would be forcibly modernised while one institution, the monarchy, remained largely ossified. But there was no grain of republicanism in Wilson. He warmed to the Queen and their weekly encounters were amiable.

Wilson's 'culturequake' was felt strongly at the *Sunday Times*. The paper remained nominally a supporter of the Conservative Party but had long since ceased to be the party's obedient organ – our coverage of the Profumo affair and a number of stories about ministerial incompetence made the change clear. One Saturday, while Sir Alec Douglas-Home was still Prime Minister, Denis Hamilton, who was usually at his country home as we put together the front page, called me when he had seen a proof of the first edition to point out that virtually every story on the front page was damning of the government. I argued that they were there because of their significance, and that any other selection would have reflected political bias, not news judgement. There was a long pause and then Hamilton said, 'So be it.' When Wilson arrived, the news pages remained equally neutral, but there was no hiding that his cultural reforms were in line with Hamilton's own views. On the monarchy we were agnostic. Tourism was becoming an important part of the economy and the royal family was, at least, good for that business. One member of the family, though, often seemed to be waging a personal war against journalists: Prince Philip.

The extent of his peevishness became clear when we assigned one of our best young reporters, David Leitch, to cover a visit Philip made to Morocco. It was not a formal state visit. His host was one of Morocco's royal princes, Moulay Hassan. The highlight was a polo game in Rabat between a Moroccan team and a guest team led by Philip. Leitch knew nothing about polo but watched the game with an American he had met the day before (Leitch suspected he was from the CIA) who seemed to be an expert. Philip's team won – the American suggested that the result was a diplomatic fix – and he was presented with a silver trophy by Moulay Hassan. 'The guy's a real bastard with a horse,' the American said. Later Leitch was invited to a reception at the British embassy in honour of Philip.

This was the scene of one of the most extraordinary encounters between a reporter and a member of the royal family. Philip had noticed Leitch the day before, at another event, and when they were introduced by an embassy official, Philip said, 'I knew you were a reporter the moment I clapped eyes on you, can smell 'em a mile off.' Before Philip arrived in Morocco, he had been staying with aristocratic friends in Italy. The Italian press had run stories about how much time Philip spent away from the Queen, part of a familiar narrative in European reporting that the marriage was under strain. Without any further preamble, Philip barked at Leitch, 'I've just made sure the proprietors of three bloody Italian newspapers never get into society again.'

Trying to dodge the artillery, Leitch asked if Philip had enjoyed the polo game. Philip was momentarily diverted and muttered that 'these Arab ponies are not all that they are cracked up to be' but then resumed his tirade, ranting about 'filthy lies' about himself and the Queen, and being stalked by Italian reporters 'hanging in the trees'. Then, pushing his face at Leitch, he continued, 'Not that your people are much better than the Italians. I suppose you're going to write the same bloody lies as the Italians.'

'I don't know what lies you are talking about,' Leitch responded, now openly incensed.

'Of course you know. These bloody lies that you people print to make money. These lies about how I'm never with my wife. You know very well, don't pretend that you don't.'

At this, Leitch replied with both barrels: '*My* newspaper doesn't go in for that kind of story. We don't print lies, and we also try to avoid boring our readers. Your presence here is of no possible interest to anyone, except perhaps the Hurlingham Polo Club, so I am writing nothing about you at all.'

With that, Leitch bowed his head in the manner of a duellist departing victoriously from a shoot-out and walked off.

The age of deference was definitely over. Before Leitch left the embassy, the ambassador, using a subtle diplomatic code, made clear to Leitch that he thought Philip's outburst was beyond the pale. Leitch didn't file a story (he kept the episode for his memoirs). When he described it to us at the time, nobody was really surprised. Philip was a loose cannon, prone to gaffes in public, like referring to 'slit-eyed' Asians and other racial stereotypes from the days of colonial bigotry.

*   *   *

Together with the growing impact of the paper's magazine under Mark Boxer, where Tony Snowdon was thriving as a photographer, the paper's investigative reporting helped build a rapid growth in circulation. It also increased the appetite for long-form journalism. Television executives were noticing. Granada, the Manchester-based commercial broadcaster, had become a serious rival to the BBC with a weekly programme, *The World in Action*. They decided they wanted to try the Insight style of reporting and lured away one of my two founding colleagues, Jeremy Wallington. At the same time, I had my first experience as a television commentator. The rebellious cadre inside the BBC who fathered *That Was the Week That Was*, led by the virtuoso producer Ned Sherrin, still stung by the way that show had been killed off, came back on the air with a new version with a clunky title, *Not So Much a Programme, More a Way of Life*. It was a mixture of sketches and opinion provided by guests and presented by David Frost. It lacked the openly insolent edge of its forerunner and lasted only one season, but appearing on it as one of the guests changed my career.

Frost was one of those rare beings who seems to arrive intuitively prepared for a new age – in his case, television. His connection with the television camera was almost preternatural: as he spoke to it, it became his own possession. I had some sense of this from watching *TW3*, but now, seeing it from inside the studio as he wrangled a variety of talents and ad-libbed easily to keep the show moving, it was more fully revealed. As he interviewed me, it was like we were having a private conversation without any of the surrounding technology intervening. I was there to give a journalist's view of the week's news, but Frost wanted more, to make the conversation about journalism as I saw it, as somebody who was impatient with the laziness of a lot of reporting – particularly the political reporters spoon-fed by party officials. (This provoked some angry responses in Fleet Street.)

It turned out that Frost had similar ideas about television journalism. It was still too much in the hands of reverential 'clubbable' chaps who were not interested in speaking truth to power. After several on-air interviews, Frost wanted to continue the conversation away from the studio, and we swiftly felt like members of a vocational confederacy – but confined to a membership of two. Frost was in discussions with the BBC and his agent about a new series of satirical sketches on British attitudes to the class system. It became a classic: *The Frost Report* ran for twenty-eight episodes and made stars of John Cleese, Ronnie Barker and Ronnie Corbett. Its success established Frost as a talent-enabler and national phenomenon – but it fell short of satisfying his ambition. He was frustrated by now being automatically typecast as a satirist. He really wanted to be a television journalist, and some of the more pompous BBC news presenters used 'satirist' as a disqualifier for anyone with ambitions to be taken seriously as a journalist. At the same time, I had become tantalised by the idea of what television journalism would look like in the hands of Frost. We had to wait two years for the chance to find out.

In the meantime, in 1966, I left the *Sunday Times*. The patriarch of the *Daily Mirror* group, Cecil Harmsworth King, had orchestrated an unprecedented series of mergers to create the world's largest magazine company, the International Publishing Corporation. Hugh Cudlipp became the editorial tsar of both the tabloids and the magazines and then asked me to become executive editor of the magazines – all 200 of them. I agonised over taking the job. The *Sunday Times* had made my reputation. Denis Hamilton was a remarkable editor who had taken a big gamble allowing Insight unfettered development. There was no limit to the paper's role in leading a new golden age of journalism. My colleagues argued that it would be crazy to give this up to take on the problems of a hastily improvised magazine colossus with no element of serious journalism. But Cudlipp was persuasive: a chance like this would never occur again; he would give me carte blanche to modernise the magazines – and a lot more money. Plus, it transpired that on the executive floor there was a butler who maintained for every executive a cellar stocked with the finest clarets. That should have been a warning about a relaxed style in management. And before taking the job I should have asked a few more questions than I did, particularly about the main occupant of that floor, Cecil Harmsworth King, great-nephew of Alfred Harmsworth, founder of the *Daily Mail* and creator of the species, the mass-market Fleet Street daily.

Almost immediately, I fell under King's baleful glare. Cudlipp had persuaded him that I was the kind of Young Turk the company needed, but he decided to take a closer look for himself. He directed that I should accompany him on a three-week tour of the company's North American businesses, ranging from publications to paper mills, paint factories and a hydroelectric plant in the far reaches of northern Labrador, on the brink of the Hudson Bay. The trip began in Washington with a dinner given for King at her home by Kay Graham, the proprietor and publisher of the *Washington Post*. She had invited half the members of Lyndon Johnson's Cabinet. King and I were seated at separate tables. I was seated next to Johnson's head of National Security, McGeorge Bundy. We struck up an instant rapport and had an animated and good-natured discussion about the Vietnam War, which I boldly criticised while he attempted to defend it. I noticed that King was watching this exchange without being able to hear it. As we left the house, King was clearly displeased and said, 'You know, they came here to listen to what I had to say, not what you had to say.' Disastrous start, obviously, but I didn't care. Things slowly thawed as we progressed through New York, where we met American editors and publishers, the paint factories in northern New York State and then to the paper mills and the power plant in Labrador. But something about me was still bugging King. It turned out that he felt that I required a final understanding of his power – and my lack of it. One morning at breakfast, out of the blue, he suddenly said, 'You know, I can think of nobody better qualified to run this great business of ours than me.' Well, OK, he was the boss. I survived the test, to Cudlipp's relief.

*　　*　　*

Early in 1966, the talks with Frost took on more urgency. I was on holiday with my family on the small island of Comino, between Malta and Gozo, when he suddenly arrived. We took a long walk along a rugged, thyme-scented path above some cliffs. The BBC were not interested in his ideas – basically they told him to stick to satire – but the commercial station in London, Rediffusion, was. They were prepared to take a huge risk: a one-hour peak-time programme five nights a week – live. Frost had enlisted one of the creators of *The Frost Report*, Tony Jay, as an adviser, and Tony had added a daring new idea. Not only would the show be live but it would have a studio audience. They were thinking of it as a nightly public forum for debate about the day's news, each one featuring an interview with a maker of that news. Would I join Tony as an adviser, specifically to provide guidance on the news and how to respond to it? That would mean sitting in on the morning conference and then, in the evening, being at the studio at Wembley to make the final decisions. To do this I would have to moonlight from my new job at IPC. The programme would be called, in the proprietorial style that he liked, *The Frost Programme*. It would launch in seven months, in September. As long as Cudlipp agreed to the moonlighting, I would do it – and Cudlipp did.

*   *   *

At 9.15 a.m. on 21 October 1966, in the Welsh mining village of Aberfan, children in the Pantglas Junior School had just returned to their classrooms after morning prayers and lustily singing 'All Things Bright and Beautiful'. The village sat in a shallow valley and the school was directly below a small mountain that, like many others in Wales, had grown larger by being used as a dumping ground for slag waste from coal mining. A bank of grey fog clung to the valley. Suddenly the whole school began to shake as though in the first moments of an earthquake. There was an inexplicable roar of terrifying power. Unseen because of the fog, a large part of the mountainside was bearing down on the school and within thirty seconds obliterated a farmhouse and all its occupants and then the school. Millions of tons of mine waste – a crushing sludge of slag, rock, earth and water – sealed the school like a tomb.

A few hours later, Tony Snowdon received a call from a friend in Cardiff. By then the scale of the tragedy was becoming clear. Scores of children and their teachers were beyond rescue, buried beneath the sludge as suddenly as were the citizens of ancient Pompeii by volcanic ash from Vesuvius. Tony told Margaret that he had to go immediately to Wales. She asked why. 'Because I'm Welsh,' he answered. He arrived at 2 a.m. the following day and was shattered by the scenes of desperation and grief. There was nothing to be done at the site;

it would take days and require specialised equipment to reach the bodies. Tony spent many hours with stricken parents and talking to survivors in hospital. In a note to Margaret, he wrote, 'It was all so awful seeing grown men, really tough miners, crying and crying. One turned to me and said: "I've lost both mine – Tony, you'll understand, because you have two as well."' The final toll was 116 children and twenty-eight adults.

During the course of the day, Tony was joined by Prince Philip and they went to the site together. They looked as ashen as the scene itself, with still no trace of the school buildings and the acrid stench of oozing coal waste and the pervading sense of impotence in the face of such a merciless force. Within forty-eight hours there were the beginnings of public murmurings – *where was the Queen?* This was the most harrowing peacetime tragedy the nation had seen since she came to the throne. Should she not join those giving comfort to so many to whom her presence would surely have been signally valuable? The press office and her advisers urged her to go. She resisted. There was never any public explanation of why she waited until a week later, when the last bodies had been recovered, to go. Then she spent just two hours with Philip, talking to parents, visiting the site and laying a wreath in a cemetery where eighty-one crosses marked the graves of children. 'As a mother, I'm trying to understand what your feelings must be,' she said, tearing up. 'I'm sorry I can give you nothing at present except sympathy.'

Responses to a tragedy of this size can't be a considered a matter of protocol or tradition or policy. They should be spontaneous – as demonstrated by Tony. But the Queen was unable to react spontaneously as he had. Something paralysed her. The phrase 'I'm trying to understand what your feelings must be' was stark in its self-confession and spoke to a rigidity in her emotions. She could not, at least, be accused of making a calculated public relations decision. Later the palace said she feared her presence would have got in the way of the rescue effort. But, as her advisers knew, it was a PR disaster. Of course, her tears were not of the crocodile variety. Even the most disciplined bureaucrat would tear up at such a scene. But the impression was left that there was within the Queen a cold core that suggested a deficit of empathy. Afterwards she was aware that she had failed in a very public way. The problem would recur in an equally public way when Princess Diana died, albeit as she faced a wholly different kind of tragedy much closer to home.

Aberfan was the result of scandalous dereliction by the state bureaucracy that ran the mines, the National Coal Board. This was compounded by a heavy-handed response from the Wilson government. Five days after the event, the government appointed a tribunal to investigate what happened. Wilson's Attorney General, Elwyn Jones, then imposed a gag order on the press, barring any investigative reporting and threatening editors that if they persisted they would face a charge of contempt of court. By then *The Frost Programme* had been on the air for six weeks. Critics had described it as compelling television, bringing a new interrogative quality to daily news coverage. When the government gag order was announced, I had a call from my old Insight colleague at the *Sunday Times*, Ron Hall. He told me that the paper had already been investigating the history of the Aberfan slag tip, with some inside help from the Coal Board, and that it already looked like a case of gross incompetence. Elwyn Jones, the man who imposed the gag order, had once been a journalist himself. He had also served as a junior counsel at the Nuremburg trials of the Nazi leadership. There hadn't been any previous indication of a totalitarian bent of thinking, but his behaviour here was an outrage. I talked it over with Frost, relaying the *Sunday Times* information. We decided to open the programme that night with a monologue by Frost, written by me, condemning the gag order. No Fleet Street editor had thought it worth the risk to challenge the Wilson regime so directly, but we did. We turned the contempt of court threat against the government by winding up: 'The only contempt here is the government's own contempt for a free press.' The studio audience applauded. Editors finally stirred to comment themselves.

The government's reaction was immediate. Frost had a call from the chief law officer of the Crown, the Lord Chancellor, Gerald Gardiner. Until that moment, Gardiner had been rightly seen as a leading liberal force for Wilson's social reforms. But this was a different voice. He told Frost:

> You are sailing very close to the wind. I seriously considered taking action. I want you to understand – I want your producers and the Rediffusion company to understand – that if you repeat any commentary of this nature you will face a charge of contempt of court, and that charge will be enforced.

When Frost relayed this conversation to me, we were both shocked. It seemed like such a reactionary position for a Labour government to take – the kind of automatically repressive judicial voice that belonged to another age. But we were gagged, and we knew it.

When the Aberfan tribunal reported a year later, its verdict was savage. The tragedy was the result of 'bungling ineptitude by many men charged with tasks for which they were totally unfitted'. There had been frequent failures to hear clear warnings and 'a total lack of direction from the top'. The head of the National Coal Board, Lord (Alf) Robens, accepted the findings. Robens was a party hack I had met several times and he would have been incapable of running a fish and chip shop.

In his diary, Harold Wilson wrote of Aberfan, 'The highest praise was for Lord Snowdon. He had gone spontaneously and instead of inspecting the site, he made it his job to visit the bereaved relatives, sitting holding the hands of a distraught father, with the head of a mother on his shoulder for half an hour in silence...'

It seemed to me that Wilson had left something unspoken. The one commoner in the royal family had shown a natural common touch in the midst of a great tragedy. The Queen was not expected to show a common touch, but she had held herself aloof in a way that surprised many of her subjects.

CHAPTER 16

HOW MUCH PROMISCUITY CAN A MARRIAGE TAKE?

I never forgot that it was a phone call from Robin Douglas-Home with his cryptic tip to look out for stories about a young woman named Christine Keeler that had basically led Insight to its breakthrough coverage of the Profumo affair. Since then, his career and stature had grown. He became a columnist for the *Daily Express* and wrote a biography of Frank Sinatra – he was so close to Sinatra that when he fell sick Sinatra broke away from an English concert tour to take a helicopter and visit him in hospital. The Douglas-Home family had a distinguished lineage in Scotland, going back to 767 AD, and Robin was a nephew of Sir Alec Douglas-Home, the controversial choice of Prime Minister to follow Harold Macmillan. He was married to one of the iconic models of the early 1960s, Sandra Paul. My wife and I spent a weekend with them at their cottage in Sussex. While I was at the *Sunday Times* he continued to be a very well-informed source on the strata of high life that he moved through with consummate charm and ease. What I never knew at the time was that he had fallen for Princess Margaret in a serious and ultimately tragic way.

Seven years into their marriage, Tony and Margaret had each been having a series of affairs without any of them being serious enough to force a break-up. Tony was casually promiscuous with men and women. Margaret was more reluctant and guarded and, probably, more hardened and cynical. Robin Douglas-Home was the exact opposite: an old-fashioned romantic of such sensitivity that, as he passed from one affair to another, he sometimes savoured love and tragedy as equal parts of the potion. Sandra Paul divorced him in 1965 on the grounds of his adultery. Two years later, he re-encountered Margaret after having not seen her for a while and found her desolate. Tony was away in Japan for weeks with a *Sunday Times* writer on an assignment that covered the whole country, and from there was going to New York. The reunion was accidental. Douglas-Home was still moonlighting as a cocktail pianist, now at the Society Restaurant in Jermyn Street, when Margaret walked in. It reminded Margaret of when they used to play duets and sing show tunes in her old salon, and her spirits picked up. He was invited back to Kensington Palace to join others for more nostalgic evenings of drinks and music. In Japan, Tony grew a beard to evade recognition and never called or wrote home. One evening, at the end of a soirée at Kensington Palace, when the other guests had gone, Margaret said to Douglas-Home, 'I don't know what I'd do without you.' Later they spent several nights together at Douglas-Home's Sussex cottage. Margaret sent him a note: 'Thank you for making me live again.'

Douglas-Home might have believed that he had made the greatest conquest of his life, but Margaret, grateful for solace, still wanted to keep her marriage together. This was made harder when Tony heard that she was having an affair with Douglas-Home. He called her from New York and demanded that Douglas-Home be for ever banished from Kensington Palace. This was an unusually personal burst of animus for a man who was usually complaisant about infidelity. But he knew Douglas-Home as an almost professional seducer and was livid that Margaret had succumbed so readily. Tony and Margaret were reunited in the Bahamas in a very public exhibition of harmony. Tony batted away questions about the state of the marriage and – disingenuously

– said, 'While I am away – and I'm away quite a lot on assignments for my paper – I write home and telephone like other husbands in love with their wives.' The Queen, in a note to Tony, congratulated him on a 'masterly' appearance on television and for having 'quietened things down considerably'. When they got back to London, Margaret called Douglas-Home to say that she could never see him again, followed up with a long letter in which she was notably less adamantine – 'I shall try and speak to you as much as possible but I am in fear of him, and I don't know what lengths he won't go to, jealous as he is…'

A year later, Douglas-Home took his own life at the Sussex cottage. The end of the affair had sent him into a spiral of despair and depression. Once the epitome of the suave and secure serial lover, master of his own emotions and ever confident of his attractions, he had lost the greatest love of his life. Margaret showed no emotion on hearing of his death. She had told Tony, 'He wasn't nearly as good a lover as you, darling.'

Like me, Mark Boxer knew both men. He also knew about the affair long before I did. When he relayed some of the details, I said I had never seen that side of Tony – the jealous and vindictive cuckold. Mark agreed; there had, he said, been a similar affair earlier when Tony had been on a long assignment for the magazine in India. Then it was with someone far closer to the family: Anthony Barton, an old friend of Tony's who was godfather to his daughter Sarah. Like the Snowdons, the Bartons had two children, and the two families had holidayed together in Bordeaux, where the Barton family had a prominent wine business, Barton & Guestier. Anthony Barton was not a sensitive romantic like Douglas-Home and when he jumped into bed with Margaret – at her beckoning – they both regarded it as a passing itch. Nonetheless, Barton's Danish wife, Eva, was furious when Margaret called her to confess – which was the first Eva knew about it. Tony's response was far more relaxed. Barton was no threat to the marriage and he could not himself pretend to be blameless, so it was easy to kiss and make up. The *Daily Mail*'s Nigel Dempster, who once more was very well informed of Margaret's adventures, quoted a friend of the Bartons: 'Margaret obviously enjoyed the role of *femme fatale*. She is a typical Leo – devious, destructive and jealous. I don't think Eva has ever forgiven her.' Douglas-Home, I thought, had probably felt the same way.

In any event, this view of Margaret was too simple. She had broken free of a sanctimonious regime at the palace. Tony introduced her to an uninhibited enjoyment of sex. She was fearful of losing that intensity of pleasure and willing to give him a certain amount of latitude in his own sexual tastes. They moved among openly libertine couples. Kenneth Tynan, for example, delighted in inviting them to some titillating amusements at his home. One evening, Tony and Margaret were there with Harold Pinter and his then wife Vivien Merchant and Peter Cook and his wife. Tynan put on a show of blue films, one of which was Jean Genet's notorious *Un Chant d'Amour*, which dived into the carnal details of a group of convicts making love to each other and with themselves. Rampant penises abounded. There were signs that this might have gone too far for Margaret, until Peter Cook began ad-libbing a voiceover that presented the film as a television ad for the phallic Cadbury's Flake bars. Everybody collapsed into laughter.

Margaret was also a victim of a syndrome I knew well: being a *Sunday Times* widow. Tony's long absences on assignments for the paper were serious opportunities for him to make his mark on stories where his personal security was not at risk. I knew of other marriages under strain where correspondents and photographers were sometimes away for months. The Vietnam War, for example, made the names and reputations of a number of the paper's correspondents and photographers. (Wives could become actual widows, as in the tragic case of Claire Tomalin, whose husband Nicholas, one of the finest of the paper's writers and a close friend of mine, was killed during the Arab–Israeli War in 1973.) Margaret was unhappy about these assignments but was unable to curtail them, leaving Tony with a feeling that she never really understood or respected the call of a vocation.

Douglas-Home's death was an awful consequence of Margaret's very powerful allure. At the very least, it struck me as a sign that Tony and Margaret were careless about enjoying themselves at the expense of others. Indeed, I saw in them a likeness of Scott Fitzgerald's rogue couple in *The Great Gatsby*, Tom and Daisy Buchanan: they were 'careless people ... They smashed up things and creatures and then retreated back into their money or their vast carelessness, or whatever it was that kept them together ... and let other people clear up the mess they had made.' The ultimate question in my mind was: how much promiscuity can a marriage take?

* * *

While the Snowdons' marriage headed for the rocks, so did the nation's economy. The Wilson government found that trying to prop up the pound at the level expected of a world power was an impossible task when, in reality, the country was no longer a world power. But the strength of the pound was indelibly tied to the national psyche to an irrational degree and, as it sank, Wilson was viewed by many as unequal to the needs of patriotism and British self-esteem. Consequently, the Queen found herself at the centre of what might well have been a constitutional crisis, involving the core reason for the very existence of the monarchy – that after all alternatives are exhausted, it provides a head of state free of political alignment and intrigues. Who, for example, would want a military man at the top instead of the Queen?

This question might have occurred to Earl Mountbatten in 1968 before he found himself involved in a demented plot to unseat Harold Wilson in a coup and create a 'government of national emergency' with himself at the top. Even today some crucial details of what happened remain either lost or obscured. This problem has, inevitably, helped to feed conspiracy theories about some 'deep state' revanchist movement against democratic governance. One way of trying to bring some clarity is to look at the people involved. They make a strange alliance. I knew two of them well, and they both left self-serving and conflicting accounts. All in all, the whole cast of conspirators is unimpressive. Anyone planning a serious coup d'état would not have taken any of them seriously, least of all Mountbatten – and part of Mountbatten's problem was that he took himself far too seriously.

The plot begins in the mind of one man, Cecil Harmsworth King. You will remember him as the eminence who created the magazine colossus IPC, where I was hired as the executive editor. He was also the supreme authority overseeing the *Daily Mirror* group – which is what makes him instrumental in this story. Even more fundamental to his role is that in 1965, in the first year of the Wilson government, King had been elected as one of eighteen members of the Court of the Bank of England and in March 1968 became one of four non-executive directors of the Bank's Committee of Treasury. This placed King in a unique and privileged position where he could see in detail the financial condition of the country. And that condition was dire. The previous November, Wilson had been forced to devalue the pound, reducing its value against the dollar from $2.80 to $2.40, a cut of 14 per cent. Devaluation always inflicted a psychological blow to national pride beyond its fiscal impact. Wilson struggled to appease the shock by saying that it did not mean that the pound 'in your pocket or purse or in your bank has been devalued'. In one day, the Bank of England had spent £200 million trying to shore up the pound before submitting to devaluation. Wilson was an economist. He was also a realist and he knew how deep his problems were. Three years earlier, he had inherited a deficit of £800 million from the Tories. But he hadn't anticipated the combined impact of a Middle East crisis that closed the Suez Canal and a series of crippling strikes at home.

Now, some five months later, as King inspected the Bank's books, things looked even bleaker. Moreover, he regarded Wilson and his government rather as a headmaster regarded delinquent pupils under his own charge. The *Mirror*'s support had propelled Wilson to power and now King wanted to pull that support. He wanted to go further – to replace the elected government with a new one of men he thought could save the nation from a coming calamity. Then he heard that Mountbatten shared the same idea. With Hugh Cudlipp's assistance, he arranged to meet Mountbatten at his London home at 4.30 p.m. on 8 May 1968 – an encounter that lies at the centre of the conspiracy and remains disputed in details. Cudlipp and King arrived to find a fourth participant, invited by Mountbatten: Sir Solly Zuckerman. Of the quartet, Zuckerman was the least likely to be a conspirator. He was chief scientific adviser to the Wilson government and had advised Prime Ministers since the Second World War, when he had been the leading advocate of strategic bombing. Zuckerman towered over the others in the room in intellect – it was said of him that 'he didn't suffer fools gladly … he didn't suffer them at all'. He must swiftly have felt that he was now trapped in the company of fools. King launched into an apocalyptic prediction of imminent political and social collapse: in Cudlipp's summing up, 'the government would disintegrate, there would be bloodshed in the streets, the armed forces would be involved'. At the end, King asked Mountbatten if he would agree to head a new administration 'in such circumstances'.

According to Cudlipp, Mountbatten turned to Zuckerman and said, 'You haven't said a word so far. What do you think of all this?'

Zuckerman's response is key to all subsequent versions and is portrayed rather like the stage directions of a Restoration comedy:

Zuckerman gets up, goes to the door. Halfway out of the door, he loudly declaims:

'This is rank treachery. All this talk of machine guns at street corners is appalling. I am a public servant and will have nothing to do with it. Nor should you, Dickie.'

Cue Mountbatten's private secretary, John Barratt, descending from an office above and reaching a landing where he is in earshot of Zuckerman; Barratt notes Zuckerman's words verbatim for future use.

Exit, a few minutes later, King and Cudlipp.

King, it turned out, had written in his diary a version of what happened in those crucial few minutes, and this account introduced the Queen:

Solly seemed embarrassed by this and hurried away … After Solly had gone, Mountbatten said he had been lunching at the Horse Guards and that morale in the armed forces had been so low. He said that the Queen was receiving an unprecedented number of petitions, all of which have been passed on to the Home Office. According to Dickie, she is desperately worried over the whole situation. He is obviously close to her and she is spending this weekend at Broadlands.

Mountbatten, according to King, then asked King if there was anything he should do, and King advised

that there might be a stage in future when the Crown would have to intervene: there might be a stage when the armed forces were important. Dickie should keep himself out of public view so as to have clean hands if either emergency should arise in the future. He has no wish to intervene anyway.

The whole farrago was driven by two monster egos, those of King and Mountbatten. The others were lesser players.

Cudlipp's relationship with King had always intrigued me as I observed it and it eventually came to a breaking point in the Mountbatten affair. Until now, Cudlipp, no faltering egoist himself, had openly genuflected before King: 'His capacity for greatness was generated by three attributes' he wrote in a memoir, '…his prodigious knowledge, his grasp of world events; and his foresight.' This was silly hagiography. King read widely, even obscurely. But it was the consumption of a vacuum cleaner, not a mind. His 'grasp of world events' was voyeurism in the anterooms of the great, seldom tempered with any kind of scholarship. His foresight, as shown in 1968, was of the dolorous variety driven by a serious patriotism gone awry. He was physically imposing and adopted the manner of the mandarin class, with a monumental conviction in his own superior wisdom. But he never knew what he didn't know and lacked that essential humility of intelligence which can be swayed by counter-advocacy. He would never have been taken seriously for very long by the editors of a serious paper, had he run one. But the *Mirror* did not have editors of that calibre and Cudlipp endured him out of a strange and yielding need to believe that a boss is a boss: 'Our areas of agreement on most matters had been wide over two or three decades but he was The Man With The Last Word' – Cudlipp's capitals in the memoir. But by 1968 Cudlipp was clearly unable to restrain King from his craziest impulses even though he shadowed him like a nervous minder. Perhaps he sensed that if he gave King enough rope he would hang himself. It turned out that King handed him that chance by ignoring his advice and making a fatal error.

Two days after the meeting with Mountbatten, Cudlipp consented to King taking over the front page of the *Mirror* to write an extraordinary personal attack on Wilson under the headline 'ENOUGH IS ENOUGH'. 'Wilson', wrote King, 'and his government have lost all credibility, all authority.' He complained that Britain had fallen behind the countries it defeated in the war – Japan, Germany and Italy. And he wound up with this: 'We are now threatened with the greatest financial crisis in our history. It is not to be removed by lies about our reserves, but only by a fresh start…'

Cudlipp failed twice to cut out the line about '*lies about our reserves*' – knowing that it was based on King's inside knowledge of the numbers from the Bank of England and the Treasury. Each time King refused. It was a wilful breach of the silence expected of members of the Court of the Bank of England and several days later King resigned from that post. The Labour Party leadership was enraged, but it was the board of IPC who decided that 'Enough Is Enough' applied more to King that it did to the Prime Minister and by the end of the month King was gone – dismissed in a personal letter written by Cudlipp, who succeeded him as chairman.

Mountbatten, meanwhile, lay low as King had advised. The mention in King's diary of an 'unprecedented number of petitions' to the Queen needed elaboration but received none from King. Who was petitioning? Were they, too, wanting to suspend democratic processes and move against Wilson? And who did Mountbatten have in mind to run a 'government of a national emergency' under him in some kind of quasi-presidential role?

The answer to the last question lay partly in something not present in any of the documentation of the time – because it was an atmospheric pressure rather than a recordable one. People were in thrall to a new idea that while politicians were failing in their competence to manage the country and bring out its real potential, there was, standing by waiting to be called, a cohort of just the talents required: the leaders of big business. I knew where this originated. Six years earlier at the *Sunday Times* magazine we did a big piece on the so-called German economic miracle, led by business tycoons at companies like Krupp, the steel makers, and Volkswagen (both had been willing collaborators of the Nazis). King's lament about the German and Japanese renaissance was from the same song sheet. As I knew from working for him, King regarded himself as model of business efficiency and admired others he believed had the same brisk realism. Business journalism was an accessory to this conceit. The serious newspapers were giving more prominence to it and, as a result, had seized on the idea that German managers were an example to the whole world and they began personalising business stories – suggesting the emergence of a new breed of British super managers.

Cudlipp noted that some of the names Mountbatten mentioned were businessmen – like, for example, the man who had taken an axe to the bloated British Rail network, Lord Beeching, who, as a result, was over-regarded as an all-purpose miracle worker. The trouble was that if you looked hard at the performance of British industries comparable to those of Germany, like cars and modern consumer products, they were woefully managed. Mountbatten also thought well of senior civil servants in Whitehall, even though they had little experience of real-world business and were easily bamboozled by business lobbyists – for example, by giving away North Sea oil drilling rights for ludicrously low sums. But there was another somewhat more sinister axis of interests that Mountbatten was also listening to as he warmed to the idea of a coup, as a result of his experience in the war. They were the old time-servers in MI5 and MI6, long skilled in unscrupulous methods of defending the realm, as well as what might be called the James Bond school of muscular patriotism, that included both Bond's creator, Ian Fleming, and his friend David Stirling, founder of the SAS.

It doesn't seem to have occurred to Mountbatten that this bizarre scheme, if revealed in all its vainglorious intrigue, presented a serious threat to the monarchy. Indeed, according to King's notes, Mountbatten had interpreted the Queen's flustered response to the 'petitions' as a sign that when she joined him that weekend at Broadlands he would be able to reassure her that, if it came to it, he had a remedy for what ailed the nation. There is no reliable documentary evidence of who actually put a stop to the scheme. The impression that Zuckerman's instinctive cry of horror, so carefully minuted by Mountbatten's secretary, put a stop to it there and then is patently false. There is an alternative theory, but it is weakly sourced. It first surfaced in a book published in 2007, *Indian Summer: The Secret History of the End of an Empire*, by Alex von Tunzelmann. Claiming to have a private source at the palace, Tunzelmann says it was the Queen herself who stopped the plot. This story was repeated, with attribution to von Tunzelmann, by Andrew Lownie in his 2019 biography of the Mountbattens. Von Tunzelmann did not answer requests from me to elaborate on her source. Since it is a classic case of one version of a story that totally transforms its outcome in favour of the royal family, it is a pity that it lacks broader authority. Nonetheless, if it was so, it must have been quite a moment. The Queen was one of the few people able to puncture the gigantic conceits of 'Dickie', the frustrated and permanently power-hungry rogue uncle. His part in the row over the family name (together with Philip's hectoring) had shown her how deeply felt his personal agenda was. Now, if this was true, she had saved him, and quite probably herself, from a truly disastrous constitutional crisis.

* * *

Meanwhile, as one Fleet Street tycoon was forcibly ejected, a new one appeared. Early in 1969 Rupert Murdoch, the scion of a powerful Australian newspaper-owning family, bought control of the *News of the World*. In order to get a foothold in Fleet Street, the young Murdoch was prepared to take on a business that he knew suffered from a malaise common to many of the London papers: poor management, chronic overstaffing and tired editorial formulas. To me he seemed like a welcome blast of new thinking, even if the *News of the World* was hardly an exemplar of great journalism. Many of his fellow Fleet Street proprietors were ossified relics of another age.

By this time, David Frost, largely because of the status he achieved as a journalist with *The Frost Programme*, had been the prime mover in a group that won the commercial television franchise for Friday, Saturday and Sunday in London. Having seen enough of the IPC magazine empire to know that it would take years to fix, I resisted entreaties from Cudlipp (sluiced by many shared bottles of fine claret) to stay and joined the company, London Weekend, as head of current affairs and executive producer of a new incarnation of *The Frost Programme*. For one of the first programmes, I suggested that we devote the whole time to an interview with Murdoch. He was still virtually unknown to the public. The timing was decided by Murdoch's decision to run a 'tell-all' memoir by the vamp of the Profumo affair, Christine Keeler. The *News of the World* promoted it as revelatory; as I knew very well from my own reporting there was nothing new in it. Murdoch paid Keeler £21,000 for the serial rights. He had not expected a hostile response to this decision but there was one, immediately. John Profumo had rehabilitated his reputation by spending the previous six years doing good works among the poor of East London. Cardinal Heenan, the Catholic archbishop of London, was one of many who protested on behalf of Profumo.

Murdoch accepted our invitation with alacrity. I met him in the Green Room and it was clear to me that he was extremely confident of his case for publishing the memoir. I cautioned him that Frost would press hard on his motivation – Murdoch claimed that Keeler's story had vital new details about how politicians had handled the scandal, which was nonsense. He had been quoted as saying 'People can sneer as much as they like, but I'll take the 150,000 extra copies we're going to sell.' It bothered me that Murdoch seemed not to know that he was facing the most forensically formidable interviewer on television. As a result, the first segment of the interview went badly for him. Frost demolished his defence and the studio audience were hostile. We didn't want a debacle: we wanted to get to the core of Murdoch's beliefs about journalism. So I did something I had never done – I went on the studio floor during the commercial break and made sure that Murdoch knew what was coming. Earlier in the day we had recorded an interview with Cardinal Heenan, who spoke forcefully on behalf of Profumo and said he thought it was shameful for him to be still pursued by Keeler. In fact, Murdoch could have argued that the real victim had been the publicly pilloried Stephen Ward, who had committed suicide. Instead, recoiling from Heenan's attack, he invented an absurd conspiracy theory that his attackers were 'members of the Establishment that don't want to be seen with Mr Profumo anywhere'.

The interview was a disaster for Murdoch. As he came off the set he headed straight for me and, jabbing a finger at me, said, 'You have just made an important new enemy.' He was equally furious with Frost. The next day he sent us a personal note that accused us of staging 'an unscrupulous ambush'. Frost replied in detail, pointing out how he had been fully briefed in advance of the line of questioning and about the Heenan interview, and that I had repeated the briefing points at the studio. There was something unexpectedly absurd in Murdoch's paranoia about an 'Establishment' stitch-up. As journalists we had a record of exposing scandals and disasters created in part by the power of the old-boy networks. Murdoch had no such credentials but for years afterwards he persisted in attacking as 'elitists' anyone who attacked him. More significantly, he did have a sure instinct for what sold newspapers and when he discovered that the royal family were catnip for tabloid readers he had no scruples about satisfying that appetite.

CHAPTER 17

A GREAT PAGEANT
AND A DISAPPEARED
DOCUMENTARY

With Charles reaching the age of twenty, the Queen decided that he should be publicly invested as the Prince of Wales – the twenty-first prince to hold that title – with a grand state ceremony in Wales in July 1969. (He acquired the title when he was nine, on the initiative of the Queen, who announced it at the close of the 1958 Commonwealth Games in Cardiff, without forewarning Charles.) The idea was encouraged by the Queen Mother, who had acted as a ready shoulder for Charles to cry on during the assault-course experience of Gordonstoun. She saw in Charles some of the inner psychological torments suffered by her husband, George VI, with whom she had developed caring skills, particularly in helping to overcome his stutter, that her daughter clearly lacked and were needed anew. 'Launching' Charles in public, she believed, might give him some of the gravitas thus far absent from his image.

There has always been something ersatz, something phoney and fabricated, about the title the Prince of Wales. For a start, there is the way it is arbitrarily imposed on Wales, whether the Welsh want their own prince or not. After Wales was conquered by Edward I, who invested his baby son with the title in 1301, the Welsh were never consulted. And there was not much loot attached to the title, not enough to encourage actual residence in Wales. The other title that came at the same time was far more lucrative: Duke of Cornwall. The Duchy of Cornwall included vast estates and properties in the West Country and London (as we shall see, Prince Charles has turned the Duchy into a multi-million-pound industry).

The Welsh title does not pass automatically to the heir to the throne. Technically, the monarch could withhold it if they felt it inappropriate, but in modern times it is taken as obligatory. And, of course, it carries great significance by ranking this prince above all others. The problem is that the princes are usually pushed into the role before they are ready for it. Charles might have been aware of this risk; he had only to look back to what happened to his great-uncle, Prince Edward.

King George V conferred the title on Edward at Windsor on his sixteenth birthday, 23 June 1910. He was then a naval cadet at Dartmouth. The King was concerned that Edward was immature – the euphemism he used was 'young for his years'. He determined that Edward would gain authority by staging his investiture as a great piece of public theatre, and that happened a year later, in the summer of 1911. A Prince of Wales hadn't been anointed in Wales since the future Charles I in 1616 (although the authenticity of that event is hazy). The idea that a Prince of Wales should actually be crowned in Wales came from David Lloyd George, the Liberal politician and fervent Welsh patriot. What ensued was an over-the-top pageant with some of the feeling of a Gilbert and Sullivan opera. The site chosen was the unoccupied and partly ruined medieval castle at Caernarfon in north-west Wales, a place that belongs more in the world of *Game of Thrones* than among occupied royal piles.

There was no precedent for how the prince should be costumed, so one was invented: a purple coat of velvet edged with ermine over white satin breeches and topped with a coronet cap. Edward protested that appearing in this 'preposterous rig' – indeed, it was like something out of *HMS Pinafore* – would make him risible to his naval colleagues, but his mother persuaded him to go through with it. Winston Churchill, who was Home Secretary, proclaimed his titles and his father duly confirmed him. Lloyd George had coached him to speak a few lines in Welsh, including 'Diolch fy nghalon I Hen wlad fy nhadau' – 'Thanks from the bottom of my heart to the old land of my fathers.'

Tony Snowdon couldn't speak Welsh (although his grandfather did), but he had proved with his response to the tragedy at Aberfan that he felt a real kinship with Wales. The Queen had given him the honorific title of Constable of Caernarfon and when I heard that she had given him charge of designing the new investiture at Caernarfon it seemed encouraging, though obviously a challenge. How do you modernise something that is essentially archaic? Of course, the only thing authentically medieval about this ceremony was the castle itself. But it seemed reasonable to assume that Tony, with his preference for functional elegance over pretension, would avoid the awful kitsch of the last investiture. This time the show was being televised, the first royal broadcast in colour. From the start, Tony was up against a couple of reactionaries: the Duke of Norfolk, who, as Earl Marshal, had the ultimate control of all state ceremonies, and the Garter King of Arms, Sir Anthony Wagner. As is usual with experts on heraldry and royal insignia, Sir Anthony was a pedant for detail. Tony chose Welsh dragons as a natural icon of Welsh lore and identity and set them on scarlet banners. He wanted dragons with knotted tails. Sir Anthony said knots were not allowed. 'Oh, come on, Garter darling, can't you be a bit more elastic?' Tony pleaded in the deliberately camp tone that I had heard in many a *Sunday Times* meeting. Garter relented on the dragons but was responsible for the worst outbreak of kitsch in the whole ceremony, the coronet to be placed on Charles's head by the Queen. Tony suggested a plain, unadorned coronet of gold as worn by the great warrior King Henry V. Sir Anthony prevailed with a much larger confection of his own involving gold, jewels, crosses, an orb, velvet padding and fleurs-de-lis. Not only was it heavy but it was too big. As the Queen slipped it on, it settled just above Charles's eyes and he had to gently nudge it back up his temple. The Queen was not amused by Sir Anthony's cumbersome coronet. Recounting the event afterwards to Noël Coward, she compared it to a candle snuffer.

Tony's acknowledged success was the centrepiece of the television ceremony, a dais of Welsh slate set on grass – he eschewed red carpets – with three simple thrones of slate for the Queen, Philip and Charles. Above this, Tony placed a large, tilted canopy of plain Perspex on cantilevered poles, a structure he had first modelled in his workshop at Kensington Palace. It was a clever adaptation of the far grander dais that George V, as Emperor of India, had sat on for the Delhi Durbar of 1911, as intimidating as Tony's version was humble – and cutting back on the pomp was Tony's real achievement. Instead of a repeat of Edward's operatic investiture, this was a great hit on TV screens across the world. In the US it gave the NBC network the highest rating it had ever had for a live event. (The BBC rebroadcast it on the fiftieth anniversary in 2019.) Tony had managed a clever balance of the medieval and modern, something that the royal family was having constant trouble achieving.

In fact, the family were still continually conflicted about how to manage this tension. The Wilson government was finally fulfilling its promise to end the archaic censorship of plays by the office of the Lord Chamberlain. However, at a Cabinet meeting, Wilson said he had received representations from the palace. According to Richard Crossman, a minister present at the meeting, Wilson explained, 'They don't want to ban all plays about live persons, but they want to make sure that there's somebody who'd stop the kind of play about Prince

Philip which would be painful to the Queen … They want to be able to ban plays devoted to character assassination.' No such restraint – other than the libel laws – was allowed to remain. And the mindset in the palace that thought it should, represented by Commander Colville, disappeared with his retirement in 1968. He was replaced by a brisk Australian, William Heseltine, who better understood what the most powerful influence on the public view of the monarchy now was – television. The Duke of Norfolk, overseeing the Caernarfon spectacular, had grudgingly conceded that television was now a fact of life: 'If people invent these things,' he said to Tony, 'you've got to live with them.' Heseltine also knew that the BBC was no longer the fawning accessory to royalty that it was when Altrincham fired his salvo in 1957. In 1966, the corporation's most-watched current affairs programme, *Panorama*, aired a special titled 'The Monarchy and Its Future'. It exposed a split in the nation's view of the royal family. Scholars of the constitution and metropolitan commentators lamented that Altrincham's critique had not resulted in fundamental changes in the monarchy – like less pomp and ritual and more engagement with real life. But the view in the hinterlands remained loyal to the point of absurdity: an unpublished survey showed that a majority felt that if the opinions of the monarch and the Prime Minister conflicted, the Queen's would prevail – that she *should* prevail.

The producer of the programme, Jeremy Murray-Brown, was asked by a publisher to commission a series of essays with the same title, *The Monarchy and Its Future*. Murray-Brown had been particularly incensed that the two most vocal critics of the Windsors, Altrincham and Malcolm Muggeridge, had been banned for years from appearing on the BBC and he asked both to contribute to the book. Altrincham, now under his commoner name of John Grigg, agreed. Muggeridge did not, saying, 'The subject bores me to death.' I was one of the other sixteen invited to join Grigg.

In a piece with the title 'The Palace and the Image Machine', I compared the Windsors to America's royal family, the Kennedys. This was partly informed by a column I had written for *The Times* on Robert Kennedy's successful campaign for a Senate seat in New York State. This article had not gone down well with Kennedy's public relations gurus. They objected to my analysis that they had packaged and branded Kennedy using the same techniques employed for consumer products. But it was true. I showed how the Kennedy clan had been transformed from tough Boston-Irish politicians of a reactionary cast into Prince Charmings, witty, enlightened and elegant. Robert Kennedy was just the latest product in the line, albeit a winning one. What would happen, I asked, if these same techniques were applied to the royals? Somewhat facetiously, I wrote:

> Would Mary Quant be appointed wardrobe mistress? Would the Queen give up the racing calendar for Len Deighton thrillers? Could Buck House swing like the rest of the town? Would there be riots in the rest of Europe calling for restoration of the monarchies to provide a new dynamic to government? Would Harold Wilson publish a book called *The Wit of The Queen*?

Having set up a straw man, I then unpicked it, arguing that the Kennedy techniques would turn the family into a grotesque fantasy. Instead, I recommended that the case for the monarchy in a rapidly changing society should be made not by amateurs, as it usually was, but by professionals able to judge the consequences – often second- or third-stage consequences – of royal activities. And I wound up by saying:

> If only the Queen could really appear as she is, in an unrehearsed, informal and involved situation discussing, for example, her ideas

of the national purpose with others who have a chance of shaping it – all this in front of television cameras – how much more value it would have than the appallingly contrived and useless Christmas broadcast.

(On long reflection, I was probably mistaken in thinking that the Queen had the intellectual curiosity to debate 'her ideas of the national purpose'.)

Malcolm Muggeridge reviewed the book for *The Observer*. Over-generously, he wrote, 'In the light of Mr Irving's contribution many of the others become irrelevant.' One of the shrewdest pieces was, in my view, by a young Indian writer, Sasthi Brata, who said:

If not exactly divine, British society still considers its monarchs above the normal run of human beings. And because there is no rational basis for this belief we call it a mystique. But such a mystique creates an unhealthy dialectic. We disapprove of the principle of heredity as a valid basis for social discrimination – in theory at any rate – yet at the apex of the social pyramid the monarch exemplifies that very principle ... The monarchy provides sanction to caste.

Unknown to me when I wrote my essay, Buckingham Palace had already decided that the royal family needed a media makeover. And they fell right into the trap I had posited of attempting a Kennedy-style rebranding. Heseltine, the new broom, argued that the Queen and her family had become 'one-dimensional figures'. Prince Philip agreed: 'It is quite wrong', he said, 'that there should be a sense of remoteness or majesty. If people see, whoever it happens to be, whatever head of state, as individuals, as people, I think it makes it much easier for them to accept the system and feel part of the system.' The error lay right there. The core quality of the royal brand *was* majesty. It was as an inexact word describing a quality of appearance and stature supposedly attained only by birth. Once reduced to acquaintance and familiarity in the form of 'individuals' or 'people', that quality would be jeopardised – the mere effort of seeming to be normal would either debase the coinage or end up looking fake. And there was no new bargain to be made in which the people would feel 'part of the system'.

In my essay, I wrote that the Queen had never pretended to be what she was not. Now, by following the urging of Philip and Heseltine, she was being lured into passing herself off as two people: the monarch and a normal wife and mother. The palace recruited a top BBC documentary director, Richard Cawston, to create an epic piece of *cinéma vérité* that would be broadcast just before the Caernarfon investiture. One strand of the conceit was to show how arduous the job of being Queen was. She would be filmed making state visits to Brazil and Chile. She would be seen greeting world leaders in London, working at her desk with state papers, taking her weekly audience with the Prime Minister, organising and presiding over a garden party. This was set alongside some of her private passions, her horses and her dogs. Filming lasted nearly a year and covered 172 locations. At first, the Queen, showing a sound instinct, was reluctant to play this new role. She had never before been asked to tolerate the constant presence and scrutiny of cameras. But on the advice of those around she relented and got on with it, as was her stoic way.

The documentary was called *Royal Family* and was broadcast on 21 June 1969. The audience in Britain was 40 million and abroad totalled around 400 million in 130 nations, but in terms of a rebranding exercise the result was a disaster. There were scenes of excruciating banality – the family trying to look folksy around the kitchen table, the Queen washing the dishes, the Queen shopping for sweets with a young Edward near Balmoral and discovering she was not carrying enough money. Some critics had fun trying to place the Windsors in the correct social bracket suggested by their performances and the locations. These ranged from chatty suburban arrivistes to stuffy county squirearchy. David Attenborough, the doyen of BBC documentarians, who was one of the producers, used his anthropological knowledge in delivering his verdict. He said that the monarchy was an institution that 'depends on mystique and the tribal chief in his hut. If any member of the tribe ever sees inside the hut, then the whole system of the tribal chiefdom is damaged and the tribe eventually disintegrates.' After its initial broadcasts, the documentary was never seen again (though snatches of it can now be found on YouTube). The Queen made no comment herself, but Princess Anne later said it was 'a rotten idea' and that the last thing the family wanted was more access by the public.

In the blunt language of marketing, nobody was buying this version of the product. There was far less reverence for it, anyway. *The Monarchy and Its Future* included some brutal cartoons of the family. In one, by the *Evening Standard* cartoonist JAK, the Queen sits in a tacky armchair with her bare feet in a mustard bath and hair in curlers reading the equestrian magazine *The Field*, with Philip standing alongside looking like a six-pints-a-night slob, and the Queen says, 'My husband and I always have Thursdays off.' Gerald Scarfe, then drawing for the *Daily Mirror*, has the Queen saddled to a rearing stallion burdened with imperial banners while Philip clings on desperately to the horse's arse.

And it was Philip who, early in November, blundered into a new controversy. While touring America, he was asked about the royal finances. He portrayed the family like a business that was going bankrupt: they were going into the red and might have to sell Buckingham Palace; the level of their public funding was based on costs as they were eighteen years ago and was falling far short of the need. In public, Harold Wilson tried to correct the picture, tactfully saying that although the accounts had been in surplus they were about to go into a deficit and to deal with this he would appoint a committee to adjust the amount. In private, though, Wilson faced outrage from three Cabinet members who were republicans: Richard Crossman, Roy Jenkins and Barbara Castle. The flame-haired Castle let rip: Philip's complaint was outrageous. Crossman backed her up, noting in his diary, 'The Queen pays no estate or death duties, the monarchy hasn't paid any since these taxes were invented and it has made her by far the richest person in the country.' Wilson, by then a devoted fan of the Queen, nonetheless agreed. He said that most rich people, having acquired wealth, devoted a good part of it to charitable work – only royalty assumed that they could keep all their private income to themselves and not spend any of it on their public duties. At the time, Wilson was struggling to establish a national prices and incomes policy, yet in public he showed no indignation towards Philip and no interest in having the royal family pay taxes. 'Harold is a steady loyalist,' wrote an exasperated Crossman.

As the royal family withdrew once more into its protective ramparts, the newest and least-known of the newspaper owners, Rupert Murdoch, launched a tabloid, *The Sun*. He was already planning this move, the second step in building an empire, when I encountered him during his fracas with David Frost. Restless with the limitations of a Sunday paper, he wanted a daily companion for the *News of the World*.

Nobody except Murdoch really foresaw the kind of paper he had in mind, least of all me. I reviewed the first issue of *The Sun* for the media industry magazine *Campaign* and dismissed it as dull and provincial. My piece was illustrated with a cartoon by Ralph Steadman, who was far more prophetic than me: he had the editor, a bloated, bibulous-looking figure, in shirtsleeves at his desk when a sub-editor bursts into his office with, literally, a shovel full of steaming shit crying out, '*Hold the front page!*' Murdoch bought the title and plant of *The*

Sun from the *Daily Mirror*. It had earlier morphed from the Labour Party's official organ, the *Daily Herald*, to a bland broadsheet under the direction of Hugh Cudlipp, who was relieved to get the paper off his hands. But Cudlipp had fatally and unwittingly enabled the *Mirror*'s future nemesis. *The Sun* was to turn out to be a lucrative foundation for the Murdoch empire, as well as the template for a radical vulgarisation of popular journalism. When Murdoch bought *The Sun*, it was selling 800,000 copies a day. Ten years later, it was selling 3.7 million copies a day (with a great deal of help from its impudent coverage of the monarchy), outstripping the *Mirror*.

CHAPTER 18

A KING TAKES HIS
SECRETS TO THE GRAVE

In the late spring of 1972, the Queen was deployed in a role that many British monarchs before her had not relished: being nice to the French. The government had successfully negotiated the terms for Britain to join the European Common Market, as it was then called, after initial indifference to the project followed by several abortive attempts to join. France had always been resistant to allowing Britain to become a member. Harold Macmillan, blaming the intransigence of Charles de Gaulle, said that the general had never forgiven Britain for winning the war – implying, of course, that de Gaulle was an ingrate since it was Britain that gave him sanctuary when France collapsed. De Gaulle, in his turn, asserted that the British could never be natural Europeans because they were too attached to their former colony on the other side of the Atlantic. The Queen proved herself able to rise triumphally above these historical antipathies. Georges Pompidou, the French President, had consented to a state visit without realising that the French people had not entirely lost their enthusiasm for monarchs. At Versailles, the Sun King's opulent creation, the Queen outshone even that setting at a banquet, her tiara aglow as she told Pompidou, 'We may drive on different sides of the road, but we are going the same way.' Riding through Paris in an open car with the

President, she suddenly looked like the Queen of France as the swooning crowds lined the boulevards.

But there was a darker side to the visit. Before she left for France, the Queen had been told that her exiled uncle, the Duke of Windsor, had terminal throat cancer. There had been something of a thaw in relations between the Queen and the Duke. Seven years earlier, she had agreed that when he died the Duke could be buried in the royal family's cemetery at Frogmore in Windsor Home Park, and that the Duchess could be buried alongside him. Four months before the Queen's state visit, Earl Mountbatten had called on the 77-year-old Duke at his home in the Bois de Boulogne and found him very ill and frail, down to 100 pounds in weight. The Duke told Mountbatten, 'There's something I bet you don't realise. If I hadn't abdicated, I'd have completed thirty-six years of my reign by now – longer than either my father or grandfather.' Now, the Queen had been told, the Duke had only days to live.

Wallis Simpson, so reviled by the royal family as the instigator of one of the most traumatic crises the monarchy had faced, steeled herself for the Queen's visit. The Duke was in bed, connected to an intravenous drip. He insisted that Lilibet – as he still called the Queen – should not see him like this. He demanded that the drip be removed, and the doctors consented. Wallis spent four hours helping to get him out of bed, dressed him in one of his signature blue blazers and put him in a chair ready to receive the Queen. He was now down to eighty-five pounds and the blazer hung loose around the shrinking body.

Wallis curtsied deeply as the Queen arrived with Prince Philip and Prince Charles. The Queen was taken to the room where the Duke sat while Wallis served tea to the others. There is no record of what was said during the fifteen minutes that the Queen spent with her uncle, but one of the doctors said there were tears in her eyes when they parted. There are conflicting versions of the Duke's last hours. Late in the night on 27 May, he asked for and was served a bowl of stewed peaches, a favourite from his nursery days. In the early morning of 28 May, Wallis was called to his bedside. In one version his last word was 'Darling', while another had him crying out 'Mama, Mama, Mama, Mama.'

A few days later, the body lay in a coffin on a specially built catafalque in St George's Chapel, Windsor, where, for two days, members of the public filed by. On the first day 30,000 people came. The queue was a mile long. By the second day the total was 57,000 people. Many women wept as they reached the catafalque. One of them said, 'I am a monarchist. By what he did the Duke preserved the monarchy for all of us. But over the years he has been shabbily treated.' That was a kind thought; Edward's weakness was that he rarely put the monarchy above his own pleasures and prejudices, as a journey back to his youth demonstrates.

* * *

It is the summer of 1924, the Roaring Twenties in New York, the setting for *The Great Gatsby* and Prohibition and Flappers and bootlegged liquor and speakeasies and the refrain 'I danced with a man who danced with a girl who danced with the Prince of Wales'. But there is a more first-hand witness of Edward as a dancing partner: 'He dances like an American and does all the dances well. He plays the drums exquisitely. Oh, he is terribly smart. He's the cutest trick.' This is Rosie Dolly, one half of the Dolly Sisters, identical twins who starred in *The Ziegfeld Follies* and seduced a succession of wealthy men in Europe and America. She was talking to a reporter from the *New York Tribune* during rehearsals for a new revue, *The Greenwich Village Follies*. The sisters arrived in Manhattan from Europe a month ahead of Edward. 'If the Prince of Wales ever kissed the Dolly Sisters, they're not telling on him,' wrote the reporter. Jenny, the other sister, had enjoyed a fling with Edward after meeting him at a party in London in 1921, but many partners had passed in the night for both of them: 'He has been reported engaged so often, I don't know … I don't think he wants to marry at all,' Rosie explained with the air of someone to whom princes, magnates and playboys of all hues were just fleeting, fickle figures in the endless carnival of life.

When the Prince of Wales arrived in New York on the liner *Berengaria*, he was immediately drawn into the world of Jay Gatsby – the actual location and the actual society that Scott Fitzgerald had immortalised in his novel, the north shore of Long Island, studded with the mansions of the very rich, the barons of steel, railroads and oil, where the sports were polo matches, horse racing and sailing. Its residents vied for his presence as though his market value as a trophy was greater than any of the commodities they traded in – one millionaire spent a staggering $1.5 million on a party for 1,200 where Edward was the guest of honour. And then he disappeared.

Prohibition introduced a new level of thrill for New York club life – and risk. Public figures needed to know where, among the wide choice of nightspots selling booze, they would be safe from a sudden arrival of the New York cops and the scandal of being taken away in a paddy wagon. Connoisseurs of this scene tipped off Edward that the club du jour was Texas Guinan's El Fey Club. Mary Louise 'Texas' Guinan was a remarkably versatile talent who, among other things, moved from being a showgirl to become one of the first women to direct silent films. But she found her true calling in the speakeasy, first as a singing star and then, because she was able to embody the quintessence of the hard-nosed, fast-talking, hard-drinking 'doll' of the age, as the hostess of the club on West 47th Street – the 'Fey' in the name was an amendment of the name of the owner, a gangster called Larry

Fay. Guinan also had a flair for talent spotting: Ruby Keeler, Barbara Stanwyck and George Raft were all discovered while dancing at the El Fey. Her classic catchphrase was 'Hello, sucker! Come on in and leave your wallet on the bar.' Edward, along with Dickie Mountbatten and others in his entourage, found her irresistible and went to the club several nights in a row.

Guinan, in turn, like Rosie Dolly, thought the Prince of Wales was 'the cutest trick' and called him Eddie. Then, early one morning when the place was at its most riotous, Prohibition agents burst through the doors. According to Guinan, she had enough warning to scoop Edward off the dance floor and into the kitchen, where she put him in chef's whites and told him to fry eggs. Mountbatten was told to masquerade as a drummer in the band. Guinan is the only source for this event, and her account came long afterwards, so it may well have been self-servingly embroidered. But for one detail: the Prince of Wales gave her a vanity case studded with diamonds in gratitude. The New York dailies of the time followed the royal progress in the same breathless, uncritical way they covered movie stars, and there was no hint of scandal. Just think about it: if the tabloids of today were to catch the slightest whiff of a current Windsor prince romping through the underworld of Manhattan as Edward did, the scandal would be cataclysmic.

There was one person in the royal entourage who was appalled that a future king was so careless and wanton: Tommy Lascelles. Here is the first appearance of the man who was to become the stern moralist of the Margaret and Townsend affair. He arrived in New York as the prince's assistant private secretary – in effect, the minder with the thankless task of keeping scandals at bay on behalf of the King and the royal household. What must have concerned Lascelles was that Edward's behaviour was not a final burst of youthful dissipation and indiscretion: the main traits of his character were already fully formed and all too clear. As a young man, Lascelles was already 'old guard' – raised in an aristocratic tradition of what was needed in those who served the court, the very essence of probity and self-discipline. He was also far superior to his master in intellect and cultural sophistication. We can only imagine how annoying it must have been for Edward to be shadowed by such a serious scold. However, it's not necessary to imagine how Lascelles felt. He left the prince's household in 1929 and made it known that it was because he could barely stand the sight of the man he served. 'Words like "decency", "honesty", "duty", "dignity" and so on meant absolutely nothing to him,' Lascelles said. He did return to royal service in the last year of George V's reign and then, as we have seen, rose to become private secretary to George VI. Lascelles was as loyal and admiring of George VI as he was embittered by Edward's inadequacies as a monarch and a human being. The bitterness was mutual. During his long passage from the throne to exile and, eventually, death in France, the Duke of Windsor always spoke of Lascelles as a nemesis. But Lascelles knew many skeletons in the Windsor cupboard, including the fact that Edward's wayward ways were no worse than those of his brother George, the Duke of Kent.

*   *   *

At the end of the Battle of Britain in 1940, Churchill saluted the small band of victors: 'Never was so much owed by so many to so few.' The Royal Air Force had matched in glory Nelson's victory at Trafalgar. It therefore seems counter-historical to discover that only a decade earlier the RAF harboured men who, rather than confronting fascism, worked to build a concordat between Britain and Nazi Germany. The Duke of Kent, who wore the RAF uniform, was a prime mover in this effort. The more that is discovered about George's pro-German advocacy, the more obvious it becomes that history's view of the Duke of Windsor as a single rogue admirer of Hitler is mistaken. Even though the records of George's role have been assiduously purged, there are enough clues to see how prolonged and serious it was and that in his avidity to avoid war at any cost he was every bit the equal of the Duke of Windsor.

The trail begins with one of the most elusive yet instrumental figures of the whole saga, Frederick Winterbotham. During the First World War, when the fledgling air force was called the Royal Flying Corps, Winterbotham commanded a squadron in which one of the pilots was Baron Wilhelm de Ropp, a member of a noble family from the German Baltic coast, who had settled in England in 1910, become a naturalised British citizen and married a British woman. After the war, in 1920, de Ropp, who was by then shaken by the speed and success of the Soviet Revolution and fearful that it might envelop Europe, returned to Germany, settling in Berlin with his wife. At some point he became a close friend of Alfred Rosenberg, one of the leading ideologues of the right-wing *Völkisch* movement that, under Hitler, morphed into the Nazi Party. Subsequently, Rosenberg introduced de Ropp to Hitler. Largely through the linkage of Rosenberg, de Ropp and Winterbotham, contacts between the Nazis and people sympathetic with them in Britain began long before Hitler came to power.

In 1928, Prince George, having bailed from the Navy, much to his father's disgust, became the first member of the royal family to work as a civil servant: he was given a job at the Foreign Office, where his linguistic range was an asset. A year later he became the first member of the royal family to qualify as a pilot, and found his true medium in the air. He became a member of the Guild of Air Pilots and Air Navigators, a vocational club organised on Masonic lines, and because of his status and glamour he moved easily among the top echelons of British aviation. Together with his day job in Whitehall, this meant that his political connections were wider than those of any other member of the royal family – and an obvious target for anyone wanting to reach that family.

Depending on how the light fell on him, George could seem to have very different personalities. By day, he was the upright junior Foreign Office official; by night, he was alternating between the pursuit of famous women – his conquests included the African-American dancer Florence Mills, Gloria Swanson and Tallulah Bankhead – and the pursuit of young men, with a preference for Aryan blonds, one of whom described him as 'artistic and effeminate' and strongly perfumed. This double life was conducted under the close watch of his brother the Prince of Wales. Edward's serious efforts had ended George's drug habit but the two of them shared handsome bachelor quarters within St James's Palace, in York House, far enough away from their broody father in Buckingham Palace for the debauchery to be discreet.

In 1930, Winterbotham became head of the Air Intelligence Section of MI6. Weimar Germany was still observing the post-war ban against rearming, a ban that Hitler had no intention of honouring. Air power was already viewed as the new superweapon and the air forces of Europe, particularly those of Britain and France, were leading its development. However, Winterbotham's predominant interest was in Germany. He had established a bond with his former German adversaries because of a strangely chivalrous code they shared: the man-on-man combat of the war had been conducted like a knightly jousting. Each side honoured the other's dead with special burial services. Winterbotham's German contacts included some of the war aces who would create Hitler's powerful Luftwaffe.

The value to Germany of this cliquish association was clear in a report from Alfred Rosenberg to Hitler in 1935:

The attempts to find people in England who were eager to

comprehend the German movement date back to 1929. Our English agent [he's referring to de Ropp] in Berlin then made possible my first journey to London in 1931. There it was possible to make a number of contacts which worked out well for Anglo-German understanding. In the forefront was Squadron Leader Winterbotham, a member of the Air General Staff, who was entirely convinced that Germany and England must move together to ward off the Bolshevik danger. The outcome of the various discussions was the widening of the group amongst the Air General Staff, and the Royal Air Force Club became the centre for fostering Anglo-German understanding.

Along with a number of the conduits used to reach Hitler personally as the Nazis sought to 'educate' members of the British royal family, Rosenberg's influence should be carefully measured for its importance. Rosenberg had been in Hitler's inner circle a long time. When Hitler was jailed for five years in 1924 for leading his failed putsch (he was released after nine months), he left Rosenberg in charge of the party – probably because he presented no threat as a successor. But Hitler had long rejected Rosenberg's personal version of National Socialism as a political religion, almost a spiritual cult. For Hitler, it was a hard-nosed secular system based on science, albeit a perverted view of science. As far as Hitler was concerned, the only permissible cult was himself. Nonetheless, Rosenberg could credibly pass himself off as an authoritative agent of the Führer. And so it was that Winterbotham's most immediate contact, his old flying companion de Ropp, because of his closeness to Rosenberg, also became a credible player in the game.

And by 1933, with Hitler now in power, we find that de Ropp is visiting London openly enough for him to place a wreath woven in the shape of a swastika on the cenotaph to the war dead in Whitehall.

More importantly, Winterbotham's initiative has taken de Ropp directly to the two Windsor princes, George and Edward, so that he can lay out to them what to expect from the new Nazi regime as it ruthlessly consolidates its power. The only journalist present at that meeting (working for Beaverbrook's *Evening Standard*), Sir Robert Bruce Lockhart, who was also a former British counter-intelligence agent, noted in his diary that Prince George was 'strong in the German camp'.

A year later, Winterbotham was allowed by the Germans to make a tour of Luftwaffe bases with de Ropp's help and afterwards met Hitler. This policy of openness was a calculated tactic of German propagandists that followed a two-track course, playing up how formidable the Luftwaffe would be while assuring the British that Hitler believed that Germany and Britain were natural allies against Bolshevism. The legendary American pilot Charles Lindbergh was so swayed by this tactic that he said that there was no way that Britain or America could equal German air power. In London, the same fear had been expressed by the once and future Prime Minister Stanley Baldwin, who told Parliament, 'It is well for the man in the street to realise that there is no power on earth that can protect him from being bombed. Whatever people may tell him, the bomber will always get through.'

As an exercise in psychological warfare, Hitler had cause to believe that he had already won a war against Britain without fighting it, and the royal family had been frequently subjected to the same theme. In January 1935, Rosenberg noted in his diary that, using the 'Air Ministry' as a channel, de Ropp had again met 'unobtrusively' in London with the 'King's adviser, Prince George', for three hours, and that George had then reported to his father, George V, in a move that, according to Rosenberg, 'contributed very greatly to strengthening the pressure for a reconstruction of the Cabinet and mainly towards beginning the movement in the direction of Germany'.

Bear in mind that this is happening simultaneously with the promulgation by the Nazis of the notorious Nuremburg Laws decreeing that Jews were now defined as being not of German blood, and marriage between Jews and German 'nationals' was forbidden. Two British officials, Eric Mills and Frank Foley, went to Berlin to negotiate the resettlement of German Jews in Palestine. They reported to the Foreign Office in London that 'German policy is clearly to eliminate the Jew from German life, and the Nazis do not mind how this is accomplished. Mortality and emigration provide the means.' Mills wrote in a private letter, 'I knew that the Jewish situation was bad, I had not realised as I now do that the fate of the German Jews is a tragedy … The Jew is to be eliminated and the state has no regard for the manner of his elimination.'

That was not a message that the royal princes wished to hear. In fact, the question is – what exactly did the two princes want to hear from Berlin that would reassure them? '*Want to hear*' is valid in the circumstances because there was clearly a natural bias – almost an anxiety – to see Nazi Germany as a wholly compatible ally of Great Britain against Bolshevism, no matter what atrocities were under way. In this, the princes were far from alone. They shared their wishful thinking with the large body of influential people in Britain who were ready to choose appeasement over confrontation. But unlike those people, whose views were openly discussed and promoted and are a matter of historical record, the Windsor princes took care to be far more clandestine as they worked their backchannel to Berlin and visited their German relatives.

In 1936, the one year that he was King, Edward continued on the trajectory he had followed with his brother with even greater urgency, but it was no longer furtive. There was, for example, a detailed record of the previously mentioned conversations he had had with Charles Edward, the Duke of Saxe-Coburg-Gotha, a grandson of Queen

Victoria, who had joined Hitler's Brownshirts. The King, he reported to Hitler, 'had a sincere resolve to bring England and Germany together'. More worryingly, some of those around him saw an intention in him to wrest more power to himself and away from the politicians. Sir Henry 'Chips' Channon, the snippiest diarist of the time, noted, 'The King ... is going the dictator way, and is pro-German against Russia ... I shouldn't be surprised if he aimed at making himself a mild dictator...'

But it was Edward's open embrace of Nazi Germany and Hitler during a visit there, now as the Duke of Windsor, in October 1937 that sealed his reputation as a dupe – or worse – of fascist propaganda. He was twice seen giving the full Hitler salute to guards of honour lined up for his inspection and then, with Wallis Simpson, he met the Führer at the Berghof, his Bavarian retreat with its vast window overlooking the Untersberg, the massif that straddles the border of Bavaria and Austria and conveys the mystical effects of a Wagnerian Valhalla, in accord with Hitler's sense of his own epic destiny. Inevitably, it was Hitler who dominated the encounter: the Duke and Duchess looked like supplicants to a demi-God.

As Edward became far too conspicuously a tool of the Nazis, his younger brother was far more circumspect but no less committed to an Anglo-German peace pact. He was given cover by Neville Chamberlain's surrender to Hitler's terms at Munich in September 1938. It could hardly be argued that it was treacherous for the Duke of Kent to persist in backchannel contacts with the Nazis while the Prime Minister himself had turned out to be such a willing appeaser. It must also be remembered that the 'peace at all costs' lobby that encircled Churchill as he came to power in 1940, led by Lord Halifax, had as few scruples about living with Hitler as the Duke did. In fact, Halifax supported a peace plan that the Duke of Kent delivered to his German relative, Prince Philipp of Hesse, barely a month before the outbreak of war in September 1939, hoping for an opening for him to see Hitler. And all of this was going on with the assent of the third brother, the King, George VI, who backed Chamberlain and, at least for a while, regarded Churchill as a reckless warmonger. In the light of what we now know, it's clear that three Windsor Kings were successively riding in the same train to a rapprochement with Hitler: George V, Edward VIII and George VI, and from the beginning in 1929 it was the Duke of Kent who set the course and provided the staying power. The courtier who said, as I have noted earlier, that it was lucky that the Duke died a hero's death in a plane crash in 1942 must have known all of this.

As Andrew Roberts says in his Churchill biography with acute clarity, 'The important point about Churchill in 1940 is not that he stopped a German invasion that year, but that he stopped the British government from making peace.' And one has to ask, what kind of peace would that have been? How would the royal family have complied with it? The communications between the Duke of Windsor and the Germans before he was exiled to the Bahamas suggest that he held out a hope that if Britain capitulated, Hitler would have put him back on the throne. Was he really prepared to depose his brother George VI? When the Americans released the German Foreign Office documents disclosing efforts by the Nazis to suborn the Duke before he was sent to the Bahamas, this idea was dismissed by the Duke as a German fantasy. Nonetheless, there is strong evidence to the contrary. While the Duke and Duchess waited in Portugal to be shipped to the Bahamas, an American diplomat in Lisbon, Herbert Claiborne Pell, had dinner with them. Shocked by what they said, he sent a top-secret telegram to Washington, reporting, 'The Duke and Duchess are indiscreet and outspoken against British government ... They say whether Churchill likes it or not [they] desire to make propaganda for peace.' When Edward abdicated, Hitler said, 'There is no other person in

England ready to play with us.' But whether the House of Windsor really had any future in a Britain subjugated to German conditions is impossible to know. Nobody among the appeasers ever advanced a model for how Britain could continue as a parliamentary democracy while Hitler had absolute power over Europe. The fate of France, after she capitulated, was to be partitioned. Northern and western France, including the entire Atlantic coast, were under German occupation. The rest of the country was under the puppet regime at Vichy. The first Vichy government, under the 84-year-old Marshal Pétain, was a sad bunch of neutered relics. Even if Britain were not occupied, a similar assembly of defeatists under Halifax would have been contemptible. On Hitler's order, the great battleships of the Navy would have been scuttled. No Spitfire would have left the ground. Is this what the Windsor princes thought was a price worth paying for their version of peace?

In 1972, there was one man in Buckingham Palace who knew this history well, some of it intimately, and was trusted by the Queen to keep it to himself: Anthony Blunt. That arrangement would not last.

CHAPTER 19

A YEAR OF DISGRACE

Margaret Thatcher became Prime Minister in May 1979 – not only the first woman to occupy that role but the first to be welcomed by a female monarch. They were almost exact contemporaries in age, although obviously of very different backgrounds and temperaments. Despite Thatcher's public demeanour as 'The Iron Lady' set on introducing a new discipline to the management of public affairs and, in particular, to the performance of torpid British institutions, she was a loyal monarchist. She identified her own rise with the example set by the Queen: in 1952, she wrote in the *Sunday Graphic*, 'If, as many earnestly pray, the accession of Elizabeth II can help to remove the last shreds of prejudice against women aspiring to the highest places, then a new era for women will indeed be at hand.'

On 6 November 1979, the royal shroud of secrecy that had so far continued to protect Anthony Blunt suffered an intrusive jolt. Andrew Boyle published the first really deep investigation into the background and effectiveness of the five Cambridge spies, *The Climate of Treason: Five Who Spied for Russia*. The identities of two of them, Blunt and Cairncross, remained undisclosed. However, Boyle had been given their names by former American intelligence officials. In the prologue to his book, Boyle wrote that without their guidance, 'I would never have stumbled on "Maurice" or "Basil", the code-names given to the Fourth and Fifth Men in the conspiracy'. The choice of 'Maurice' for

Blunt was in itself part of a subtle and typically British insider's game. It was the title of the last of E. M. Forster's novels to be published, posthumously in 1971, an unusually explicit account of a loving relationship between two men. Forster's decision not to publish it in his lifetime reflected two basic fears: the fear suffered by such lovers involved in what was then a dangerously illicit relationship – and Forster's fear that it revealed too much of his own private life. Malcolm Muggeridge was one of several former spooks who held the view that gay men were, in one respect, ideally suited to the life of spies because they knew how to conduct secret lives. But, he argued, the other side of the coin was that they were also risky because of their vulnerability to blackmail. This was, he said, the nature of the kind of private hell that gay spies were assigned to – except that in Blunt's case he was able to use another kind of coercive knowledge to his own advantage.

I had known Boyle since 1963 when he was the producer of one of BBC Radio's highest-rated news programmes, *The World at One*. On the day that *Scandal 63* was published, he put me on the air to talk about what we had discovered of the hidden world of the Profumo affair. He invited several BBC reporters to the studio because, he told me, he felt that the corporation's strict ideas of journalistic neutrality had inhibited their own reporting of the scandal and he hoped that in future they might follow our example of showing less respect for the old-boy network and its ability to cover up its delinquencies. Eventually BBC journalism found a new and more incisive voice, and Boyle was a forerunner of that change. We kept in touch and when his book appeared I asked him why the 'Fourth and Fifth Men' were still not nameable. The publishers had been advised that the risk of an expensive defamation case was too great. But *Private Eye* had long since perfected a technique of exposing cover-ups with satirical stories that were a kind of coded truth-telling. They ran a mock *Spectator* article headlined 'THE FOURTH MAN' with the byline Anthony Blunt.

The newspapers still held back, although they knew the truth. And then, nine days after Boyle's book was published, Margaret Thatcher ended the conspiracy of silence. She replied in writing to a parliamentary question about the damage done by the Cambridge spies. She said that Blunt had acted as a recruiter for the Russians at Cambridge and had passed a string of secrets to Moscow between 1940 and 1945. It was obvious that Thatcher wanted no further mercy shown to Blunt: she added in a debate the following week that he was 'contemptible and repugnant'. There followed a cascade of abuse from the newspapers. The *Sunday Telegraph* alleged that Blunt had been responsible for the deaths of forty-nine British agents working behind enemy lines in Europe. It was not true, but the *Telegraph* refused to retract the story. More odiously, there was an outbreak of rabid homophobia. Blunt was accused of being a paedophile and the editor of the *Sunday Express* called him 'a treacherous communist poof'.

Fleet Street's tone had not much changed since 1952, when the *Sunday Pictorial* ran a two-part report headlined 'EVIL MEN' suggesting a kind of deeply hidden freemasonry of gay men: 'Most people know there are such things – "Pansies" – mincing effeminate young men who call themselves queers. But these obvious freaks and rarities represent but the tip of the iceberg. The problem is far greater than most people realise and the time has come to tackle it.'

Later, I came to know some of the men (they were always men) who wrote and published this drivel. They reflected a strange crossbreeding of British attitudes. In their homophobia, they spoke for a British bourgeoisie who feared that 'deviants' threatened children and were an offence to nature. And yet some of these same people were campaigners for social justice and reforms – unless those reforms included decriminalising homosexuality between men. They were sometimes hypocrites, too: as editors, they hired and promoted writers they knew were gay but whose attitudes in print were nonetheless like their own.

Thatcher herself did not run with this level of vitriol. But there was no mistaking her tone of moral abhorrence when she addressed Blunt's sustained acts of treachery. It was in keeping with the Manichaean simplicity of her moral code – she once said to a journalist, 'I am in politics because of the conflict between good and evil and I believe that in the end good will triumph.' To her, there were no nuances to soften the Blunt crimes. And it was now evident that the Prime Minister's description of Blunt contrasted starkly with the Queen's treatment of him. The palace had readily provided a safe haven for him once he was unmasked, and that tolerance had given him cover after he retired. He had enjoyed fifteen years of freedom during which he had been able to continue to earn the respect of his peers in the art world and move around in society without blemish. It was as though a devastating act of treachery carried no cost. But Thatcher never revealed whether she thought the royal family's cosiness with the Russian mole was a kind of willing consent to overlook his sins, nor did she press to know why they might have been so generous to him. In fact, their protection of Blunt suggested that the Queen would much have preferred that he not be 'outed' – ever.

Broaching such a difference with the monarch would not, in any case, have been in character with their relationship. The Prime Minister was always deferential to the Queen in person. Indeed, one courtier said she was 'excessively reverential'. She always arrived fifteen minutes early for her weekly audience with the monarch. She always set time aside to watch the Queen's Christmas message to the nation. There were admittedly times when the Prime Minister's singular efficiency in affairs of state was hard to reconcile with the Queen's traditional recreations. When Thatcher went to Balmoral during the Queen's summer break, she was not, as was the habit with male Prime Ministers, ready to join in the shooting and fishing. And she had no interest whatever in horse breeding or racing.

For the first time, Blunt was now experiencing the hyena-like howls of the homophobes in addition to being exposed as a wartime traitor. But he was not without friends. Brian Sewell, the art critic of the *Evening Standard*, regarded Blunt as both a mentor and a peerless art historian. He spirited Blunt away to a flat in Chiswick. This kind of loyalty of one man to another in the face of a vengeful mob was to be expected of Sewell, a vituperative critic who hated much of modern art and offended many of the modish London curators. He wrote several brilliant pieces for me while I was an editor at *Condé Nast Traveler*, one of which involved a motorcycle tour of renaissance Italy while he was in his seventies that also included some extracurricular amours.

Blunt spent the remainder of his life as a virtual recluse. He died of a heart attack in 1983, at the age of seventy-five.

It has to be said that Blunt's suffering was far less than that of a man who, in great contrast to him, could lay claim to have done more than any other single person to win the war for Britain: Alan Turing, who cracked the German Enigma codes and was a father of the modern computer. On the very same evening in 1952 that the Queen arrived back from Kenya following her father's death, two detectives arrived at Turing's home in Manchester. Turing confessed to having an affair with a much younger man, Arnold Murray, and was charged under the draconian terms of 'gross indecency contrary to Section 11 of the Criminal Law Amendment Act 1885'. Between 1931 and 1951 there had been a five-fold increase in these prosecutions, a regime that George V apparently approved of, because he is recorded as saying, 'I thought men like that shot themselves.' After barbarous treatment that included being injected with male hormones (a quack 'gender-reversing remedy' for male homosexuals), Turing committed suicide in 1954 by eating a cyanide-laced apple.

Like many thousands of others, Turing had not enjoyed the magic curtain that shielded Blunt for decades from punitive Victorian laws while the police were ramping up their hunt for 'poofs'. As for George V, who had one son, the Duke of Kent, who was a free-roaming bisexual and another, Edward, whose sexuality was, to say the least, confused, was he really so blind to the double standard that the monarchy seemed to accept as a birthright? In her handling of Blunt, Elizabeth II was surely complicit in that long-established arrangement and displayed no regrets when it was exposed to view.

It took the imagination of Alan Bennett to put into words what many people wondered and none would ever know: how did the Queen and Blunt converse?

In a play and then a film, *A Question of Attribution*, set in the period after Blunt confesses to being the Fourth Man but before he was outed, Bennett has a scene where the Queen arrives home unexpectedly early from a public engagement and finds Blunt removing from the wall a painting from the royal collection – he says he wants to study it because of problems with its provenance. The Queen calls it a fake, but Blunt disagrees – all he is prepared to say is that it is an enigma. There is a sense that both of them are practised in the peculiarly British art of avoiding candour in favour of innuendo. Was this really a kind of established system in the palace of using semaphores in order to leave unsaid things between them that would cause pain? Whatever their relationship had been, to the Queen, Blunt remained the man who knew too much.

CHAPTER 20

THE LONG AND
SCANDALOUS LEGACY OF
DICKIE MOUNTBATTEN

At 11.45 a.m. on Monday 27 August 1979, a Bank Holiday, a 29-foot fishing boat, *Shadow V*, drew alongside some lobster pots that had been set down the day before a few hundred yards beyond the harbour wall at Mullaghmore, County Sligo, Ireland. At the wheel was Earl Mountbatten, now seventy-nine years old, slightly slowed down by age but still with the unmistakable bearing of a naval master and commander. At that moment, just as *Shadow V* became still and swayed gently in the swell, the boat was ripped apart by the explosion of fifty pounds of gelignite that had been planted on it the night before by the Provisional IRA and detonated remotely from a clifftop nearby. Mountbatten's legs were severed and most of his clothes were stripped off by the explosion that killed him instantly.

For the woman he frequently called 'my niece, the Queen' and her family, the shock of his death was as violent as the blast itself – he was the only relative to die during the prolonged IRA terrorist campaign. The assassination had reputedly been ordered by Martin McGuinness, later instrumental in ending the Troubles and in crafting and carrying out the Good Friday Agreement.

Given the perspective of time, Mountbatten's death can be viewed as one of the most fundamental turning points in the Queen's reign. The more I looked at the tangled web of her family's inner allegiances and conflicts, the clearer it became that this had so far been the story of two royal families, not one. The primary family was seemingly embodied in the Queen, her father and her mother – sturdily conventional to the point of dullness. But this family was always dogged by the second, which lived grudgingly in the shadows of the first, and they were far from conventional. They were principally embodied in Dickie Mountbatten and Prince Philip, with past associations that went back to the Duke of Windsor and his brother the Duke of Kent. As we saw in the corrosive dispute over the royal family name, Mountbatten displayed a strong hereditary attachment to the Teutonic forebears of the Windsors that had the blood fervour and pride of a medieval royal clan. One of his former military aides said of Mountbatten, 'He was different because he was Hanoverian. He had a Teutonic determination.'

This skilfully manipulative man was always on the alert for any opportunity to advertise his influence on the Queen, whether real or imagined. When it came to the education and cultural guidance of Prince Charles, it was more real than imagined. That is just one reason why Mountbatten left a legacy that is still highly contentious. For the Queen, the consequences of living with this family dichotomy have been profound, never completely shaken off or forgotten, recurring in unpredictable ways.

We now know with much more certainty that the salient characteristic of Mountbatten is that he spent most of his life living promiscuously as a bisexual without fear that he would be exposed. Later in life, he was happy to confess that he and his wife Edwina spent a lot of time hopping in and out of other people's beds – but not that many of his bed mates were men. The absence of this knowledge has crippled understanding of who he really was and, crucially, of how he used his power and influence both within the royal family and in his continuously active public life.

As with the royal family's engagement with the Nazis in the 1930s, a continual effort has been made to block access to the Mountbatten archives. These range from the private diaries of Dickie and Edwina to extensive political papers covering his military service. Mountbatten himself believed that the rewriting of history was not something that was best left to others. He was so sensitive about his wartime legacy that while he was still alive he made sure that his own version of events went on the record while contrary evidence was removed. And when it came to his scandalous sex life, he knew that as long as he was alive both the draconian British libel laws and the conventions of authorised royal biographies would protect him.

As it has turned out, Mountbatten's sex life was far too extensive and incontinent to be bottled up by the archivists. As soon as he was dead the truth was out – and kept coming in a steady stream of revelations until all restraint ended with the publication in 2019 of Andrew Lownie's biography *The Mountbattens: Their Lives and Loves*. Lownie carefully collects as much anecdotal evidence as he can without any hint of needless keyhole salacity on his part. In fact, the salacity is there not in Lownie's commentary but in some of the passages he quotes, as, for example, this from *Private Eye* soon after Mountbatten's assassination:

News that Lord Weidenfeld has signed up naval historian Richard Hough to write an intimate family portrait of Earl Mountbatten raises speculation as to just how 'intimate' a portrait this will be. Will it, for example, reveal that the old sailor, particularly in the last nineteen years of his life following the death of his heiress wife Edwina Ashley, was also a raving queen?

The *Eye* went on to note 'rollicking all-male frolics' at Mountbatten's London home and his 'preference for young servicemen' that could 'do wonders for a young officer's career'. Lownie follows this with a description from another source of 'the tiny mews house ... awash with young, muscular and suspiciously good-looking Naval ratings bustling about the place to no apparent purpose'.

This is 1979. Society's final acceptance of gay marriage and total transparency about gay lives is as far away, it now seems, as a distant planet. 'Raving queen' reveals a lot about the prejudices of the time – and how far prejudice is a symptom of taboos: when something is suppressed by a taboo, it takes on a furtive quality that feeds the kind of bigotry that freely uses phrases like 'raving queen'.

In the last eight years of his life, Mountbatten had a steady gay relationship with a man Lownie interviewed, whom he describes, somewhat patronisingly, as 'handsome, smartly dressed and well-spoken' as though to indicate a lover unlike the rough trade among the naval ratings. The man was in his seventies 'but looks considerably younger'. He said he met Mountbatten at least once a month – 'sometimes for a chat, sometimes for more. He was a great mentor to me, introducing me to all sorts of useful people...'

However, the problem posed by Mountbatten's life as we now know it is not his bisexuality but how far he exploited his unique position of power and influence to procure lovers. Lownie quotes him boasting, 'Why do you think I'm Colonel of the Life Guards? We have such beautiful boys.' That does sound openly predatory. But there could be two sides to the transaction: as his lover said, Mountbatten could provide useful introductions to other people.

Mountbatten had felt free to use this power for decades. Lownie found a 1944 Federal Bureau of Investigation report on Mountbatten and Edwina that described them as 'persons of extremely low morals' and went on to allege that Dickie was a homosexual 'with a perversion for young boys'. This document should be viewed with some serious caveats: for example, it was addressed to the FBI director J. Edgar Hoover, who, when it came to sexuality, was a monstrous hypocrite. Despite being gay himself, he had a long record of punitive witch-hunting, particularly against gay people and anyone of left-wing tendencies. His agents knew that and went out of their way to accuse people on scant evidence and hearsay. Hoover didn't like vigorous heterosexual behaviour, either: as late as 1963 he had his agents mining the Profumo affair for every scrap of lascivious detail they could find on the British political class – as well as pursuing a rumour that John Kennedy, the President he then served, had used call girls supplied by Stephen Ward, which was not true.

A number of the encounters noted by Lownie involve sources that he acknowledges are dodgy and go back as far as the 1930s so are impossible to corroborate. But there remain others that are credible and squalid, including the trafficking of young boys from a home in Belfast to a hotel near the harbour in Mullaghmore during Mountbatten's summer sojourns there. One of these boys, who was sixteen at the time, clearly remembered having oral sex with Mountbatten in a hotel suite two years before his assassination took place; it is therefore highly likely that the IRA, which had many pairs of eyes tracking Mountbatten's movements in Ireland, knew about this traffic and would have cited it as one of their justifications for choosing him as a target.

You can only be as reckless and careless as this in the pursuit of sex if you feel entitled to it almost as a birthright. Throughout his life, Mountbatten had that belief in his own freedom and power to do as he wished. He liked to boast about his closeness to the Queen while he was, in fact, showing contempt for the traditional values that she and the monarchy itself were assigned to uphold. As with so much of the Windsors' private lives, the roots of Mountbatten's sexual preferences go back to that period when London society was as decadent as Weimar Berlin – and when Anthony Blunt was at Cambridge.

At Cambridge at that time, homosexuality and the belief in an open-minded, elitist aesthetic were combined in the Apostles, a self-selecting intellectual group with some of the characteristics of a cult. Both Blunt and Guy Burgess were members. The group's antecedents went back to before the First World War, when Lytton Strachey, who became a bestselling popular historian, and the economist John Maynard Keynes developed the idea of 'a new monastic age'. Part of this was to be the general acceptance of a new style of love between men that they called 'the higher sodomy'. Strachey predicted that it would take a century before sodomy would be accepted not as a sin but as a pure form of manliness and transcendental love. (This wasn't misogynism in another form: women were regarded as equals.) Strachey and Keynes, with all the passion of their own youth and dreams, saw the Apostles as fertile ground to be tilled. But the ravages of a world war and the reality of unchanging moral codes sobered up the dreamers. Nonetheless, the idea that there was a purer form of manliness to be achieved without women lingered on. (By the 1950s, the Apostles had a different cachet. Jonathan Miller, who was elected to the fraternity, said it helped in the seduction of girls: 'One would say, I'm an Apostle, get your knickers off.')

Both Mountbatten and Prince George, the Duke of Kent, moved in circles where these ideas were discussed – and practised. And they both lived in the protected bubble of royalty where they need not fear the law as they did so. Dickie Mountbatten was no intellectual, and as a successful womaniser he was surely no believer in an exclusive higher sodomy, but that didn't matter; he had the freedom to fuck as he wished. And, in fact, there was a direct link from Prince George to Blunt. In the early 1930s, Buckingham Palace got wind that one of the prince's boyfriends in Paris had a cache of personal letters that named a network of lovers and was talking of making them public. Two detectives were sent to Paris by the palace and they burgled the man's flat and retrieved the correspondence. Among those revealed as the prince's lovers was Blunt – who was five years younger than the prince. It was the Blunt case, when it broke open, that suddenly brought the discussion about homosexual loyalties and networks much closer to Buckingham Palace. But Blunt wasn't a traitor because he was gay; he was a traitor who happened to be gay. His companion in crime Philby was not a 'raving queen' but a raving womaniser. One was not umbilical to the other.

In 1988, in his groundbreaking book on Blunt, *Mask of Treachery*, John Costello gave a picture of Buckingham Palace before and during the Queen's reign that was unusually revealing:

> Homosexuality was not a drawback when Blunt started to work his way into royal favour. Membership of the royal household has traditionally provided homosexuals with the same comfortable security as the cloistered enclaves of an Oxbridge college. This applies not just to the courtiers upstairs, but also to many members of the male staffs in the royal palaces.

The rule, Costello wrote, was to 'know but not openly acknowledge'.

Costello went on to give this secret network its own precise locus beyond the palace gates, though not too far beyond, citing Whitehall, Knightsbridge and the barracks of the Household Cavalry and the Guards: 'The principal players ... were observed making discreet visits to the London pubs where guardsmen were for rent ... A pub called the Packenham was the favourite haunt of Blunt and the royal set in pursuit of illicit male sex.' And, warming to his theme, he adds a line from a bawdy ballad: 'I want to be like the boys at the Packenham and go about whackin' 'em and stickin' my jack in 'em.' The army would correctly resist the impression given by Costello that some of its most prestigious barracks were little better than male brothels.

Mask of Treachery remains a work of serious forensic investigation, but passages like these carry too much of the whiff of the casual stereotyping of gay communities that still prevailed in the late 1980s – in tone, it was all of a piece with *Private Eye*'s readiness to mock Mountbatten after his death. The phrase 'illicit male sex' already had an anachronistic ring, since consensual sex between men over the age of twenty-one in private had been decriminalised by the Wilson government in 1967. Roy Jenkins, as Home Secretary the father of the reform, who was himself discreetly bisexual, argued that the criminal law should no longer serve as an instrument to stigmatise men for life. He said, 'Those who suffer from this disability carry a great weight of shame all their lives.'

Of course, Fleet Street had been as complicit in the composition and enlargement of the Mountbatten legend and as blind to his secrets as anyone. Two of the bosses I worked for, Beaverbrook and Cecil King, were aware that Mountbatten was bisexual, though neither of them could have known just how predatory he became. Ironically, Beaverbrook ran a personal vendetta against him not because of this but because one of Mountbatten's female conquests was at the same time a mistress of Beaverbrook's. Beaverbrook had a well-informed personal intelligence service on London's gay networks. One of his best sources was Tom Driberg, the originator of the *Express*'s William Hickey column and later an influential member of the Labour Party. Driberg was not in the same league as Mountbatten in seeking rough trade, but he was one of the people who knew enough to call Mountbatten 'Mountbottom'. As for Cecil King and the *Daily Mirror*, they, too, maintained for decades the fiction that Mountbatten deserved his place in the pantheon of war heroes – why else would King have summoned him to provide what he obviously thought were Mountbatten's sterling martial virtues to his crackpot coup against Harold Wilson? But, once spurned by Mountbatten, King suddenly turned against him and openly ranted to anyone who would listen about Mountbatten being a pervert and Edwina being a nymphomaniac.

The final judgement of Mountbatten by history must be that he was a disgrace to the house he insisted should be called Mountbatten-Windsor. He was a narcissist with a particular love of military uniforms – a sartorial fetish for which the upper ranks of the Royal Navy provide particularly glorious regalia. More consequentially, he was a vainglorious self-promoter who, through using the patronage of his class and the royal family, was able to pass himself off as a charismatic leader of men and icon of the aristocratic virtues while actually being, in the words of historian Andrew Roberts, 'a mendacious, intellectually limited hustler'. Indeed, one of the mysteries of Mountbatten's reputation is why Churchill, usually a ruthless judge of his military commanders, allowed Mountbatten such scope in the Second World War when, as Roberts wrote, he had been 'promoted wildly above his abilities, with consistently disastrous consequences'. In his Churchill biography, Roberts says that when Churchill was writing his memoirs in 1950 he accepted without question Mountbatten's version of the catastrophic 1942 raid on Dieppe, a version that falsely absolved Mountbatten of the responsibility of planning it.

Then there is the final public endorsement of the idea that he was a great public figure. Mountbatten's state funeral at Westminster Abbey on 5 September was, with the Queen's consent, carried out according to his own design. It was as elaborately staged as the funeral of a monarch, down to a nineteen-gun salute from the King's Horse Artillery.

Whether the Queen ever fully understood how toxic Mountbatten was to her family's reputation, we will probably never know. There must have been some kind of reckoning between them after the attempted coup against Harold Wilson. Without doubt, though, Mountbatten's

most lasting influence on the Queen's family was through the immediate male line: first his grooming of Philip and steering him towards
the future Queen and then, repeating much of the same formula, on
the upbringing of Charles, where he exerted almost as much influence on the heir's psychological and physical development as Philip;
there was really no space between Mountbatten and Philip in what
they thought was necessary to build the character of the next King.
But now Mountbatten was gone, and with him a distinct era of the
Queen's reign – while Charles was about to follow Mountbatten's
advice to find himself a suitably young and innocent bride.

CHAPTER 21

THE RADIANT ONE

Early in September 1973, Princess Margaret was at a loose end. Tony was away making a film for the BBC – he had left a few weeks earlier, on her forty-third birthday. They were barely on speaking terms anyway. One of her oldest friends, Colin Tennant, invited her to a house party at his baronial family seat in Scotland, Glen. Tennant and his wife Anne hurriedly searched for an available male guest to provide company for Margaret. They found Roddy Llewellyn, who was nearly eighteen years younger than Margaret. He was a son of minor landed gentry in Wales with a casual, low-paid job at the College of Heralds where he could pursue an interest in aristocratic family trees. In appearance, he was superficially similar to the young Tony, with fair hair and an easy, engaging manner that had made him popular with older women. As soon as Margaret set eyes on him, she was smitten. Llewellyn was the final straw for Tony – and also a sexual reawakening for Margaret. Once their affair became public, it was a gift to the tabloids. Llewellyn was ambushed outside his humble basement flat in Fulham and, captured by television crews, came across like a man in the grip of a kind of dizzy wonderment – diffident, gracious and obviously careful not to play up to a role that, inevitably, some of the tabloids were ready to pin on him: Margaret's toyboy. No royal marriage had ever before broken down as publicly as Margaret's, nor with such a flagrant flouting of convention.

Naturally, people wondered what the Queen made of her sister's fling, but it was impossible to tell. Some Fleet Street editors decided to subject Margaret to what we would now call slut-shaming: they wrote pompously that she should choose between Llewellyn and her royal duties and, if the former, that she should no longer be funded by the civil list. But by far the greatest consequence of the affair was that any lingering restraint on the stalking of royals by reporters and photographers was cast aside. The way was cleared for future legions of paparazzi with one tabloid image that appeared in Murdoch's *News of the World* of Margaret and Llewellyn enjoying a state of rapture on a Caribbean beach. With this, Margaret discovered that the old respect for the privacy of the royal family was finished – particularly for the royal women of the following generations.

Throughout the rest of the 1970s, a team of two happy hacks in particular set the pattern for what would follow. They worked for Murdoch's other paper, the mother of all tabloids, *The Sun*. One was the reporter Harry Arnold and the other Arthur Edwards, the photographer. Fleet Street had often thrown up reporter and photographer partnerships in the past but none so assiduous in pursuit of the royal family: Arnold and Edwards applied to Buckingham Palace the same art in the cultivation of contacts I had previously marvelled at when I was at the *Daily Express*, where it was directed at Scotland Yard and the security services. Royalty had become a far more competitive commercial market than that, and Arnold and Edwards had burrowed deep into the lower orders of those who served the Queen and who, over a pint or two in a pub and using a reward system based on the results, were ready with actionable tips.

The funny thing is that when Edwards landed one of his biggest scoops, he was unaware of it.

In July 1980, Prince Charles was playing polo at Cowdray Park, in the heart of upper-crust Sussex. For months, the tabloids had been pursuing fanciful stories about who would become the greatest boost to newspaper sales in the future of royal family coverage: Charles's bride and future Queen. None had so far produced anything approaching a credible candidate. Arthur Edwards turned up at Cowdray Park and took a few stock shots of Charles at play. Among the entourage with Charles was eighteen-year-old Lady Diana Spencer, who had just met Charles at a weekend house party. There was no close contact between her and Charles as Edwards snapped away, but she was caught in the same frame in one or two shots. When the polo game photographs were developed, the prints were filed away at *The Sun* without being used.

Two months later, Edwards and Arnold were doggedly sticking to a career that involved never losing track of the royals, this time lurking in the undergrowth above a river near Balmoral where Charles was fishing. Suddenly, Edwards realised that Charles was not alone. There was a girl sitting beneath a tree close by: Diana. Edwards recognised her from the Cowdray Park crowd. He fired off some shots of Charles fishing, but Diana, again, was carefully avoiding contact and when she realised that she was being snapped, she melted away. It was enough. Harry Arnold, a master of building a big story on the basis of few facts, filed a front-page splash headlined 'HE'S IN LOVE AGAIN'. The 'again' referred to a previous girlfriend who had briefly been thought a contender. Thus for the first time the young woman who would be 'Lady Di' broke into print, given that moniker by Arnold. Nine days went by before another paper, the *Daily Mail*, confidently confirmed that the radiant teenager was a serious prospect and, inevitably, it was Nigel Dempster, using his trademark name-dropping technique, who had found convincing sources: 'The two happily married women who influence Prince Charles on personal matters, Lady Tryon and Camilla Parker Bowles, have both given the heir to the throne their approval over his new girlfriend.'

The mention of Camilla Parker Bowles carried no significance at the time; her role as part of a social screening system was assumed to be normal.

But few things would remain normal any longer. Diana herself was soon complaining: 'The whole thing has got out of control. Everywhere I go there is someone there. If I go to a restaurant or just out shopping in the supermarket they are trying to take photographs.' By the turn of the year, the pursuit of Diana became invasive of the whole royal family, culminating in what *The Observer* called 'The Siege of Sandringham'. As usual, the family was at their Norfolk estate for Christmas and New Year. Obtusely, the palace press office failed to do the one thing that would have left the papers with no excuse for lingering in the undergrowth: confirm that Diana was a guest and request that the royal house party be granted its usual privacy. The Queen herself, photographed while out walking with one of her grandchildren on a pony, glared at the pursuing posse and said, 'I wish you would go away.' Charles was less polite. He walked up to a cluster of photographers and said, 'May I take this opportunity to wish you all a happy New Year. And your editors a particularly nasty one.'

These were opening skirmishes in an ineluctable ethical shift in the coverage of the royal family. Diana was not solely the cause, but her arrival multiplied the effects. The market for royal stories worked like any other commodity market when driven by demand: the people who supplied the commodity would have been derelict not to have responded to the rise in demand. The international reach of Margaret's rebellious life had shown that the royals were no longer of only parochial interest. Simultaneously, media owners were becoming more globally ambitious and not confined any longer to print and the Fleet Street news cycle. Rupert Murdoch was always ahead of his British rivals in this respect. Murdoch instinctively understood news as a commodity; with *The Sun* he had built a tabloid gold mine by catering to unbridled mass-market sensationalism and, as often as not, royal stories were gold coinage. Murdoch called his company News International for good reason – he was going to internationalise news, in print and now on television, in its most marketable form and as he framed it. And his kind of news was in the course of discovering one of its most profitable subjects: Diana.

At that time, though, early in 1981, during the encirclement of Sandringham, neither side yet properly understood what was happening. *The Sun*, for example, attempting to bring decency to the scrum, editorialised, 'Nobody wants to ruin the Queen's holiday. The press is not there to persecute her. Its natural and legitimate goal is to photograph the lady who may be the next Queen of England.' The *Daily Mirror* went further, aptly exploring one of the classic paradoxes of celebrity – that the more somebody resists it, the more they acquire it: 'If Lady Diana Spencer is to be the future Queen of England, she cannot expect to be Greta Garbo as well.'

Months before her marriage, Diana was already exposed to a tension that nobody of her age would find easy to handle. On the one hand, she was learning – or trying to learn – the etiquette of life inside the glass cage and in a family that had a clannish resistance to any form of personal disclosure. On the other hand, the outside world, waking up to her glamour, was demanding to know every personal detail about her and her life that could be discovered.

The wedding in July 1981 sealed both Diana's role as a media superstar and her fate. Billed absurdly as 'the wedding of the century', it reached a weightless level of theatricality: Diana arrived in a glass coach and left, with Charles, in an open carriage. It was the apotheosis of the series of public pageants that began with the televising of the coronation in 1953, and it attracted a global television audience of 750 million. This time the setting was St Paul's Cathedral. The change seemed to bring the occasion closer to the people than was possible in Westminster Abbey: St Paul's, Wren's masterpiece of the English baroque sitting atop a hill that had once been at the heart of Roman London, has always been more closely woven into the fabric of every-day, working, cosmopolitan London – seen by the people of the city as an accessible, almost secular shrine rather than one locked into the establishment symbolism of Westminster. There are amazing photographs from the Blitz showing the dome surrounded by a ring of fire. Twenty-eight bombs fell on the cathedral, including a 500-pounder, yet miraculously, like Londoners themselves, it survived as a defiant, unbreakable force. (I first noticed this St Paul's effect when I directed the *Sunday Times* coverage of Winston Churchill's funeral in 1965.)

Whether by chance or design, the special aura of the cathedral helped to imply that the next King and Queen of England might, like the ceremony, be closer to the people than any of their predecessors. The couple also, by mutual agreement, changed the wedding vows so that Diana did not promise 'to obey'. And, for at least that day, her radiance made it seem that this was also a magical love match, an impression sealed when they kissed as they stood at the centre of the family on the balcony of Buckingham Palace.

Having convincingly played their fairy-tale roles to a truly besotted audience, Charles and Diana then expected to be allowed privacy when not performing public duties. At around the time Charles first met Diana he had bought himself a grand new home, Highgrove House, in Gloucestershire, which should have provided ample privacy since it was set in a 347-acre estate. A few months after the wedding, it was announced that Diana was pregnant, and she and Charles assumed that while she was at Highgrove the photographers could be kept at bay. But someone tipped off the tabloids that Diana had an addiction to wine gums and would sometimes slip away from the estate to buy the sweets in a shop in the nearby town of Tetbury. Photographers from *The Sun* and the *Daily Mirror* caught her in the act of satisfying her appetite and had to share the big scoop the following day.

Astonishingly, on the basis of this relatively trivial intrusion, the Queen herself chose to intervene – the one and only time that she attempted to rein in the media feeding frenzy that was now insatiable for Diana stories. Every national newspaper editor, as well as the editors of BBC News and Independent Television News, were summoned to Buckingham Palace by the Queen's press secretary, Michael Shea. Editors of the serious papers respected Shea. He was a refreshing departure from the usual palace gatekeepers. He had a doctorate in economics and before arriving at the palace had served for fifteen years as a diplomat, with a left-leaning reputation. All the editors answered the summons except Kelvin MacKenzie of *The Sun*. He claimed that the time clashed with a meeting he had to attend with his boss, Rupert Murdoch. It wasn't true; MacKenzie, who had been editor for only a few months, was indicating his indifference to the Queen's concerns in a way that no other editor had the gall to do.

Not surprisingly, the best account of the meeting came from another Murdoch editor, Harry Evans of *The Times*: 'We walked from the snow-covered forecourt along the red carpets, past the marble busts of monarchs and into the white and gold of the 1844 Room, named because of its occupation that year by the Emperor Nicholas of Russia.' Shea warned them that Her Majesty was not amused by the treatment of her new daughter-in-law and wished to express her feelings directly to them. Before the editors were ushered into the presence of the monarch, Shea tried appealing to their inner family instincts by reminding them that Diana was twenty years old, suffering from morning sickness because of the pregnancy, and in anguish over what amounted to harassment by the tabloid hacks. He portrayed the photographers as the major villains, as though they were trespassing beyond limits set by their editors, and cited the precedent of several freelance photographers who, two decades earlier, had taken shots of Princess Margaret water-skiing on a royal estate watched by the Queen, who was sunbathing. On that occasion the freelance photographers involved had been publicly rebuked by the Press Council, the normally toothless watchdog of Fleet Street's ethics. The editors were happy to offer them up as sacrificial offerings. They stopped assigning work to them, basically putting them out of work. Shea, reported Evans, 'put it all with brilliant diffidence: on the one hand the attitude of the photographers, on the other the views of an anxious mother-in-law, a human dilemma rather than an issue of state'. But Shea did not appear to grasp the reality that staff photographers, not freelancers, were now part of an integrated professional industry of celebrity pursuit in which the royal family carried the same commodity value as Hollywood stars. Moreover, unseen and unsummoned behind the assembled editors were proprietors like Murdoch who believed that as public figures funded by the people, the royals were not entitled to greater levels of privacy than movie stars.

From the 1844 Room, the editors were moved on to the Carnarvon Room for their audience with the Queen, who had chosen to bring Prince Andrew with her. Andrew was twenty-one years old and presumably the Queen thought this would be a good opportunity for him to get a first-hand sense of the kind of people who would be directing the coverage of his own life as he went forth into the world. Evans, on introduction, found himself telling the Queen about an incident in which the Soviet leader Leonid Brezhnev had been trapped up a tree during a bear hunt. 'I was struck,' Evans reported, 'as everyone is, by her superior knowledge of affairs.' The Queen told the editors that she shared Diana's distress and expected them to change their ways and allow her to enjoy a private life. In the only moment that betrayed how little of the old deference towards the Queen remained, the editor of Murdoch's *News of the World*, Barry Askew, suggested that if Diana really wanted privacy she could send a servant out to Tetbury High Street to buy her wine gums. The Queen smiled thinly and replied, 'Mr Askew, that was a most pompous remark.' Nervous laughter followed.

Nothing really changed as a result of this unusual encounter. Both sides were talking past each other – any sense of them having a common civic interest in constraint had long since disappeared. Some of the papers published pieties that rang with ambivalence and insincerity, like the *Daily Mail* saying, 'We shall respect her privacy while at the same time not depriving our readers of the pleasure of sharing her charms.' Others, like the *Daily Telegraph*, sought to put themselves above the stink of the tabloids: 'How tragic it would be were over-zealous intrusions by some sections of our profession come so to prey on the mind that a figure enjoying much public affection felt driven to draw back and shelter from the lights.'

We are looking here at a phenomenon in an embryonic phase, when none of those engaged in its emergence could have known the size it would reach – least of all Diana herself. The only certainty was that there was no going back: with Diana's appearance, the customs of the past in the relationship between the monarchy and the media vanished almost overnight. Once more the world was changing and once more the monarchy was woefully unprepared for that change. The future tabloid ethic would be defined by the editor who could not be bothered to answer the summons from the palace, Kelvin MacKenzie of *The Sun*. He was an unapologetic believer in aiming at the lowest common denominator. He described his target reader as 'the bloke you see in the pub, a right old fascist, wants to send the wogs back, buy his poxy council house. He's afraid of the unions, afraid of the Russians, hates the queers and the weirdos and the drug dealers.' MacKenzie didn't just identify the perfect bigot – he *was* that bigot, and the man who could give Murdoch the convention-busting tabloid he wanted.

From that morning at Fort Belvedere in 1936 when Edward VIII, looking at the *Daily Mirror*'s front-page splash of the Wallis Simpson story, lamented, 'It's too bad' to these early skirmishes involving Diana – all of this was to become, in terms of the monarchy's coexistence with the media, mere prologue.

CHAPTER 22

A LAST LUNCH WITH TONY

Of all those cast members caught up in the teeming dramas of the Queen's family, Tony Snowdon was the most redoubtable. Lesser mortals might have been too battle-damaged by the experience to hold their lives together as well as Tony did. He began like a novitiate called from a real and normal life into a closed world with the characteristics of a ritual-dominated holy order – at the time, a daring experiment for him and them. A marriage that began endowed with all the ceremonial furnishings of a national fairy tale had gone through a very public, slow-motion descent into a nightmare. It could be said that Margaret and Tony were both too demanding of each other as lovers to ever be satisfied and that, in the course of this ferocious engagement, other people and other things would get smashed up until everybody retired exhausted, if not embittered. But Tony was neither exhausted – as, for a while, Margaret was – nor, as far as I could ever see, embittered. More remarkably, his talents flourished and brought their own prosperity and celebrity – though they were generously assisted by his royal status.

Professionally, Tony remained himself and in full. There was no doubt of this when we met for what would turn out to be the last time. In 1987, I joined Condé Nast in New York as a founding editor, with Harry Evans, of *Condé Nast Traveler*. The Condé Nast building on Madison Avenue was alleged to be – by the rest of Manhattan's magazine establishment – the home of an invading British magazine mafia. Anna Wintour had just taken over the editorship of *Vogue* while Tina Brown was transforming an ailing *Vanity Fair* into a journalistic powerhouse and would soon do the same for the *New Yorker*. Tony had been there first, long before, working for Diana Vreeland at *Vogue*, and he owed a lot to the mentoring of Condé Nast's demanding editorial tsar, Alexander Liberman. Our objective was to bring great writing and photography to the relatively moribund world of travel magazines and when we assigned Martha Gellhorn, legendary Hemingway muse and war reporter, to write about Wales, where she lived, it was obvious who should photograph the story: Tony.

I flew to London and we had lunch at the Launceston Place restaurant, close to the house he now lived in, a handsome Georgian villa. London is a collection of villages and this quarter of Kensington was aesthetically pure Tony – an expensive but not flashy urban village. In fact, the Queen had bought the villa for him, paying £75,000, after the formal separation agreement between him and Margaret was signed. Tony had invested a lot of his time and skills in restoring the apartment at Kensington Palace. Launceston Place had none of the regal trappings of a royal palace, but, once more, Tony directed a personally selected team of craftsmen to bring the house into line with his own standards and tastes. In a way, the house was a metaphor for his own readjusted life, from the grand scale to the elegant but more modest villa that now included his studio. I knew that he made far more money from working for advertising agencies than from journalism, but his ties to Condé Nast, both in London and in New York, remained important to him.

He was fifty-seven now. I had known him for nearly thirty years and the young Tony was still present in the mature Tony – the same quickness of mind, asperity of opinion, keenness to do good work. He wanted to meet Martha Gellhorn; the idea of such a worldly and accomplished American writer settling in Wales intrigued him. He was waspish about the latest issue of *Condé Nast Traveler*, shrewdly spotting that there was a 'blind' cover line, 'How to Shop Like a Princess'. 'Why', he pressed me, 'did you not put her name on the cover? Everybody else is.'

The 'her' was of course Diana. There were six pages inside describing all of Diana's favourite shops in London. Some of the text was puerile: 'No guided tour of London can guarantee a sighting of the world's favourite princess, but *Condé Nast Traveler* can offer the next best thing, a consumer guide.' There was a picture of a satin slipper, as purchased by Diana, actual size. Tony ridiculed this as 'closet sniffing'.

Of course, he had skewered me. We were trying to have it both ways – to ride the wave of Diana adoration while not wanting to look like a celebrity magazine. I heard a note of animus and asked, 'What do you think of her?' He paused. 'Well, I must ask you not to repeat this, but I really don't believe that Diana is aware how dangerous it is to be more famous than the Queen. She... she enjoys it too much.' It was the only indiscretion he permitted himself. Otherwise he still punctiliously referred to Margaret as Princess Margaret as he always had, and it now sounded like respectful detachment. The only time he wanted to look back on was our early days at the *Sunday Times*. 'It's not the same paper now,' he said. 'Murdoch can't stand being outshone by anybody, so he only appoints sycophants.' (A year later he moved to the *Sunday Telegraph*, where his contract guaranteed him £35,000 a year, three times what the *Sunday Times* paid.)

He was still impatient with the mediocrity of British industrial design – he had recently quit working for the Design Council because of its choking bureaucracy and he was waging a personal campaign against British Rail over their failure to accommodate disabled passengers. This included, with typical Tony precision, the fact that train doors were twenty-two inches wide while the average width of a wheelchair was twenty-five inches. In an interview with the derelict chief of British Rail conducted for British *Vogue*, he described how a disabled student in a wheelchair had been locked in the luggage van at the rear of a train without access to a toilet or any heating. It was one of Tony's virtues that instead of using his title and status for his own advancement, he used that power on behalf of the powerless – and he enjoyed using it that way. He did this far more effectively and consistently than any other member of the royal family.

Alongside Tony the saint there remained Tony the rake. He was working with Marjorie Wallace, a campaigner for reform of the care of mentally ill people. He asked me about her because he knew she had worked on the *Frost Programme* team. She had had an affair with a close friend of mine, resulting in the breakdown of his marriage, and was living with him as his partner. On the one hand, I said, I was not a fan of her behaviour with him, but on the other hand she always attacked anything she did with great energy and was really putting enormous effort into her campaign and getting results. Tony agreed – and as he did, I could see that he thought I was being pompous in my reservations. I could also see that Marjorie Wallace was closer to him than I realised. Some years later they did become lovers. But at this time Tony appeared settled into his second marriage to Lucy Lindsay-Hogg – former wife of the accomplished film director Michael Lindsay-Hogg – whom he had first met in 1972. Unknown to her, however, since 1977 Tony had been having an affair that would last twenty years, with Ann Hills, a journalist who, though herself married, was a very public promoter of open marriages and wrote a book advancing the therapeutic value of extra-marital affairs. Nobody could accuse her of not practising what she preached.

Tony's ability to keep this secret reflected how good he was at compartmentalising relationships. This quality did not endear him to Margaret, who was wilfully unguarded in her affairs, as she had been with Anthony Barton and Robin Douglas-Home. She and Llewellyn had amicably ended their affair in 1980, after she spent some weekends with him in a hippie commune he had helped to found. Margaret claimed that she never dropped people, while Tony frequently did. She told Nigel Dempster, 'I pressed him to keep up with his old chums, but the funny thing about Tony is that he is a friend-dropper. After the marriage nearly all his old friends vanished and I never saw them again. I'm not like that, I don't discard people.'

Of all Margaret's friends, the most constant and influential was Colin Tennant, the Scottish aristocrat whose weekend house party had inadvertently triggered her pursuit of Llewellyn. Two things underpinned this friendship: Tennant's wealth and the affection his wife Anne had for Margaret. When Tony and Margaret married, Tennant gave Margaret a wedding present of a prime piece of land on the Caribbean island of Mustique. Soon Margaret was asking Tennant to build her a house there, which he did. At the same time, he had formed a property company to sell off another 100 sites for prices of up to £40,000. Mustique was one of a number of islands colonised by British aristocrats who used them for winter avoidance (and, sometimes, for tax avoidance). This level of exclusivity began to disappear as people like Tennant developed the land for a new generation of self-made millionaires. As Margaret moved into her own Caribbean retreat, knowing that her presence there added a cachet to the island, it was becoming a livelier winter scene, including rock stars and some more shady new money. Tony disliked Mustique from the start, calling it 'Mistake'. It represented an adamant dividing line between his tastes and Margaret's – a dividing line that became increasingly public with their estrangement. As far as the Queen and Buckingham Palace were concerned, Tony's term was altogether too uncomfortably accurate.

CHAPTER 23

TWO WOMEN AT THE TOP

After seven years in office, Margaret Thatcher had gathered to herself as much power as one person in a parliamentary democracy is able to acquire, short of leading a coup. Few male Prime Ministers had consolidated their grip on their party and the country as completely as she now had – Churchill had behaved like a warlord, but he was never as confrontational as Thatcher. Between 1984 and 1985 she broke the miners' union with a pitiless ferocity that sometimes gave the country the appearance of a quasi-police state. Metaphorically if not actually, she had emasculated even the stoutest members of her Cabinet. In 1976, before she came to power, she made a blistering attack on the Soviet Union, warning that Russia was hell-bent on world domination and if Britain did not understand this (at the time Harold Wilson was negotiating a trade treaty with Moscow) it would end up 'on the scrapheap of history'. In response TASS, the official Soviet news agency, called her 'The Iron Lady'. Instead of insulting her, the label was all too predictive. By 1986, any foreign leader who had met her left knowing how 'iron' she was, as did the British people.

Inevitably, we became more and more curious about the relationship between the Prime Minister and the Queen. For the first time in history, two women were – nominally at least – the figureheads of the nation. Queen Victoria had been the last monarch to exercise consequential power over her Prime Ministers, although she knew the limits. Elizabeth II represented the 'placebo theory' of the monarchy – it worked even though it actually had no power. It had no power because it was above power. Harold Macmillan, always keen to uphold this theory, did so in his memoirs by complimenting the Queen on how she 'conscientiously performed' the duty of reading all the official papers sent to her every day in the red boxes. 'The Queen', he wrote 'has the absolute right to know, to criticise, to advise.' With Margaret Thatcher in Downing Street, those last two duties would have become difficult if not impossible to offer. Thatcher did not see her own ascent as a triumph of feminism. The politics of gender were irrelevant to her, too modish and too limiting. She understood power and how to use it. One feminist critic said of her that she was not setting out to prove that a woman could be as tough as a man 'but that she is not under the governance of Venus, that she is a stranger to the exactions and weaknesses of the heart'. Hugo Young, an astute biographer, said, 'Without discarding womanhood, she had transcended it.'

And yet… was there really a stark psychological gulf between these two women? As was shown in the Aberfan disaster, the Queen had trouble displaying 'weaknesses of the heart' – *displaying* being the fair term because it doesn't exclude feelings. The Queen was always conscious that even if the woman felt pain and emotion, the monarch should be economical with both. After all, her sister had no control over either and was less and less able to conceal the fact. Like Thatcher, the Queen had iron: an iron discipline about being regal in the way that she had been taught to always show that quality. She was condemned to a life of upholding regality. She was so drilled in this discipline in public that it was impossible to tell if this was also the private woman – the whole or a part of her. As a result, she and Thatcher both came across as cold, though with the Queen the coldness was passive and with Thatcher aggressive. And they had one more thing in common: they were both philistines. There was no more poetry in Downing Street than there was in Buckingham Palace. Thatcher's approach to politics as a form of action – of getting things done – was relentlessly forensic. She studied chemistry at Oxford under Dorothy Hodgkin, a Nobel laureate, and trained as a barrister, where the total mastery of a brief was a religion with her. Infamously, she said that there was 'no such thing as society' – it was too abstract a concept. The Queen did have one consuming interest that in a way was scientific – the breeding of horses. Some of the men she most admired were those who schooled her on the chains of insemination that led to a winning thoroughbred. Needless to say, this was not a subject she could discuss with Thatcher as a means of finding common ground.

Both Downing Street and the palace had so far been amazingly successful in keeping the reality of the relationship between Prime Minister and monarch out of sight. Part of this was, of course, an established protocol. When leaks had occurred during past premierships, they were usually deliberately managed to convey a healthy level of comfort between the two institutions, as in the account of Churchill and the Queen having a good laugh together behind closed doors. This time, though, the fact that it involved two women, one a virago and one a benign enigma, suggested that the pressures might build up to a point where the veil might well slip – and slip it did, suddenly, and very noisily.

In July 1986, the *Sunday Times* splashed a story saying that on a wide range of issues, domestic and foreign, the Queen was at odds with Thatcher. But, according to the paper, the most explicit of the Queen's complaints was that Thatcher was 'uncaring, confrontational and divisive'. Many of her subjects would have agreed, but, if true, this was an unprecedented violation of a code of discretion that had held fast for the thirty-four years of the Queen's reign. Of course, it was absurd to believe that during that time the Queen had never been upset by the actions of a Prime Minister – for example, Anthony

Eden's invasion of Egypt on false pretences. But all her Prime Ministers had known, until now, that she would never reveal what she really
thought. The *Sunday Times* story went further. It suggested that the
Queen had actually wanted to have her disaffection revealed – and
that it extended to foreign policy, particularly Thatcher's reluctance
to deal with apartheid in South Africa. The palace moved swiftly to
debunk the story. Within hours of its publication, the Queen called
Thatcher to assure her that that the allegations were completely false.
Michael Shea, the press secretary, admitted that he had talked to the
paper's political editor on the normal basis of providing off-the-record
guidance for a story that he understood to be about the changing
role of the monarchy. Aside from his day job, Shea was a compulsive
writer of political thrillers, publishing more than a dozen of them.
He was also no lover of Thatcher. It was never confirmed that – egged
on by the reporter – he had transplanted some of his own political
views into his briefing. In any event, he had overstepped the mark
and left the palace the following year, taking a job as head of public
relations for an industrial conglomerate. The paper's editor, Andrew
Neil, enjoyed the controversy he had triggered, although he was surely
sophisticated enough to know that the Queen, no matter what her
frustrations, would never sanction such a breach of protocol. She was
given complete deniability and thereafter her meetings with Thatcher
were unclouded by any sign of rancour.

Indeed, courtiers noted that when Thatcher appeared for her weekly
audiences with the Queen, her curtsies were lower than anyone else's.
For all her steely ascent to the top of politics, Thatcher still felt obliged
to genuflect in the presence of a woman who had been at the top long
before her and would remain there long afterwards. The wife of one of
her Cabinet ministers said Thatcher had a 'Queen Bee complex' in the
company of other women – implying that if she could make it, they,
too, should show the same determination. Given an actual Queen, she

couldn't behave that way. There seemed to be a residual sense of class in these encounters. Ferociously upwardly mobile herself, Thatcher had little time for the classes beneath her, but the monarchy was in a class of its own, secure behind ramparts that she had no intention of storming.

Then a funny thing happened. Once she had smashed one layer of national institutions, particularly any remnant of the idea that the state should control the means of production, Thatcher the destroyer became Thatcher the atavist, bringing her more into line with an aversion to change similar to that of the Queen. She thought it a mistake to have abolished capital punishment; likewise to have decriminalised homosexuality. Most of all she emerged as an unreconstructed jingoist, a feeling intensified by fear that British sovereignty was being jeopardised by overreaching federalists in the European Union. The English Channel held for her the same value as a bulwark against alien Europeans as it had for Churchill in 1940. She feared German aspirations most of all. When Helmut Kohl, the German Chancellor, boasted that a German football team had beaten the English at their own game, she snapped back that the English had 'beaten the Germans at theirs twice in the twentieth century' – an incredibly wounding thing to say to a man who represented Germany's rehabilitation as a European partner.

Thatcher's jingoism so completely reflected the Queen's own world view that in 1982, when she went to war against Argentina over the Falkland Islands, the Queen – against the advice of some courtiers – consented to Prince Andrew joining the naval task force sent to the South Atlantic. This was the last outing of gunboat diplomacy, made possible only by American logistical support. Andrew was co-pilot on a submarine-hunting helicopter aboard the aircraft carrier *Invincible*, and returned home to be greeted, along with the rest of the force, like a war hero. Afterwards the commander of the force, Admiral Sandy

Woodward, confessed that 'to have a royal anywhere near the front line is a bloody nuisance ... You have to take extra precautions that he doesn't get shot down.' Defending the operation, Thatcher quoted the Duke of Wellington: 'There is no such thing as a little war for a great nation.' Prince Philip heartily agreed. He thought it had been a jolly good show for the country – and proved that Andrew was worthy of the family's long record of naval service, including his own. Thatcher, it turned out, shared another trait with the Queen – a deep anxiety for the safety of sons. Usually bereft of emotion for those in peril, the Prime Minister was in a tearful panic when her own son disappeared for days during a car rally in Africa. Like Andrew, he was hailed as being up to snuff when he reappeared without a scratch. And, as would become even more obvious later, Andrew could do little wrong in his mother's eyes.

If Thatcher respected the monarchy for being an untouchable in a class of its own, it was, nonetheless, changing in subtle ways. Its original inbred homogeneity was breaking down. Tony, the first commoner to marry into the family, remained fully embraced as a family member after the collapse of his marriage, and his children were welcome and lively additions. But Diana was a different kind of interloper. Her family's credentials in the pantheon of the British aristocracy ran far deeper than those of the Windsors. The Spencers could be traced back to 1478 and were intertwined with the Churchills, making them part of the great tradition of a warrior aristocracy unmatched in illustriousness by any royals. In fact, to purists of royal bloodline theory the Windsors were neither aristocrats nor authentic native royalty: they were parvenus. In this nativist view, the problem begins with the Hanoverians and specifically the German-born King George I, who reigned from 1714 to 1727, and his immediate successors, who were accused of split loyalties between the British and German kingdoms they ruled. There is no need to get into the steamy tangle of the early Georges, their mistresses, their inattention to duties, their family feuds. Their lasting influence seems to be a strange case of regressive genes, as it persisted over the generations. Here, for example, is James Pope-Hennessy, during his 1957 trawl of the Queen's close relatives, on the third of George V's princes, Henry, the Duke of Gloucester (whom I have so far omitted from the narrative due to his irrelevance): 'Prince Henry is one of the finest and most authentic specimens of the race available for study today. He is tall and bulky, and his head is wonderfully Hanoverian, flat at the back and rising to the real pine-apple point of William the Fourth.' (Henry was the quintessential blockheaded blimp. Among his wisdoms delivered to Pope-Hennessy: 'Funny shape for a country, Holland. Damn funny shape.') And here is a senior civil servant on the problems of advising Prince Charles in the matter of his marriage: 'The trouble is that Charles is a Hanover-ian' – in this case meaning that he was petulant and self-indulgent. These supposedly Hanoverian afflictions will turn up again.

Three days after the *Sunday Times* story about the Queen and Thatcher, the royal family admitted another infusion of outside blood. Prince Andrew, now dubbed Randy Andy by the tabloids because of his priapic adventures, married Sarah Ferguson, a commoner. As it would turn out, she was a very common commoner. The pairing of these two confirmed a significant pattern in royal family mating procedures. Fergie, as she was instantly known, was the daughter of Major Ronald Ferguson, formerly a cavalryman in the Life Guards and now a farmer but, more to the point here, an equestrian who played polo with Philip and was Charles's polo manager. In another twist, polo had cuckolded Major Ferguson: his wife took off for South America with a dashing Argentinian polo player. In 1973, Princess Anne had married a horse-man, Captain Mark Phillips of the Dragoon Guards. And Charles had first been sighted with Diana while playing polo, although Diana was not really herself ever a member of the horsey set.

Elites tend to control the talent pool they depend on to perpetuate their family lines – that's why for generations the family trees of European royalty were so inbred. But the Queen's children were circling in an orbit that was unusually narrow, dominated by her own great equestrian passion and its preferences in the kind of people she liked to be with. This was a marked departure from her father's cohort, which had been shaped in war and more broadly gathered from the political and military leaderships. And, as we have seen, after the war George VI deliberately brought in outsiders like Peter Townsend to counter the influence of the courtier class, exemplified by Lascelles.

Of course, it was only natural that, living under the constant pressure of public life, the Queen wanted to find her own unchallenging comfort zone where she could feel at ease among people with a common interest. That is why the equestrian world was so attractive to her. Consequently, a new kind of identifiable sub-class of the rural bourgeoisie emerged that, with royal patronage, flourished in the southern shires – as it does to this day: Kate Middleton, the Duchess of Cambridge, is a quintessential member of it. It also produced a thriving marriage market, involving many of the same families who had propelled their daughters into the debutante ring when that was still a way of getting a royal audience and nod. Now, showing up at Royal Ascot in a silly hat inspired by Cecil Beaton's *My Fair Lady* wardrobe had acquired the status of the great debutante summer ball. Beyond British shores, this set had a magnetic attraction for those who saw it as the epitome of high society, particularly if they, too, were horse breeders. This was strikingly the case in America, where the Queen spent five private holidays that all included the upper-crust horse country of Kentucky. One courtier reported, 'She felt very much at home in Kentucky … There was an atmosphere of informality and gaiety I never saw in England … Guests were all from the horse world; conversations rarely strayed from thoroughbred topics.' There was a similar affinity with the sporting life of the Gulf state sheikhs. (Grifters among the royals, like Andrew in his later years, were happy to use this attraction to engineer highly remunerative pay-to-play contacts.)

Closer to home, the Queen displayed an open bias towards those who were happy in the saddle – she immediately warmed to Fergie for this reason, while she was visibly annoyed that Diana was averse to field sports and had broader cultural literacy and interests. (Though, ironically, the Queen had told Margaret that she could never be seen in public with her and Roddy Llewellyn because the liaison was too risqué even though Llewellyn's father was a renowned equestrian.)

Alas, the outcome of all three of the horse-borne romances was divorce. Princess Anne's marriage faltered early. She and Mark Phillips were officially separated in 1989 and divorced in 1992. While Anne was cruising on *Britannia*, she met and fell in love with Timothy Laurence, one of the ship's officers, and they married in 1992. This turned out to be the most stable of the Queen's children's marriages, and Anne the most grounded of the children. Fergie and Andrew, mutually unfaithful to a vigorous degree, were separated in 1992 and divorced in 1996. And, of course, Charles's marriage to Diana soon became the most drawn-out and scandalously public rupture in the Windsor family.

But it was more than that. Diana almost single-handedly provided the oxygen for the development of industrial-scale celebrity journalism at the precise moment that all the pieces were in place to make that happen. One of the principal architects of this change was Rupert Murdoch. Once Kelvin MacKenzie took over *The Sun*, he moved swiftly to follow Murdoch's wish for a far looser boundary between news and entertainment. One of Murdoch's advantages over his Fleet Street competitors was that he saw Britain from the perspective of an outsider. Mocked by the 'pommies' as 'the Dirty Digger', he was actually more worldly than they were. When he bought the *News of the World*, his formidable mother, Dame Elisabeth, was worried that the paper was too vulgar. Murdoch told her that the lives of the average Brit were so miserable that they needed more entertainment. Now Murdoch had two editors who had a jaundiced view of the monarchy: MacKenzie and, at the *Sunday Times*, Andrew Neil. The men were very different, however, and operated at a different level of journalism: MacKenzie went for the lowest common denominator, while Neil, an erudite and combative Scot with some of Murdoch's aversion to elites, catered to a far more sophisticated readership. But he knew the value of embarrassing the monarchy, as he had done with the vastly overblown story about the Queen and Thatcher. This was really a more literate version of a tabloid scoop. Murdoch approved of this trick because, as far as he was concerned, there were no limits on the coverage of the royal family.

But did Murdoch actually want to see the end of the monarchy? Asked this in 1991, as the theatrics of the Diana and Charles soap opera were reaching their hysterical middle act, he replied:

> I'm ambivalent about that. I think you'd have to say No, because I don't think the country has the self-confidence to live without it … But is the system holding the country back in this new competitive open global village that we talk about? Is it inhibiting the country's growth? I think it's debatable at least. And I think there is nothing wrong in debating it. But if you show yourself even to be thinking about it, that makes you a figure of hate there, because some people get very excited about it.

Parsing Murdoch's words, two things stand out. The first is that he is still speaking as an outsider looking in, and suggesting his ingrained paranoia about being 'a figure of hate'. The second is fundamental to his own ambition to rise far beyond being a parochial British media baron: 'in this new competitive open global village'. To do that,

Murdoch would successfully transform his own business into a global empire, to a large extent by exporting his new amped-up formula for celebrity journalism as it had been incubated in his British papers. And they had found their superstar: Diana.

CHAPTER 24

THE MOST FAMOUS PERSON IN THE WORLD

Diana had no precursors in the level of her celebrity. In the course of a few years she became the most famous person in the world when it was possible for the first time for fame to be truly universal. While many others were struggling to explain this phenomenon, she was still trying to understand it herself. At first it seemed to grow exponentially without any effort by her. Like someone trying to stay alive while snatched up in a fast-moving current, she had to fight to keep her head above water – until suddenly she mastered the forces at work and learned how to control them for her own purposes. She became, in a sense, the devil's apprentice: able to learn new destructive powers and deploy them as she wished without care.

It was the royal family's misfortune to play host to this spectacular person. But then Diana's powers could not have existed without their antithesis, and the royal family provided that at many levels. Put simply, she was everything they were not. She was beauty and they were the beast. She was vulnerable and they were strong and cruel. She was the future and they were the stubborn past. She was generous of spirit and they were mean. She readily embraced people and they shrank from any signs of intimacy. She was a lone force of nature and they were a disembodied institutional force of reaction. And at the most basic level, the camera loved her and she could love it back from any angle and it wanted more, more, more while the royal family glowered and fled.

The point is not that this portrait is unfair, which it is. The point is that this was the public's perception at the time, created with the latest tools of media management and spin. The juxtapositions of character are too absolute, but they contained just enough recognisable truth to be accepted at face value. Once established, these impressions were impossible to dislodge. The tabloids were infatuated. A popular narrative was being built from the ground up, the ground being the tabloids. It was noted early, well before Diana and Charles were married, that a bias in favour of Diana had developed among reporters and photographers. In a perverse way, the Queen's gentle reprimand of the Fleet Street editors actually helped form this bias. While it did not inhibit the pursuit of Diana – a few months later, two tabloids were censured by the Press Council for publishing pictures of a six months' pregnant Diana with Charles on a Caribbean beach – the idea of Diana at bay gave her the virtue of seeming vulnerable, an idea that carried over when murmurings of tension in the marriage surfaced, with the added twist that any fault must lie with Charles.

Higher up the media food chain, the same nascent sympathy for Diana combined with the same instinct for her future market value. Before she moved to New York and worked her magic on two moribund American magazines, Tina Brown was bringing back to life the near-dead *Tatler*, originally a house journal for the genteel aristocracy, creating what became, in effect, the first upscale celebrity glossy magazine for the age. In her diary, she noted a windfall for *Tatler*'s editorial fortunes…

Lady Diana Spencer's emergence, rise, and conquest of Prince Charles and the British public. It was the twentieth century's biggest social story since King Edward VIII traded the throne for

Mrs. Simpson in 1936. Lady Di's world was *Tatler*'s world. She was nineteen; most of our staffers were only a few years older ... We were able to write about her world with insider-y insolence. *Tatler* became the go-to shop for every nuance of the royal romance. The Di story would be to *Tatler* what O.J. Simpson later was to CNN.

This was a remarkable example of editorial clairvoyance. And it had an effect beyond the world of glossy magazines. Diana provided a far deeper and more rewarding subject for study than the normal population of celebrities. She ultimately acquired the same aura and potential for literary investigation as Marilyn Monroe, whose life was tortured enough to merit the extended attention of Norman Mailer. This quality elevated the danger she presented to the royal family. Any serious biographical pursuit of Diana inevitably led to her supposed tormentors – the Windsors and their familial skills, or lack thereof.

To me, as all this was happening, there was something familiar in the evolution of Diana's celebrity. I was researching the life of T. E. Lawrence for a project that became an Emmy-winning television drama, *A Dangerous Man: Lawrence After Arabia*, starring a young Ralph Fiennes as Lawrence. In the early 1920s, Lawrence was, by any measure, the most famous man in the western world. But his fame was not created by his own hand – after his exploits in the desert he might well have returned to his earlier quiet life as an archaeologist and explorer of the ancient world. He was discovered in Arabia by the American journalist and war propagandist Lowell Thomas. Thomas shot enough footage to stitch together a documentary, *With Lawrence in Arabia*, and it premiered at Madison Square Garden in New York. The film was an excitable version of the desert war in which Lawrence became an almost mystical heroic figure – and the audiences loved it. It became such a sell-out attraction that Thomas took it on a road show across America and Europe, including London. At first, in the face of this blizzard of myth-building, Lawrence feigned embarrassment and modesty. But suddenly he realised that fame at this level was capable of becoming a political weapon. This was the core of our film: Lawrence exploiting his fame at the Paris Peace Conference of 1919 as he attempted to honour the promises that he (and the British government) had made to grant the Arabs independence from British and French colonial rule. That promise was reneged upon and Lawrence, judged by the politicians to be a dangerous influence, was banished from Paris. Politically neutered, he went on to consolidate his status as a tragic hero by writing his masterpiece, *The Seven Pillars of Wisdom*.

In Diana's case, there was no literary masterpiece but, instead, thousands of adoring profiles and, finally, an electrifying biography in which she, like Lawrence, became very dangerous to a rival force – the monarchy. (Martin Charteris, the Queen's private secretary, used those very words, *very dangerous*, about her.) Lawrence was a keen student of the media mechanisms that made him so celebrated; so was Diana. Nigel Dempster told Tina Brown that Diana 'spent hours studying her press clippings almost as if she's trying to figure out the secret of her own mystique'. Whether she at first understood it or not, the greatest consequence of her mystique was that eventually the royal family lost control of the narrative – and would never really recover it, at particular cost to the Queen herself.

The turning point came in 1992, when the Queen reached her fortieth year on the throne. Again it was the *Sunday Times* that rattled the family's composure, this time with a far more credible and devastating story than the supposed rift between Thatcher and the Queen. The paper had already led a public outcry about the extravagances of Andrew and Fergie. Now it delivered the inside story of a marriage from hell, the ten years of a battle of attrition between Diana and Charles that had scenes so full of vitriol that they could have sprung directly from the script of *Who's Afraid of Virginia Woolf?* Over two weekends the paper serialised a book written by Andrew Morton, *Diana: Her True Story*. Morton had developed the killer instincts of tabloid journalism by working at the *News of the World*, but he combined those with a natural fluency for storytelling in a longer form; in Diana he discovered a perfect subject for both. It was obvious that the clinical details of his book could have come from only one source – Diana. But Diana was now a very confident dissembler and denied any involvement.

Through the medium of Morton's book, Diana established the basic text of her victimhood. It included all the tropes that she used until she died – especially those portraying a woman wronged, a woman scorned, a woman made ill by a merciless husband and in-laws. The key to all her suffering was the triangle of her, Charles and Camilla Parker Bowles. In her later startling public catharsis, an interview on the BBC's *Panorama* programme in 1995, Diana delivered the immortal line 'There were three of us in this marriage, so it was a bit crowded.' In this version, Charles was reduced to a cynical stud who, having produced 'an heir and a spare' rather as in the cold functional mountings that his mother so carefully orchestrated for her horses, then reverted to the loins of the one true love of his life, Camilla. Two days after the second instalment appeared in the *Sunday Times*, the book came out, and it was an instant bestseller. At the same time, Charles and Diana were summoned to Windsor Castle to be told by the Queen and Philip that they should make a new effort to save the marriage for the sake of the monarchy, their children, the country and its people. As usual, Philip advocated the stoic dogma of Gordonstoun that Charles should tough it out and Diana should meekly obey, a view he reinforced in stern letters to Diana. Diana was taken at her word that she had not talked to Morton. (Only after her death did Morton reveal just how completely she had collaborated with him, very deliberately allotting to each of the players the roles that reinforced her own version of history.)

Behind the fevers of a conspicuously failing marriage there were other more fundamental breakdowns in the family's cohesion that got little attention. One of the more serious problems was brought about by Charles. The heir was proving to be increasingly difficult to work for. He went through four private secretaries in seven years. Moreover, he was intent on building his own power base separate from that of the palace, with its own hierarchy of priorities dictated by his personal whims, which were many. For example, suddenly convinced that he needed outside advice on staffing, he sometimes delegated authority to the most bizarre people. One of these was the obscenely cigar-chomping television jester Jimmy Savile, later to be exposed as one of the most predatory paedophiles in the country. A bewildered candidate for the post of Charles's private secretary was told that he had first to be vetted by Savile. Afterwards Charles sent Savile a box of Havana cigars, a gift from Fidel Castro, with a note saying, 'Nobody will ever know what you have done for this country, Jimmy.'

Andrew and Fergie were another problem, with their marriage breaking up. One of the persistent puzzles about the Queen's judgement was the way she seemed always ready to indulge Andrew. She readily handed over £3.5 million for him to acquire a fifty-room mansion. Fergie, meanwhile, always drawn to big spenders, was caught by the tabloids enjoying the close attentions of a Texan millionaire. In fact, watching the Andrew and Fergie show through the years, they seemed to me to fulfil the definition of that wonderful piece of slang, naff. They had no awareness of their own exuberant naffness – a strain of vulgarity that shed all sense of propriety and taste. The Queen put up with Fergie's blatant infidelities as she did with Andrew's cupidity: when the *Daily Mirror* ran a ten-page story with photos showing a topless Fergie having her toes kissed by a lover during a holiday on the French Riviera while with her two young daughters, Philip blew his stack but the Queen continued to see her, because (according to someone close to the family) she wished to remain close to her grandchildren.

To the blind eye was soon added a tin ear.

On 20 November 1992, a fire broke out at Windsor Castle and quickly consumed a number of state rooms and the magnificent St George's Hall. Because some of the rooms were being restored at the time, priceless paintings normally hung in them had been removed. A hastily assembled volunteer force moved swiftly to remove other artwork, furniture and valuables, but the structural devastation was substantial. The Queen arrived from Buckingham Palace in mid-afternoon and stood in the middle of the main courtyard as the roof of St George's Hall collapsed. One of the visual paradoxes of Windsor Castle is that the Norman battlements, so grim to behold as they were intended to be, enclose some of the most exquisite national architectural treasures. The Queen felt far more attached to the medieval glories of Windsor than she did to the Victorian kitsch of Buckingham Palace. There was also the symbolic tie of the place that gave its name to the family in 1917 when they needed to reassert their Britishness. As a result, the ravages of the fire seemed to reach deeper into the Queen's emotions than the human damage that the year had so far inflicted on her family. Seeking solace with her mother, and receiving it, she thanked her: 'It made all the difference to my sanity after that terrible day.'

However, the fire brought to a head the ambiguity in the owner-ship of royal palaces. Windsor Castle was, without doubt, a national treasure. Did that mean that the nation should pay for its restoration? John Major was now the Prime Minister and he was ready to accept that it should, even though it was estimated that the restoration would cost as much as £40 million. The Queen took it for granted that the money would come from the public purse. But the people had other ideas. Led by the *Daily Mail*, there was a highly vocal protest: not only should the family pay for the restoration but it was also about time they paid taxes.

The spontaneity and ferocity of the response caught the Queen off balance: photographs of her standing in a raincoat and wellies in the courtyard looking shattered were expected to make her seem sympathetic, but the cold reality of life outside palaces was that people who lived in grand style should not bring out a begging bowl when some of their rooms burned down. Major, usually a level-headed realist, had also made the same misjudgement of the national mood. Both of them had apparently missed the Diana Effect: months of exposure to what came across to the people as marital misbehaviour among the rich and famous had evidently harmed the image of the monarchy, and the Queen had now witlessly added to the disenchantment.

Even then, she didn't get it. Four days after the fire, she presented herself as the victim. She appeared for a lunch at the Guildhall, ancient seat of the burghers of the City of London and gathering place for the nation's bankers and industrialists, arranged to mark the fortieth anniversary of her accession. She delivered a speech remembered for two sentences: 'Nineteen ninety-two is not a year on which I will look back with undiluted pleasure. In the words of one of my more sympathetic correspondents, it has turned out to be an "*Annus Horribilis*".'

She went on in a tone of wounded complaint that 'moderation and compassion' were absent in 'those whose task it is in life to offer instant opinions on all things great and small'. Almost wistfully, she added, 'Scrutiny ... can be just as effective if it is made with a touch of gentleness, good humour and understanding.'

Although her plutocratic audience at the Guildhall applauded, the people did not. And the seriousness of their hostility was finally acknowledged in a series of concessions: the Queen and Charles would voluntarily pay income tax on their private income from the Duchies of Lancaster and Cornwall (although, as we shall see, this was not the windfall for the nation that it appeared to be); the Queen would reimburse the government the official expenses of Andrew, Anne, Edward and Margaret; and the state rooms at Buckingham Palace would be open to the public in summer with an admission fee to raise money to pay for the Windsor Castle restoration. In fact, the opening of the state rooms generated enough to cover much of the final cost of £37 million and the rest came from cost savings.

On 9 December of the *Annus Horribilis*, John Major announced that Charles and Diana would be separating. Somewhat bafflingly, he added that they had no plans to divorce, that the succession was un-affected and that 'there is no reason why the Princess of Wales should not be crowned Queen in due course'.

For the tabloids, Diana was already Queen. Michael Shea called the tabloids 'a cancer in the soft underbelly of the nation', but he spoke for the palace, not the people. Diana connected with the people in a remarkable way that the Queen could not and on the same level as the tabloids. The pulling power that was pure gold for tabloid front pages also had a more worthy halo effect, making her a huge fund-raiser for any cause she backed, and she supported scores of charities. She was also ready to engage in causes that others lacked the courage to champion. For example, the Aids epidemic of the 1980s created a plague-like panic that stigmatised its victims. To demonstrate that the virus was not transmitted through touch, she deliberately shook hands with an Aids patient without wearing gloves. She did the same in a leprosy hospice in Indonesia. (Margaret also visited Aids victims but did not invite photographers along.)

Diana had also become a cultural asset to the nation. She caught and reflected an undercurrent of the 1990s not seen since the 1960s – that London and Britain were again cool. British music, movies and fashion had a new zest. John Major's Tory government attempted to ride the new wave. 'London is universally recognised as a centre of style and innovation,' announced the Department of National Heritage. 'Our fashion, music and culture are the envy of our European neighbours. This abundance of talent, together with our rich heritage, makes "Cool Britannia" an obvious choice for visitors from all over the world.' There was little doubt that the most photographed woman in the world, Diana, with little effort and a natural gift for style, was the principal diva of British cool.

But John Major was definitely not cool. Steve Bell, *The Guardian*'s political cartoonist, indelibly nailed Major's suburban insecurity by always portraying him wearing Y-fronts on top of his trousers. Moreover, the Tory Party had no idea what cool was. There was, however, a new face in politics who really got it – indeed, 'getting it' was part of his brisk vocabulary. In July 1994, Tony Blair was elected leader of the Labour Party. As his personal press officer Blair chose the political editor of the *Daily Mirror*, Alastair Campbell. Between them, these two had the talent to imprint a completely new face on their party, as in New Labour, with the same techniques of rebranding that an advertising agency might bring to a 'new and improved' soap powder. Within months of taking over the party, Blair demonstrated his ideological flexibility by flying to Australia to see Rupert Murdoch and address a meeting of his top staff. The idea was to try to get a pledge of *The Sun*'s support in the next election, due in 1997. Murdoch was interested. He saw a winner – if Blair could really pull off his plan to move his party from the left to the place where they both thought the majority of the country now lived: the centre.

Blair had another target for radical change: the monarchy. He suggested that the Queen had to make a choice. The monarchy could either retreat into isolation and the old hierarchical order or follow the Scandinavian model of looking like a modern family living more modestly and engaged in good works. One of Blair's gifts was to conceal how moderate his views really were, but he led a party that had a rump of republicans in the tradition of Willie Hamilton – including his own wife, Cherie. He had carefully calibrated his own position. He didn't want to abolish the monarchy. At this point he had no way of judging whether it had the capacity to embrace any change.

Charles didn't like the Scandinavian allusions and invited Blair to his London home, St James's Palace. Like most people meeting Blair for the first time, Charles succumbed to his charm and reasonableness. He was also pleased to discover a shared concern about the environment and education. It was not the time for Blair to explain that he had no interest in having any of the royals involved in policymaking or even trying to influence a government's policies – something that Charles could never stop hoping to do. But there was another member of the royal family, albeit alienated, whose causes and public good works impressed Blair, as did her chic: Diana. As Blair and Campbell appropriated 'Cool Britannia' as part of their own message, they shrewdly saw that Diana's classless gift of connection was something they needed to acquire if they were to win.

That gift of connection and communication largely explained why, when Charles and Diana were finally divorced in 1996, the media bias against Charles and in favour of Diana persisted and, if anything, became stronger. It seemed that Diana's halo could survive any number of sexual adventures. Physically, she was becoming more voluptuous. In her early years of celebrity, she was a stunning beauty but gauche and shy. Her beauty had a touch of the androgynous that suggested a David Bowie-like ambiguity. As she matured and after the births of her sons, she became more like a super-toned Hollywood star. She was also far more self-assured about her seductive powers.

The first to fall for her was a police bodyguard, Barry Mannakee. Diana was suffering postpartum depression after the birth of Harry. Mannakee was thirty-eight and married. The affair began in 1985 and ended in 1986 after it was discovered by another bodyguard. Mannakee was transferred to other duties. He died in a motoring accident not long afterwards. Immediately on the heels of that affair, Diana began a five-year fling with James Hewitt, an officer in the Household Cavalry, who resembled the kind of adorable rascal familiar in Victorian novels and, after it was over, Hewitt betrayed all in a book by Anna Pasternak that read like one of those novels. Hewitt was followed by James Gilbey, heir to a gin fortune, who called her 'Squidgy' during an affair that lasted a year. This was a *cinq à sept* kind of romp without any depth. Oliver Hoare, the next lover, was very different. As unlikely as it may seem, the role assigned to Hoare by the tabloids was that of the Freudian archetype, the older man who 'awakens' the latent whore (no pun intended). The evidence for this is based largely on another of Diana's bodyguards, Ken Wharfe. The life of a bodyguard in Kensington Palace appears to have been an awkward balance of body protection and keyhole intelligence-gathering. In fact, taking Wharfe at his word, keyholes were often not required because one of Hoare's innovations was al fresco sex in the palace bushes. Another, bondage, needed more discretion. Hoare was sixteen years older than Diana and a father of three, a dealer in Islamic antiques, with the looks of a practised ladykiller. When his aristocratic French wife threatened divorce if the affair was not ended, Hoare complied. Diana was distraught. She made more than 300 late-night 'hell hath no fury' calls to Hoare, causing his wife to complain to the police, who traced them to Diana. She fumed, but it was over.

Until now, Diana's lovers had come from the world familiar to her; her next big affair opened up strikingly different horizons. In November 1995, a photographer from the *News of the World*, acting on a tip, found her at the Royal Brompton Hospital at midnight. Rather than dodging him, she said she was there comforting patients. The photographer called the paper's royal correspondent, Clive Goodman, who was still in the newsroom, and connected him with Diana. Diana told him that she regularly spent up to four hours a night at the hospital with terminally ill patients. Goodman composed a story that appeared four days later headlined 'MY SECRET NIGHTS AS AN ANGEL'. Diana was a natural consoler of the sick, but that role was a cover. She was developing an intense attachment to Hasnat Khan, a 37-year-old heart surgeon from Pakistan. Khan's family, living near Lahore, were upper caste and belonged to an ascetic Muslim sect: Khan, despite his distinction as a top-flight surgeon, was an ascetic himself, spurning all the luxuries that Diana took for granted. She submitted to his humility with all the passion of an apostate, spending days at his one-bedroom flat in Chelsea, washing the dishes, vacuuming and ironing his shirts. When Khan's father learned of the affair, he was unimpressed. 'He is not going to marry her,' he said. 'We are looking for a bride for him. She must be from a respectable family.' Khan had no illusions, either. He said, 'She is from Venus and I am from Mars.' After two years, he terminated the affair. Diana had met a persuasive life force greater than herself – a culture and a faith totally outside anything she had known – and once she saw and felt it, she wanted more of it.

If Charles had gathered as many lovers as Diana, he would have been stigmatised as a serial lecher. And once back with the real love of his life, Camilla, he was monogamous. Is there a double standard here? Diana's affairs were flagrantly public. More than that, she managed to present them as the inevitable and deserved compensation for being dumped by Charles. But she was a bad loser. With both Hoare and Khan she found it hard to accept rejection because she could not really believe that any man was beyond the range of her mesmerism. At the age of thirty-six and after all these messy and turbulent romances, she remained the most famous woman in the world and, certainly, the most effective celebrity activist. In January 1997, she was photographed walking across a minefield in Angola during her powerful campaign to get old minefields cleared across the world.

Hundreds of children were needlessly being killed or maimed every year. Her greatest quality was making people feel that by their own efforts the world could be made a better place.

This feeling was shared by the architects of a new kind of mobilising political evangelism, Tony Blair and Alastair Campbell. When Campbell first met Diana socially, he swooned, noting in his diary, 'There was something about her eyes that went beyond radiance. They locked on to you and were utterly mesmeric … Her whole face lit up when she spoke and there were moments when I had to fight to hear the words because I'm just lost in the beauty.'

Later, in a conversation with Blair, Campbell said that Diana believed that the royal family needed fundamental changes but they were not capable of making them – 'no matter how many times they relaunch'. They mused that it might be better to jump a generation in the succession, passing over Charles and elevating Prince William.

New Labour won power on 1 May 1997 in a landslide victory. As Blair had hoped, Murdoch had swung his daily tabloid, *The Sun*, behind New Labour. That endorsement delivered nearly half a million votes, or about 2 per cent of the popular vote. It was not enough to be decisive but enough to make Blair and Campbell anxious to keep Murdoch onside – something Buckingham Palace fervently wished it had the power to do. Soon afterwards, Blair's office had a taste of Charles's rigid self-importance. Blair had written to Charles, opening with 'Dear Prince Charles,' and closing with 'Yours ever, Tony'. One of Charles's staff immediately called Downing Street to instruct that the correct form was to open with 'Sir,' and close with 'Your obedient Servant'. That left no doubt that Blair's breezy informality was at odds with the protocols of an institution he was beginning to feel needed a big shake-up. A few weeks later, Blair invited Diana and her sons to his official country retreat, Chequers. A completely captured Campbell noted that Diana would be a real asset to Blair's modernising crusade – 'a big part of New Britain'. At the beginning of July, Blair and Campbell were with Charles in Hong Kong for the official handover of the colony to China. This was when Charles sailed home on *Britannia*, its last foreign voyage before being decommissioned. He arrived in Hong Kong on a British Airways flight, complaining about his seat in Club Class: 'So uncomfortable ... Such is the end of Empire.' Blair, Campbell and some of their staff were flying in First. Getting to see Charles more closely, Campbell was uncharacteristically forgiving: he was 'a fairly decent bloke, surrounded by a lot of nonsense and people best described as from another age ... surrounded by luxury, people fawning on him, and yet somehow obviously unfulfilled'.

Not long afterwards, an Italian photographer, Mario Brenna, couldn't believe his luck. He was not one of the paparazzi who pursued and staked out locations for shots of the royals. His normal beat was fashion and he was based in that enclave of the super-rich, Monaco, where late in July he spotted the 200-foot luxury yacht *Jonikal*, owned by the Egyptian mogul Mohamed Al Fayed, who had been enterprising enough to take over one of the Queen's favourite stores, Harrods, when it was failing and make it a success again. Brenna had read that Diana was joining the yacht as a guest of the Fayeds for a Mediterranean cruise, but there was no sign of her in the harbour.

Two weeks later, Brenna was in Sardinia when he spotted the yacht anchored in a remote bay. He attached a long lens to the camera with enough magnification to focus and clearly identify two figures on the deck of the *Jonikal*: Diana and Fayed's 42-year-old son Dodi. They were massaging each other with sunscreen with the easy familiarity of lovers. Unaware of being observed by Brenna, Diana seemed to be enjoying a new level of personal freedom. The paparazzi did spot the pair in other locations and Diana consciously gave them a chance to see her in flattering ways – for example, sitting on the edge of a diving board with her long legs dangling above the brilliant water. A young woman who was one of the yacht's crew of sixteen noted that Diana was a very different person in public and private – in private she was 'being in the moment and actually living'; in public, she played the icon and knew every way to satisfy the expectations of her. But Brenna had caught a few moments of something that was not deliberately staged – a shameless intimacy. His pictures were put up for auction to the world's tabloids. The *Sunday Mirror* paid £300,000 for them and splashed them over ten pages. The North American rights went to the Canadian weekly *Globe* for $210,000. It was later estimated that Brenna's worldwide royalties for that one shoot earned him $3 million.

The distance between the pictures of Diana in protective armour stepping warily through an Angolan minefield and of her on the deck of the *Jonikal* was seven months in time but, in terms of her saintly image, an abyss in terms of sensibility. Who was she, really?

CHAPTER 25

WHERE IS THE QUEEN?

Before *Britannia* was finally docked, to become a floating museum, she carried the Queen and members of the family on a final cruise around the Western Isles of Scotland. It was August. The Queen had recently celebrated her seventy-first birthday, and at the end of the cruise she was now able to take her summer holiday in the place where she most felt at home, Balmoral. But even there it was impossible for her to escape family tensions. For months Charles had been attempting to overcome his parents' resistance to making Camilla his wife. He wanted to assert his rights as heir and Camilla was indispensable to his future life. 'I won't be trodden down any more,' he told an aide. He deliberately organised a spectacular party for Camilla's fiftieth birthday in July. This did nothing to ease the Queen's doubts about his judgement. There was also the almost daily pursuit of Diana's adventures with the Egyptian playboy.

Measures of the monarchy's popularity were not very scientific and tended to rely too much on spontaneous reactions to particular events, all of them reported in the tabloid vernacular. For example, in a poll following a BBC programme about the younger royals, Charles was voted 'the most hated' of them, just above Camilla. Sixty thousand viewers said that if Charles married Camilla he should not succeed to the throne. Another poll early in 1997 suggested that support for the monarchy as a whole had slipped to 66 per cent, whereas it had previously held steady at around 75 per cent. Since her misreading of the public mood after the Windsor Castle fire, the Queen had become noticeably more cautious and less sure of how to respond to events.

Early in the morning of Sunday 31 August, there was an urgent call to Balmoral from the British embassy in Paris. Diana and Dodi Al Fayed had been critically injured in a car crash. A few hours later, news came that Diana was dead, at the age of thirty-six. Two institutions were immediately propelled into an uneasy partnership, the Crown and Downing Street, and that partnership exposed two starkly different approaches to a crisis of national sentiment.

Looked at more than two decades later, what followed over a week or more looks like an outbreak of collective hysteria. From the outset, the terms of the national sentiment were set by Diana. In death she was far more consequential than when alive. Part of it was articulated best by Charles that morning at Balmoral when he said, 'They're all going to blame me, aren't they? The world's going to go completely mad.' For years, Diana had worked in communion with her supposed tormentors, the tabloids. She fed them the script and they ran with it. The halo never slipped. The frugal and dedicated surgeon Hasnat Khan had been immediately followed by Dodi, a man whose life was as self-indulgent as Khan's was selflessly beneficent. That might, at least, have given pause to the adoration of Diana. But it didn't. It's just possible that Diana, on the rebound, allowed herself to recklessly go on a sexual binge with Al Fayed and exhibit her pleasure deliberately to distress Khan – or Charles. But facile pop psychology doesn't really solve the moral issue. It wasn't just a matter of appearances but of self-abasement and reputation by so blatantly parading her sudden pleasures in the careless world of superyachts and a playboy companion. Her time with Al Fayed lasted six weeks and, amazingly, left her reputation unblemished.

Tony Blair had been in office only four months and barely knew the

Queen. But he and Campbell had already been schooled in the royal family's dysfunctions through their experiences with Charles. At the time, I could see that they came with the full toolbox of marketing and media manipulation skills that I had somewhat flippantly advised the royal family to adopt in my 1969 essay. It had worked for them. The Labour Party that they took over was much like the monarchy – stubbornly out of touch and the prisoner of legacy rituals. But focus groups and deep polling don't actually produce charismatic leaders, and the party had been lucky enough to elect just such a leader – and he had been smart enough to reinforce his own instincts with Campbell's more cynical grassroots knowledge of the party. Now they faced, in the Queen, a head of state who was not charismatic and could not grasp what was happening to her.

The Queen's first public statement was terse and robotic: 'The Queen and Prince of Wales are deeply shocked and distressed by the terrible news.' The effect was exacerbated when she took William and Harry to the regular Sunday service at the nearby Crathie church and no mention was made of Diana's death in the prayers. After that, it was impossible to reverse the impression that the Queen, as she had seemed during the Aberfan tragedy, was coldly aloof from public feeling. There was one simple and offensive symbol of her attitude: no flag flying at half-mast at Buckingham Palace. In fact, the Union Jack never flew there, only the royal arms, and then only when the monarch was in residence. By Wednesday, when the empty flagpole was seen around the world as inexplicable, the Queen and Philip still rebuffed advice to fly the Union Jack at half-mast. By Thursday, the tabloids were in full cry: 'WHERE IS OUR QUEEN, WHERE IS OUR FLAG?' demanded *The Sun*.

Within hours of Diana's death, Charles flew to Paris with Diana's two sisters to bring back her body and arrived at the RAF airfield at Northolt on Sunday afternoon to be met by Blair. Thus was the Prime

Minister seen with Charles in what was obviously a state of mutual and natural grief as the coffin, draped in Diana's personal standard of red, gold and blue, was carried from the plane to be taken to St James's Palace, where it would rest on a catafalque in the Chapel Royal. Blair had already seized the moment with a phrase that cut through all the palace's confusion to the essence of how the country itself felt – Diana, he said, was 'the People's Princess'. Blair hadn't invented the term. It was coined by a *Sunday Times* writer, Anthony Holden, in a biography, but Campbell had retrieved it from memory and after Blair used it he noted in his diary, 'The phrase had really taken hold and was becoming part of the language immediately. We have to be careful though that it doesn't look like we are writing our script rather than hers.' The 'hers' – of course – meaning the Queen's. Blair and Campbell were acutely aware of the danger of becoming the obvious controllers of the message, a concern heightened on the Monday morning when the European edition of the *New York Times*, the *Herald Tribune*, ran the headline 'WORLD MOURNS THE PEOPLE'S PRINCESS'.

But it was true: Downing Street had far more nimbly and fluently caught the extraordinary popular mood than the Queen. Blair didn't really want to play the bleeding heart against the cold heart, because he was anxious to protect the Queen from herself, hoping that eventually she would 'get it'. And, to be fair to the Queen, nothing in the whole of her reign prepared her for dealing with the spontaneous combustion of Diana worship. When Charles said, 'The world's going to go completely mad,' he was right. In the great Valhalla where rested all the monarchs and warlords stretching back to the Normans, not one had, at their deaths, inspired such an incontinent sense of love and loss – not Nelson, not Wellington, not Churchill. Diana had created a dangerous level of national rapture that left the occupants of Balmoral bemused and to some degree resentful.

The Queen, it was said, could not emote. But it was not a question of a psychological disorder or shortcoming. What was happening was irrational and the Queen's view of her role and duty was always coldly rational. The person could not detach itself from the institution, and the institution had the certainty of rules. The Union Jack never flew over Buckingham Palace and the bare flagpole was a sign of how deeply rules were observed. As Campbell recorded in his diary, 'Failure to lower the flag did not help … There was a real fear that this was becoming the people against the family.' A little later, he was more alarmed: 'The mood out on the Mall was dreadful … It was becoming dangerous and unpleasant. The press was fuelling the general feeling that the royals were not responding or even caring.' Since Tuesday people had been pouring into London at the rate of 6,000 an hour. Lines formed to sign books of condolences at St James's Palace and at Kensington Palace, but the response overwhelmed the normal formalities of mourning. The most engulfing impression was of flowers – many multitudes of bouquets left outside Buckingham Palace and, particularly, at Kensington Palace. These were radiant summer days in the capital, and the tide of colour averted the danger that Campbell felt was in the air. When the Queen and Philip finally arrived at Buckingham Palace on the Friday afternoon, they were visibly stunned on seeing a bank of bouquets stacked six feet high against the railings. At 6 p.m., the Queen made a live broadcast to the nation, carefully seated to show the background of crowds outside the palace gates. 'We have all been trying in our different ways to cope,' she said. But there was, as usual, an artificial and pedestrian quality to the prose. Alan Bennett was an astute critic: the Queen was unconvincing because she was 'not a good actress, indeed not an actress at all'. The difference between Diana and the Queen was, he said, that one could act and the other couldn't. That was probably a difference that the Queen was happy to acknowledge, because she is, by nature, the least meretricious of people.

Normally, years of planning went into royal funerals. It involved layers of officials and endless committees. Even for a relatively minor state occasion like Charles's investiture at Caernarfon, Tony Snowdon had found himself entangled for months with lunatic sticklers for tradition. This time a state funeral had all been organised in a few days and much of it, after some confusion, had been adapted from plans already made for the funeral of the Queen Mother. The single most harrowing element was decided at the last minute. All week there had been much agonising over what part would be played by Diana's sons, William and Harry, who were, after all, the most direct victims of the tragedy. On Friday evening, Prince Philip suggested that they should walk with him and Charles behind the gun carriage bearing Diana's coffin. They agreed and joined the procession from St James's Palace to Westminster Abbey – a sight that wrenched at everyone's hearts.

For a national shrine, the Abbey does not have a striking location like Notre Dame in Paris or St Peter's in Rome. It sits on the western side of Parliament Square like a stranded gothic relic overshadowed by the fake medievalism of Parliament. There is no aspect from which it shines. Vast as it is inside, and full of illustrious ghosts, the Abbey seems introverted and its spirit unable to reach beyond its walls. That all changed on Saturday 6 September 1997. Walls came down. Pomp yielded to spontaneous celebration. Two thousand people were inside the Abbey for Diana's funeral service. The pews were heavy with the rumps of the great and the good. The organ's piping energy rose with the choir's voices to provide that potion of patriotism and liturgy embraced in eighteenth-century hymns, that holy union of God and Britannia, that is so loved in England. Tony Blair, a believing Christian, read from First Corinthians. But it was left to the plump, flock-headed Elton John to deliver the most rousing anthem, an adaptation of 'Candle in the Wind', in which the original line 'Goodbye

Norma Jean' was replaced by 'Goodbye England's rose'. (How apt that the original object of desire and reverence was the elusive Marilyn Monroe.) John was so nervous that he might flub and sing the original line that he had a small teleprompter placed to his left.

All of this was relayed by speakers to the crowds outside and shown on giant video screens. The Abbey's doors were opened to amplify the effects. I watched it from America, along with 2.5 billion people around the world and 31 million in Britain. It was an extraordinary moment. It gradually dawned on me that something new was happening, something enormous that didn't have any design to it – it was spontaneously filling the air beyond the Abbey as Elton John's elegy did, just as the tsunami of flowers from Kensington Palace to the Mall had magically signalled London's mood. The death of the People's Princess had produced the People's Pageant. The people had taken over the sacraments and recast them in their own voice. Earlier in the week, Alastair Campbell had noted in his diary, 'There was a lot of pressure building against the Queen and the family … There was a real change among the public.' Now it was clear that the public had moved far ahead of the monarchy in understanding the moment and setting the terms of how it should be remembered.

One eulogy delivered inside the Abbey was discordant. Diana's brother, the 9th Earl Spencer, had walked behind the carriage with Philip, Charles and the two boys. He was an unfamiliar face to the crowds, pulled rudely out of a private life by fate. His anger was palpable. It was first vented on the tabloids: 'It is a point to remember that of all the ironies about Diana, perhaps the greatest was this – a girl given the name of the ancient goddess of hunting was, in the end, the most hunted person of the modern age.' But then he seemed to find a more immediate adversary, the royal family, addressing Diana directly: 'I pledge that we, your blood family, will do all we can to continue the imaginative and loving way in which you were steering these two exceptional young men so that their souls are not simply immersed by duty and tradition but can sing openly as you planned.'

Nobody before had ever presented the obvious friction between Diana and the Windsors as one rooted in bloodlines. Outside the Abbey, in the combustible new mood of the day, there was applause. For the Queen, highly sensitive to her own family's tangled loyalties of blood, a reminder that the Spencers were a family freighted with the breastplates and battlements of medieval England was in itself offensive, never mind the idea that the spirits of William and Harry were in danger of being smothered by 'duty and tradition'. The Queen's aides immediately made it clear that she thought the remarks were gratuitous.

After the service, the Queen returned to Balmoral. The royal standard on the flagpole above the palace was lowered. In its place, the Union Jack rose to half-mast. Better late than never. The Queen's advisers thanked Tony Blair and Alastair Campbell for the way the Downing Street staff had helped the palace manage the public mood swings. But afterwards Blair said that whenever he tried to discuss future change 'the blinds came down'. He told Campbell, 'They are very different people in a very different age. They believe things should pretty much stay the same, and they want them to stay the same.'

In fact, of the ten Prime Ministers who had so far served the Queen, four were determined agents of change. Macmillan, Wilson, Thatcher and Blair all, in their different ways, moved the country on with permanent changes. As we have seen, Macmillan's carefully cultivated mask of an Edwardian grandee concealed a radical realist. His 'wind of change' speech in Africa was ahead of where much of his own party were in accepting decolonisation. He astutely used the Queen to bring Kwame Nkrumah onside and her imprimatur sealed the success of his policy. Wilson was less in need of royal endorsement. He brought social and cultural freedoms that were long overdue, yet not much relished in the palace. Thatcher was an uncompromising ideologue who smashed some things up regardless of how she was loathed for doing so, while unleashing a new kind of capitalism. But she was meticulously deferential to the monarch and, at heart, a true believer in the monarchy. But now Blair gave up on any idea of taking the monarch along in his own transforming agenda.

And so at this moment it seemed that the monarchy was less an institution than it was the last stand of a ruling caste, fighting to preserve an ossified world and left with the freedom to decide its own relevance, or lack of. It was the Queen herself who made the final call on that. In contrast, the reforming Prime Ministers faced a far more formidable challenge. In order to effect change they had to carry their party, Parliament and the people with them.

*   *   *

On the Saturday morning, as the gun carriage carrying Diana's coffin passed Buckingham Palace, the Queen and Princess Margaret stood near the gates to pay their respects. The Queen and others bowed their heads. People noticed that Margaret did not. Margaret's private life had suffered many of the same invasions as Diana's. Her affairs – most notably the bizarre romps with Roddy Llewellyn – were just as flagrant as Diana's. After all, Margaret had been the first princess to break loose and rattle the cage and, in her day, attained a Hollywood level of celebrity. But she had never approached Diana's power to sell tabloids and nobody would ever call her the People's Princess. She probably felt, like Norma Desmond in *Sunset Boulevard*, that she had once defined what stardom meant, only to be replaced by a supernova. Whatever the cause, Margaret, after an initial friendship, had tired of Diana and she was at serious odds with the Queen over Diana's successor, Camilla, whose cause she had taken up. Little more than a year after Diana's death, Charles, supported by Margaret, was pressing his mother to accept that Camilla would be his future companion for life. During a tense meeting at Balmoral, his mother not only called Camilla 'that wicked woman' but made it clear that she wanted nothing to do with her. To Charles's distress, the Queen blamed Camilla for provoking the break-up with Diana. Margaret, meanwhile, was happy to be seen partying at Highgrove with Charles and Camilla, thereby exposing for all to see where her sympathies lay in the deepening family rift.

But, as Charles must have realised, being supported by Margaret might be seen as the kiss of death. By now Margaret was hardly a model of constancy in love. She was earning a new kind of notoriety, largely due to her long winter sojourns to Mustique. The tiny island became a place where she could be the centre of attraction to a group of hedonistic admirers, some respectable and some not. Always behind the festivities was the man who had turned a mosquito-infested jungle into prime Caribbean real estate, Colin Tennant – or, more accurately, Lord Glenconner, as he became when succeeding to the family title in 1983. In her 2019 memoir, his wife Lady Anne wrote, 'I married all of my husband. Colin could be charming, angry, endearing, hilariously funny, manipulative, vulnerable, intelligent, spoilt, insightful and fun.' Fatally, he was too ill-disciplined to actually make a fortune out of founding the entity that owned the island, the Mustique Company. He sold control of it in 1976 and continued to mismanage and dissipate his family's money thereafter, to the distress of Anne, who remained one of Margaret's most devoted friends – a fealty she shared with a small number of other blue-blooded royalists who developed a remarkable level of tolerance for Margaret's needy island habits. In this supposed nirvana were the seeds of tragedy.

The Queen had long been disturbed by what she called Margaret's 'guttersnipe life' on Mustique. In 1978, the year when Margaret's marriage was formally ended, her partying habits with Roddy Llewellyn on Mustique coincided with another parliamentary review of the civil list. Willie Hamilton again rose to complain of Margaret's excessive allowance and public debauchery. He was backed up by another MP who called her 'a royal parasite'. Even worse, Margaret was incautious about some of the company she kept on Mustique, people who were drawn to her to enhance their own celebrity while further damaging her reputation. One of these was from the dodgy world of London's East End crime gangs, John Bindon. While Bindon was in prison on a murder charge (he was acquitted after pleading self-defence), he boasted that he was an intimate of Margaret's and had photographs from Mustique to prove it. The story was made more salacious by Bindon's claims about the spectacular size of his member and willingness to display it to anyone who requested proof. After his acquittal, Bindon sold his story, and the photographs, to the *Daily Mirror* for £40,000. The somewhat grainy photographs proved that Bindon had been partying with Margaret, though nothing else. She claimed that the encounter was fleeting and casual, but the damage was done, and the 'Bonking Bindon' story passed into the seamy folklore of the island, along with many others that did no credit to Margaret. Tony loathed Glenconner; he blamed him for surrounding Margaret with people who added to her notoriety, and, at the same time, he was left to explain the Mustique scandals to their children, David and Sarah.

It remains hard to fathom why Margaret allowed herself so readily to be the subject of scandal. Her self-directed transformation from the warmest, most vivacious and most culturally literate member of a family not otherwise noted for any of those qualities to the tetchy and star-crossed figure of her later years was ineffably sad. She drank too much and she had been a heavy smoker all her life. The physical toll showed. The once hourglass figure bulked up. Her face recorded the cost of too many hangovers.

Early in 1998, at a dinner party on Mustique with the Glenconners, she had a stroke. She was flown back to the King Edward VII Hospital in London and, after a two-week stay, made a moderately good recovery. But it was a precursor. In 1999, back in Mustique on another winter escape, her feet were badly burned when she turned on the wrong taps in her bath. The effects of the stroke had slowed her reactions. Anne Glenconner, alone, was left for weeks to nurse her until she was able to fly to London. Even then, Anne had to call the Queen to explain that Margaret was in too much pain to endure an eight-hour flight. She returned at supersonic speed on Concorde. John Larkin, her regular British chauffeur and confidant, a delightfully unaffected Cockney, was shocked to see her bandaged feet and how frail she was. Larkin devised a special vehicle so that, wheelchair-bound, she could visit a series of specialists to guide her recovery. She would never return to Mustique. Her villa, Les Jolies Eaux, was sold by her son David for £2.4 million. In January 2001, she had another stroke, and in March a third. That summer, in a rare public appearance to mark the Queen Mother's 101st birthday, people were shocked to see her in a wheelchair with her left arm in a sling and her face masked by oversized dark glasses. On 8 February 2002, she had a fourth stroke, and died a day later at the King Edward VII Hospital. She had given the faithful Larkin instructions to burn all the correspondence between her and her mother. He collected it, stuffed into a large plastic rubbish bag, put it in a bin and lit the match. 'It went up, *whoosh!*' he recalled.

The divergence in the characters of the Queen and Margaret was evident early on. It lay partly in the natural variety of siblings and partly in Elizabeth's assigned destiny as monarch. From the day Elizabeth became the next in line to the throne, she went twice a week to Eton College for her lessons in constitutional history from the bachelor vice-provost, Sir Henry Marten. Marten was an engaging teacher with a flair for humanising history, but for Elizabeth it was a tough six-year endeavour. Margaret, meanwhile, was having an altogether brighter time with Marie-Antoinette de Bellaigue, a Belgian vicomtesse educated in Paris, who was enlisted to teach the two princesses French literature and history. Called 'Toni' by them, she spotted in Margaret someone who yearned for a broader cultural experience than her sister. (In that age the two princesses were given home schooling without any chance to continue to a university, which was considered unsuitable for them.) Toni took Margaret on a careful and systematic progress through the best art galleries and public art collections in London, providing a grounding of knowledge that she later used in buying her own collection. As a result, she also had a far deeper appreciation of the vast royal art collection than any other member of the family. Added to Margaret's natural flair for music and to her more extrovert personality, this gave her the confidence she showed when, with Tony, she built her eclectic salon at Kensington Palace – despite the view of some of the more egotistic artists that it was impertinent of a princess to have opinions on their work. In the lives of the two princesses, Elizabeth was the duty and Margaret the music – at the end, the music was too much.

Tony died in January 2017, at the age of eighty-six. He was buried in a family plot in the remote Welsh village of Llanfaglan.

Little more than a month after Margaret's death, at the end of March, the Queen Mother died.

Elizabeth Bowes-Lyon was a great beauty as a debutante. According to one of her contemporaries, men 'fell at her feet'. However, when she was twenty years old and entered into the assigned rituals of the debutante season, there was an acute shortage of eligible young men. The officer class of her generation had been decimated in the Great

War, a blow felt in many of the great houses of the land. How she ended up choosing, from the beaux available, the least self-assured of the King's sons, Bertie, the Duke of York, is one of those misty-eyed tales that from this distance seem like they are torn from the pages of period romantic fiction.

First of all, there is the gallant but thwarted heartthrob. He was James Stuart, an officer in the Royal Scots who had won the Military Cross for bravery and, when the war ended, became equerry to Bertie. Stuart ticked all the boxes for a young woman who was proud of her Scottish roots: his family was one of the tartan elite, the oldest and noblest in Scotland, and he was an Old Etonian – full of the social swagger that that college imparts.

Second comes the switch. Inevitably, Stuart and Elizabeth met and danced during the London season and created a buzz of anticipation. Then, in 1920, at a ball to celebrate the creation of the Royal Air Force at the Ritz in Piccadilly, our dashing hero introduces his boss, Bertie, to Elizabeth. From that moment Bertie is smitten and – according to Stuart's own memoirs – 'from then on he never showed the slightest interest in any other young lady'.

Third, the rejection. Literally tongue-tied and maladroit, Bertie was far from being a natural suitor, but he had an inner determination that he had found the woman with whom he wanted to share the rest of his life. In fact, this condition, inner certainties that he lacked the confidence to express verbally, was his serious affliction. And when Elizabeth turned him down, her mother, Lady Strathmore, wrote to a friend that 'the Duke seems so disconsolate. I do hope he will find a nice wife who will make him happy.'

The rejection spun Bertie into the depression of a man who felt a great love had slipped through his hands for good. It was not only that she was herself adorable but that the life she led at Glamis Castle was, compared to the penitential atmosphere of Buckingham Palace, little short of an idyll – and an idyll that this sparkling young woman embodied. Another young blood who fell in love with her recalled that 'Glamis was beautiful, perfect. Being there it was like living in a van Dyck picture.'

And then, of course, the happy ending: bolstered by a pep talk from a friend, Bertie worked up the courage to propose again, but at the next attempt was again rebuffed until, with one final effort during a walk in the woods of a country estate, she said yes.

Given the oppression of his upbringing, the wildness of his brothers and the royal duties that he frequently felt were irksome, Bertie was really lucky in love. They married in 1923 in a ceremony at Westminster Abbey – the first time for more than six centuries that a King's son had been married there. Elizabeth Bowes-Lyon was to become more than a wife and mother. She was his rock. She understood his inner demons and managed them, including his stutter. They had no expectation that the Crown would end up on Bertie's head. When it did, Elizabeth provided much of the fortitude that the King needed for the terrible conflict ahead, and to prepare their eldest daughter for the throne. She endured to provide the same support for the first of her grandsons, the Prince of Wales, who was frequently in need of it.

CHAPTER 26

THE NEXT KING

Prince Charles is a chip off the old block. The trouble is that it's the wrong block. Of all the members of the family, he has been the most publicly dissected, his body and organs stretched out and picked over for clues beyond basic anatomy, hoping to explain his tortured path through life. And yet I have always seen in his behaviour a recognisable forebear: his great-uncle, the previous Prince of Wales and latterly the Duke of Windsor. Charles carries at least three of the Duke's traits. The most consequential is his devotion to Camilla. There are clear echoes here of the hold Wallis Simpson had over the Duke, which included the spell of a mutual erogenous zone too private to be fully understood, although in Charles's case we learned more than we really needed to know. In 1992, the *Daily Mirror* got hold of the transcript of an eight-minute telephone conversation between Charles and Camilla and published it. Charles yearned to 'live inside your trousers' and then, drifting into a familiar morbidity (you can imagine the nasal drone), suggested that after death he wished to be reincarnated as a tampon and 'just my luck … to be flushed down the lavatory and go on forever swirling round the top, never going down'. Some great loves have poetry, others have a deeper insanitary mystery. As with Wallis Simpson, there is also a strong presence of the oedipal complex. Camilla evolved naturally from the buxom lass to the matron as their attachment strengthened. Wallis Simpson never had a maternal physicality, but she had a similar palliative power over the Duke. The whole world was transfixed by Diana's angular beauty, but Charles seemed never to share this taste – all the while he was fantasising about Camilla's pneumatic embrace. In moments of spite, Diana said he was a lousy lover, but he was not to Camilla.

The second trait shared with the Duke is a deep frustration that he has unacknowledged gifts that should be put to use on behalf of the nation but are not because the politicians keep rebuffing him. Princes who live in grand country homes and palaces have a basic problem when they attempt to show understanding of and sympathy for the bottom layers of society. At its simplest, this is manifested when the royal limousines arrive in unfamiliar plebeian settings. It provided a jarring note when Edward, as Prince of Wales, went to see the ravages of the Great Depression in Wales in the 1930s, or as Charles did when arriving in his Bentley to see how the tenants of his Duchy of Cornwall estates were housed in the 1980s. These royal excursions are usually followed by a prescriptive response. In Edward's case, this took the form of top-down social engineering with an iron hand, a method he found attractive in national socialism, i.e., fascism; the other authoritarian choice, communism, was obviously anathema to him. With Charles, the prescription is more like enlightened paternalism, ideally delivered in a partnership between him and government. Between 2004 and 2005, Charles wrote twenty-seven letters to seven of Tony Blair's ministers, intervening on issues as varied as fox hunting, which he defended, and genetically modified crops, which he abhorred. The missives were known in Whitehall as the 'black spider memos' because they were handwritten in Charles's creepy-crawly script. *The Guardian* spent ten years on legal actions to get the memos released to the public, but, when they were, there was no evidence of them having had any significant influence on policies. (In 2015, a YouGov poll found that 54 per cent of the public thought it OK for Charles to speak out on issues he felt strongly about.) But, as we will see, there was one subject on which he was able to use his influence and power to overturn projects that he did not like: modern architecture.

The third trait he shares with the Duke is foppishness. In both men, an obsession with the details of the male wardrobe reached beyond vanity to narcissism. In a way, though, this trait comes with the territory. The job provides every detail of personal luxury as a vocational privilege. For every waking hour, Charles is personally serviced according to an exact regime. Michael Fawcett, a combination of butler, valet and court sycophant, became through his own example the fastidious overseer of Charles's households, from the drawing of the morning bath water at the prescribed temperature to the choice of linen and tableware for dinner. A staff of cowering inferiors obeyed Fawcett's instructions. Charles, like the Duke, saw himself as the ultimate ambassador for the bespoke Savile Row style, the sleeves ending just short of the cuff links, the trousers breaking just-so over the polished brogues. To be fair, Charles did not go to the lengths of creating his own signature Prince of Wales check or tie knot. But he is equally fussy about accessories like the silk handkerchief in the breast pocket. Charles's finesse in dressing also extends to uniforms. In this, he mirrors the taste of his long-time mentor, Dickie Mountbatten. In fact, when Charles appears in the full medal-hung carapace of a naval uniform, he now more and more spookily resembles Mountbatten.

However, Charles is far more than the sum of these parts. His full character has been shaped before the public gaze to a degree beyond that of any other member of the royal family. To his great distaste, the experiences that most determined who he is were lived in public in a relentless serial trial by tabloid. Therefore, to be fair to him, we have to ask if the Charles we think we know is the real Charles. To me, one of the most perplexing challenges is to try to figure out what century he lives in. Quite often it seems that he doesn't know himself. This wouldn't matter if his confusion remained private, but it doesn't. And sometimes it can have shocking and lasting results.

In the 1980s, Charles set out on a personal crusade against modern architecture. He was, quite rightly, critical of public housing schemes that directed people into either bleak red-brick estates or tower blocks that were poorly built copies of work by utopian modernists like Le Corbusier – the curse of twentieth-century architecture is the rash of cheap imitations of original classics. Charles decided to make his point by example. He commissioned Léon Krier, a Luxembourg-born architect, to design a model small town, Poundbury, in Dorset, on land owned by him, part of the vast holdings of the Duchy of Cornwall. He became the worst kind of dilettante, lecturing ministers, urban planners and developers on his ideas to 'liberate the common man' by providing homes and streets that were civilised without being modern – a conceptual conflict that arose partly from his susceptibility to mystics and spiritual quacks and partly from his belief that all good British architecture ended with the Georgians. Like many proselytisers, Charles didn't like being challenged and consequently gathered a coterie of sycophants around him, creating a tyrannical orthodoxy that brooked no opposition.

I went to Dorset to take a look at Poundbury. I knew the county quite well, having retraced T. E. Lawrence's years of retreat there at his cottage, Clouds Hill. It remains a picture of a pastoral England that survived the industrial revolution intact and reached a settled agricultural form in the nineteenth century, with the stirring littoral of downlands and sheer cliffs that Thomas Hardy made into dramatic forces in *Far from the Madding Crowd*. There is still little of the nouveau chic intrusion that has made the Cotswolds look like an upscale theme park for the weekend welly crowd. Poundbury sits a few miles beyond Dorchester. And what a strange place it is. While rejecting any references to the twentieth century, the architects – Krier and Quinlan

Terry – have gone on a mad exercise of reverse engineering the urban form from Victorian, Georgian and Regency sources to Greco-Roman and Venetian. But what struck me was the atavism of the housing – specifically, the windows. There was no indication that the architects had any interest in modern glazing. The houses appear to reject light rather than attract it, in the way that eighteenth-century cottages did because back then glass was too expensive for peasant accommodations. I remembered Victoria's modernising consort, Prince Albert, and his sponsorship of the Crystal Palace, the boldly innovative building that announced the arrival of industrial-scale glazing. Did Charles have any inkling of how perverse he was? Poundbury goes way beyond pastiche to create a world that has never existed outside the reactionary imagination of its patron.

This might seem not to matter too much, just a bit of a laugh to enjoy on a pleasant excursion. But it's more serious than that. It shows us a side of the man due to be the next King that has already done harm and could do a good deal more. Charles has grown accustomed to the habit of controlling public taste by royal decree. He got a first feel for exercising this kind of power in the 1980s when he prevented the construction of what, by any reasonable measure, would have given London a masterpiece of modernism.

In 1969, the Corporation of London, who control development in the City of London, approved the building of an office tower on a prime site between the Royal Exchange and Cheapside. This was not just any office tower. It was the last work designed by Mies van der Rohe, who died in 1969. This was an extraordinary coup for the City of London: Mies was one of the geniuses of the Bauhaus and this tower would have been a benchmark for all future new building in the City. It was a smaller version of the exquisitely austere bronze-tinted Seagram Building on Park Avenue in New York, built in the 1950s, in which Mies perfected the curtain-wall technology, using an exterior of sheer glass over a steel frame. For London, as in New York, he insisted on having his tower set well back from the street line by creating a piazza in front of it. Because of this, the project was delayed until the 1980s as the space for the piazza had to be bought in a series of separate parcels. It was then all set to go ahead when Charles, by then a noisy activist against modernity, damned it as a 'giant glass stump'. That was enough to kill it. When I learned of this, I was amazed that the City's burghers had capitulated so readily. I was also angry. A lot of the corporate towers that followed in the City were dreadful, including, on what would have been the Mies plaza, a building of uncharacteristic inelegance by the post-modernist James Stirling.

Mies wasn't around to call out Charles for his architectural illiteracy, but Richard Rogers, one of Britain's most acclaimed modernists, was. He had good cause. Charles effectively sabotaged what would have been another modern classic. This was a building containing 320 luxury flats and some social housing on the site of the old Chelsea Barracks. Much of the financing came from the Emir of Qatar. In 2009, at the end of a long intrigue involving developers and planners, Charles successfully persuaded the Qatari royal family to withdraw their support for the Rogers design: in other words, a stitch-up by two feudal families robbed London of another architectural landmark. Rogers wrote to *The Guardian*: 'Charles knows little about architecture … He pursues these topics because he is looking for a job … The idea that he is a man of the people fascinates me. He is a man of the rich people, that is for sure.' In the circumstances, Rogers was relatively restrained in the face of such vandalism.

I never got to ask Tony Snowdon what he thought of Charles's taste in architecture or his interventionism. There would not have been any common ground between them; Tony's record was as someone able at the same time to value the qualities of the past and foresee the opportunities of the future. He had the craft, knowledge and skills to bring Kensington Palace back to its classical glory while, at the same time, he encouraged a new wave of young architects like Cedric Price, who worked with him on his London Zoo aviary and became a seminal influence on a generation of modernists, including Rogers. More significantly, Tony actively disliked the kind of shameless opulence that Charles demanded at Highgrove and all of his quarters. One of the breaking points between Tony and Margaret was his love of Old House, a small cottage on a 900-acre estate in West Sussex. The estate had passed to the National Trust from his mother's family of wealthy bankers, the Messels. The cottage was available at a peppercorn rent when Tony made a project of it. He renovated it, doing a lot of the interior work himself, but it was too austere for Margaret. The bedrooms and bathrooms were unheated. Margaret said she had been born and bred in a castle and wasn't going to live in a cottage, even if it was handcrafted by Tony.

In his work at the Design Council and later, Tony was a force for practical innovations that had an impact on people's lives – as in his campaign on behalf of wheelchair mobility. Charles, in contrast, lacks the active and authentic empathy for people that Tony always had. Charles could never relate the realities of other people's lives to his own – on a visit to Poundbury, he told the owners of one of the two-bedroom houses, 'I have always stuck to the principle that I would not let anyone build a house here that I could not personally live in.' This is risible from a man who demands – as Margaret did – palatial comforts as an everyday natural right.

Charles's deeply felt atavism is very odd, and it suggests a clinical disorder. At some point he seems to have developed a phobic reaction to things that break clearly from the past and foretell an inevitable future. For him, these things seem to be apprehended as a personal threat, as though they are bearing down on him like a runaway train – what else can explain the intemperance of his response to something as unthreatening as a curtain-wall tower? He uses architecture to project a very personal fantasy. Poundbury, beyond its crazy mélange of styles, describes a world view of instinctive national superiority. It sets England in a notional period of ascendancy and a condition of unchallenged, genteel social contentment. In this particular fantasy, the decreed social order is topped by princely patronage. This attitude is not as crudely xenophobic as it is in the more extreme Brexit believers like Nigel Farage. Charles's version of England is not so much belligerent Little England as posh Little England. And, given its hierarchical form, it's obvious that Charles finds this England especially safe and congenial for him and his ideas of the monarchy. And what might they be?

In 2018, on the eve of his seventieth birthday, in a BBC documentary, Charles aired some of his thoughts about how he saw the role of a modern monarch. His main thrust was to assure us that he understood that, once King, he could no longer be the capricious meddler that he enjoys being as Prince of Wales: 'If you become the Sovereign, then you play the role as it is expected. So clearly I won't be able to do the same things I've done as heir … It's a different function.' But then comes the caveat: asked if he should continue to use what he calls his 'convening power', he replies, 'Well, you never know…' Indeed, you don't. And in order to see the real nature of the threat, we should return to architecture. You can actively dislike modern architecture, as many people do, without wanting to decimate it and dishonour its masters. There is a hint here of the unstable tyrant king who gathers around him an echo chamber of his own prejudices and lets loose erratic commands to rid himself of dissenters. He is that most dangerous of meddlers who combines ignorance and opinion as a guide to his actions.

What else is there to worry about? There is the issue of money and his methods of acquiring it. When challenged on this, he was forthright: 'I think it of absolute importance that the monarch should have a degree of financial independence from the state … I am not prepared to take on the position of Sovereign on any other basis.' In other words, his terms for 'taking on the position' (the job supported by public funds) depend on his being able to continue to live like a plutocrat. The arrogance is mind-boggling but typical.

As we have seen, in 1992 the Queen agreed – voluntarily – to pay taxes. But a closer look at what has turned into a goldmine for Charles, the Duchy of Cornwall, reveals that the impression left of a sudden conversion to self-sacrifice is quite wrong. In that year, 1992, Charles looked for a way to increase the Duchy's income and came up with the idea of using organic cereals from Duchy farms to make a line of biscuits named 'Duchy Originals', branded with the Duchy's portcullis as a logo. It ticked along until 2008, when the world economy crashed, and it suddenly made a loss of £3.3 million. Charles was bailed out by Waitrose – although, at the time, his office denied that it was a bailout (which it plainly was). They shrewdly saw an opportunity to marry an upscale royal franchise with an upscale supermarket's reach. The results were highly lucrative for both. Very few of the Duchy products any longer involve ingredients from the Duchy farms, but that doesn't matter any more. Charles and Camilla occasionally turn up at a Waitrose branch to promote a new line, and the power of the royal endorsement has built a fortune for them.

The Duchy franchise now makes more than £21 million a year, on which Charles pays no corporate taxes. He pays a 40 per cent income tax rate on his income from the Duchy but is able to deduct a huge sum in expenses: for example, in 2012, when the profit was £18.3 million, he deducted more than £7 million in expenses, including the costs of a personal staff of twenty-eight, among whom are butlers, valets and gardeners – as well as those of the Duchess of Cornwall, including her jewels, clothes and stabling for horses. Charles pays market-price rent for Highgrove, but all that money comes straight back to him in the

Duchy's profits without any deductions for tax – amounting, in fact, to self-dealing. The Duchy is also exempt from capital gains tax and inheritance tax.

Charles becomes very testy when it is suggested that there should be more transparency about his finances. The Duchy audits its own accounts and gives no right of access to the government watchdog, the National Audit Office. In 2005, after the Audit Office complained in a report on the Duchy's operations that 'more information and explanation need to be given to readers of the accounts, not the least of which is Parliament', Charles snapped back that the report was 'a travesty' and 'fundamentally wrong'.

Much of what is known about Charles's finances has been unearthed by the dogged efforts of Norman Baker, a former government minister and long-time Member of Parliament. Baker has also taken aim at Charles's green credentials. It is true that he has spent many years and much effort warning of the ravages of climate change – including quite valiantly delivering the message in a forty-minute monologue to Donald Trump. He does not, however, practise what he preaches. Baker discovered that when Charles made a tour of Europe to promote awareness of climate change, he flew to Rome, Berlin and Venice on a private jet, leaving a carbon footprint of 52.95 tons; using commercial flights would have reduced emissions by 95 per cent.

In 2018, the travel costs incurred by Charles and Camilla were £1.3 million and in that one year the carbon emissions generated by travel by the whole royal family doubled to 3,344 tons.

At this stage in his life, Charles can hardly change who he is. And the truth is that Charles has an overweening sense of privilege and entitlement that he feels can be properly fulfilled only when he ascends the throne. He has waited a long time – more than long enough for us to feel that that the Charles we think we know is, in fact, the real Charles, and that his character does not equip him for the throne.

CHAPTER 27

DIANA'S BOYS

As we have seen, understanding the needs of children has not been one of the royal family's strong points. Charles spent a good deal of his adult life trying to find a stable compass that was not provided in his youth. And he, in his turn, was suddenly left with the toughest task a father can face: taking care of two boys who had lost their mother – and lost her in what was, to them, an almost unbearably public way. Charles was not prepared for this and nor were the rest of the family or the archaic system that served them.

Here are a few vignettes to outline the problem.

In 1951, the then Princess Elizabeth and Philip return from a five-week trip to Canada and the United States. They are met at Euston Station by the Queen, Princess Margaret – and three-year-old Charles. As she is reunited with her son, Elizabeth gives him a short peck on his forehead and moves on. It seems to many watching that Charles hardly knows who she is.

In 1981, after announcing their engagement, Charles and Diana give a television interview at Buckingham Palace. Diana is asked if she is in love and blushingly replies, 'Of course.' Charles grimaces and adds, 'Whatever in love means.' A reporter standing by them says that Charles seems like someone from the seventeenth century. Years later, Diana confesses that this response left her traumatised.

In 1997, walking in the cortège behind his mother's coffin on the gun carriage, Harry is told by an equerry that he cannot hold his father's hand.

In 2018, during the wedding ceremony of Harry and Meghan Markle at Windsor Castle, Bishop Michael Bruce Curry, the African-American presiding bishop of the American Episcopal Church, delivers a sermon quoting Martin Luther King Jr: 'We must discover the power of love, the redemptive power of love. And when we do that, we will make of this old world a new world, for love is the only way.' Outside St George's Chapel, where thousands are listening, people sway in joy and approval. Inside, there are puzzled and awkward glances between Charles and other members of the family, as though they are annoyed that the sermon is overrunning its time by eight minutes and that they are being addressed by an interloper on a subject that is, to them, beyond public expression or discussion: love.

The ghost at the wedding was, of course, Diana. She was the one who was always ready to publicly bare the pains and burdens that came with love.

It began with Diana's own childhood, which haunted her. At one point, as her mother and the children learned from a newspaper that their father was ending the marriage and he began abusing her mother, Diana was assigned by her siblings to intervene, and she slapped him on the face, saying, 'That's from all of us.' There were no hugs and no kisses to be had in that family and she was sent away to boarding school at the age of nine. After her father's divorce, she sided with her mother and loathed her stepmother.

This was part of the traumatic memory that shaped her own approach to motherhood. She gave all her love to her boys, and after she died they were the only people who seemed still able to feel the power of that love; they were shaped every day by the loss of it. As they struggled with that loss, Charles was totally obsessed with Camilla (described at the time by a courtier as 'the laziest woman in England').

He was petitioning his mother to accept that it was his wish to spend the rest of his life with Camilla. At the same time, the future of the family and the monarchy was obviously invested in how the two boys turned out; one was heir to the throne and the other – cynically referred to as 'the spare' – was expected to help his brother to make the system seem still relevant in another century.

Diana had described Harry as being 'different altogether' from William and, as the youngest, he later admitted that he found his mother's death so difficult to deal with that he needed counselling. While she was alive, he had heard and seen things that were not easy to absorb. When he was eight years old, Diana enlisted a voice coach to help her in public speaking. She rightly sensed that she had yet to master the art of speaking naturally from a script. The coach she chose was Peter Settelen and he videotaped his sessions with her. In some of those sessions Harry is heard, off camera, larking about, and Diana calms him down. One wonders how much he took in, for these tapes were a remarkable rehearsal of the *Panorama* confessional with Martin Bashir that aired in 1995. 'I had so many dreams as a young girl,' she said. 'I had hopes that my husband would look after me, he'd support me, encourage me, say "well done" but I didn't get any of that.' She said of her first affair, with the bodyguard Barry Mannakee, 'He was the greatest fellow I ever had.' She added that she believed that the traffic accident in which he died had, in fact, been an assassination, arranged by the palace. An eight-year-old is surely sentient enough to get the drift. (In 2004, extracts from the tapes were broadcast in America on the NBC network under the title *Diana Revealed* and in 2017 they were shown in Britain on Channel 4.)

As they grew up, William and Harry were, at least, spared the first stage of the Mountbatten/Philip method of building character through suffering, Gordonstoun. After private schooling they went to Eton, which was in the tradition of Diana's family. Home life, however, was influenced by their father's increasingly uxorious behaviour, in which Camilla was becoming the diva of Clarence House, since they had moved there after the Queen Mother's death. William and Harry took to entering and leaving through the servants' entrance to avoid encountering her.

The closest the boys came to finding a place where they could be free of a royal household's constraints came about as the result of a friendship Charles had formed while he was at Cambridge, with Hugh van Cutsem, a banker who had inherited a 4,000-acre estate near Sandringham. Van Cutsem's wife Emilie had befriended Diana as her marriage began to fall apart, but later she sided with Charles. The van Cutsems had four sons of their own, and they provided an enduring companionship for William and Harry that was absent from any of the royal pastures. Not that the van Cutsem estate was in any way a step down in grandeur: van Cutsem and his wife were both part of Flemish-originated banking dynasties that established businesses in the City of London in the nineteenth century.

The van Cutsems became the epitome of grand English landowners with an interest that drew them naturally into the Queen's orbit: horse training and breeding. Hugh moved easily between the tweed jackets of the stables and the top hats and tails of the Queen's enclosure at Ascot. This gave him the manner of a toff, but he was an enlightened landowner, supporting game and wildlife conservation. The social ascent of the van Cutsems was resented by Emilie's sister, Wilhelmina, who complained, 'I sometimes think it's made them live a little bit beyond their means, but when you get in with high-powered people, that's what happens, isn't it?'

Emilie van Cutsem was happy to be a part-time surrogate mother to William and Harry, but this caused friction with Camilla, particularly when van Cutsem told Camilla that her son Tom was a bad influence on Diana's sons and, in particular, on William. This came to a head when Tom confessed to the *Sunday Times* that he had been taking cocaine at a party – he was seven years older than William and something of a mentor to him. Camilla was at first not minded to take criticism from van Cutsem, whom she called 'the Dutch cow', but they got on better terms as they came to know each other more. Two of van Cutsem's sons were so close to William that they later became, respectively, godfathers to the next generation of Windsor princes, George and Louis.

William did well at Eton, but Harry struggled. In 2005, one of his teachers at Eton, Sarah Forsyth, launched an unfair dismissal suit, in the course of which she claimed that she had been asked to complete some of Harry's coursework. Both Eton and Harry denied any cheating, but the employment tribunal, which awarded Forsyth £45,000 in damages, allowed that Harry had received special help in reaching the standard required to follow William and win a place at the Royal Military Academy Sandhurst. In being sent on to military careers, Diana's sons were recaptured by the traditional Windsor model, rather than that of Diana's Spencer family, whether they liked it or not. (Earl Spencer's promise that their souls would not be 'simply immersed by duty and tradition' but could 'sing openly' as planned by Diana already seemed from another time.) This was a vocational switch that, as usual with the family, emphasised the role of royal fathers in the way that children moved to adulthood. Both Philip and Charles could cite the virtues, as they saw them, of a spell in the military. By now it was very clear that there was nobody who could ever take the place of Diana as mother. The Queen, however, was an attentive grandmother, and the boys enjoyed the time they spent with her. It was said that she liked Harry's cheeky streak as much as she warmed to William's seriousness about his future life.

As it turned out, they both handled the challenge of military life well, although it was Harry who found among all the ranks involved in a front-line war in Afghanistan the kind of comradeship in which he thrived. In fact, as the lives of the two brothers became more independent, the differences in their characters were sharply asserted. Harry took to the army with a daredevil enthusiasm that William never displayed. They both became helicopter pilots, but William, as second in line to the throne, was more constrained by official caution about his postings, flying search and rescue missions off British coasts, while Harry was, astonishingly, eventually allowed to deploy to a warzone.

Diana once spoke of 'my danger-loving Harry' and in 2008 this trait was given its head when he served in Afghanistan as a forward air controller, directing the bombing of Taliban positions. His presence, though known to the press, was not disclosed until it was leaked by an Australian magazine, and as a result he was pulled out after ten weeks. But he was determined to return in a far more directly engaged way.

This part of Harry's life is usually treated perfunctorily, as though it served as an outlet for his wilder impulses. But, on examination, it struck me that it was actually something much more important, as a guide to the true resources of his character. Indeed, it reveals an extraordinary degree of self-discipline and proficiency under great pressure – rather akin, if you like, to a Roman legionnaire wanting to reach the distinction of centurion. To do this, Harry had to master flying one of the most fearsome weapons in the military arsenal, the Apache helicopter, regarded in the services as the most challenging machine to fly. Pilots do not so much fly the Apache as wear it – to begin with, they are fitted with a custom-made helmet that costs £23,000. Each eye is aligned with a device like a monocle, monitoring different systems, and a pilot cannot qualify before his eyes learn to work independently, a test that many fail. In effect, the experience is like morphing into a humanoid Terminator with the ability, at the press of a button, to let loose a combination of shells and rockets that can eviscerate any target. Just learning to basically fly the machine took six months, and it took another six to master its weapons systems. Because the Apaches flew low to support ground troops, they were vulnerable to being shot down, and training included survival and resistance to interrogation in case of capture.

In October 2011, after training in England, Harry flew to a remote American base in Arizona that replicated the terrain of Afghanistan. There, his instructors said he exhibited the reflexes, acuity and nerve of a natural pilot. For a break, Harry followed the macho *Top Gun* custom by heading for some rest and recreation in Las Vegas. One of his friends reported that it was 'a wild weekend with lots of chicks'. Nobody noticed. But the next time he returned to Las Vegas, in August 2012, all hell broke loose. Harry, with a group of fellow-spirits, checked into the VIP suite of the Wynn Hotel. And after a night out on the town, the group returned with a pack of young women. Harry proposed a game of strip billiards that soon became a cluster of young bodies resembling a Roman debauch. A young woman guest with a cellphone took pictures and within hours they were posted on the TMZ website, where they went viral within minutes. Harry, naked but for a Rolex watch and necklace, was clutching his 'crown jewels'. *The Sun* published the pictures, breaking ranks with other editors who held back at the request of the palace. Since they were already all over social media, it didn't really matter.

A few weeks later, Harry was in Afghanistan again, flying as a co-pilot and gunner in a squadron of Apaches. And this time, unlike his previous tour, his presence was announced. The palace and the Ministry of Defence had together calibrated the risks and decided that Harry embodied two useful qualities: he was a great recruiting agent for the armed forces, and 'Captain Wales of the Household Cavalry', as he was styled, demonstrated that the next generation of the royal family had the right stuff. And there was to be no repetition of

Prince Andrew's role in the Falklands, where protecting him was a distraction for a fully stretched battle group. That war involved intense
conventional combat. In contrast, Afghanistan was an example of the
new form of asymmetrical warfare, between an occupying army and a
light-footed, evanescent enemy.

If it proved anything, Afghanistan reinforced the advantage of the
evanescent enemy. The perils of this kind of warfare for the occupier
were easily underestimated, and they erupted soon after Harry arrived. His squadron was based in Helmand, a sprawling province of
southern Afghanistan, where the Taliban were pervasive. Camp Bastion was the largest British overseas base to be built since the Second
World War, able to accommodate as many as 12,000 troops. Indeed,
to call it a camp was misleading. It was a fortress city, an airfield and
an intelligence centre, and believed to be impregnable. But one night
in September 2012, a group of fifteen Taliban commandos, dressed
in US uniforms, breached the perimeter defences without being detected, at a part of the base occupied by the US Marine Corps. The
Taliban split into three groups, and while one group launched mortars
and rockets at the marines' headquarters, the other two reached the
flight line, where they blew up eight Harrier jump jets and a Hercules
cargo plane. In the following firefight, two US marines were killed, a
sergeant and a lieutenant colonel, and others injured.

The severity of the assault was not disclosed until much later. The
Taliban claimed that they had hoped to locate and kill Harry, but that
was unlikely, since their intelligence had identified a weak point in
the American defences and the British sector was far away. At first, the
army said Harry had been rushed to a safe house. Later they admitted
that he had slept through the whole thing. The British revealed that
only eleven of the base's twenty-four guard towers had been manned.
Two American generals were relieved of their command. It was the
worst loss of American military aircraft in a single attack since the

Vietnam War. During the rest of his twenty-week tour, Harry saw action that, he later said, involved taking bad people 'out of the game', but there was no gung-ho note in his voice. In fact, Afghanistan had left him with an intimate knowledge of war's human costs. He shared his flight home, as he later told Andrew Marr, with badly wounded men:

> One of the guys had a test tube filled with shrapnel that had been removed from his head that he was clutching while he was asleep. I spent a few minutes there just sitting with them and unable to speak to them, obviously, but that was a real turning point in my life.

A total of 453 British servicemen and women died in Afghanistan by the time Camp Bastion was closed in 2014, after eight years of operations.

Harry used the remainder of his time in the army to tackle what he called 'the invisible injuries of war'. He created the Invictus Games, a Paralympic-type international sporting event designed for wounded and disabled military veterans, an idea inspired by what he had seen in America's Wounded Warrior events. Some of the initial funding came from the Royal Foundation, a charity established jointly by William and Harry. The Games were an instant success and greatly increased public awareness of the needs of servicemen and women who suffered the physical and mental effects of war.

Harry left the army in 2015. His direct acquaintance with war might have been brief, unlike that of Mountbatten and Philip, but it permanently shaped his character – or, rather, it brought forward and enhanced parts of his character that were already there, particularly his taste for risk. It also emphasised more clearly one of his mother's qualities that she went to great trouble to instil in both boys, a natural classlessness. Early in 2020, Harry was tricked into taking a call from two Russian hoaxers who claimed to be the Swedish climate activist Greta Thunberg and her father. When this was revealed, the transcript didn't provide anything embarrassing for the tabloids to exploit. To me, the key line was: 'You forget, I was in the military for ten years so I'm more normal than my family would like to believe.'

The British armed forces of the twenty-first century were far less weighted by the class system than in the Second World War, and Harry had thrived in that atmosphere, even though the Afghanistan conflict was a curious throwback, in both its geography and its frustrations, to episodes of the old Victorian imperialism. The gutted remnants of Camp Bastion became like so many remote and remnant forts from campaigns that achieved nothing except to underline the hubris of politicians and the sacrifice of soldiers. Harry became a powerful tribune of that sacrifice and an example of its classlessness. He spoke with none of his father's Woosterish condescension. He felt things with the raw, unguarded spontaneity of his mother.

Mothers, sons, daughters, wives, fathers… William and Harry grew up amid a raging confusion of family values and failing marriages and somehow came through as real people. Their surest bond was between themselves and, for a while, William played both elder brother and surrogate father. He was as circumspect as Harry was rebellious. That was just as well, because his destiny offered no choices. And it helped that he was lucky in love. After a long – and briefly broken – courtship, he found in Kate Middleton a steady and redoubtable companion. Kate was a commoner, but privileged, too, attending a private school with fees of £30,000 a year. There was some petty tabloid snarking about her mother having been 'an airline hostess' – using as a pejorative the 1960s term for jet-set party girls rather than the appropriately contemporary one of flight attendant. In fact, Kate's parents had built a successful business of their own and slipped easily into the extended family of the Windsors. In short, William and Kate were the wholesome and totally acceptable face of the next Windsor generation, never straying from the Queen's own comfort zone. Indeed, polls consistently showed that a majority of the country would prefer that the royal succession passed directly to William – which is constitutionally impossible.

Harry took far longer to find his companion. For a while, he was happy in the life of a tearaway bachelor. His consecutive girlfriends were always glamorous and often of the Sloane Ranger variety who naturally inhabited the same ski slopes, the nightclubs, the Mediterranean hot spots and the privileged London grazing cantons that he did. It was, however, apparent that although they saw Harry as fun they also had a heightened level of vigilance about what was entailed in becoming a Windsor wife. They couldn't have one without the other, so they tended to drift away and settle for something quieter. That was until the summer of 2016 when, on a blind date in London, Harry met Meghan Markle. She was of a different quality: worldly, socially engaged and not easily deterred by the strangeness of the Windsors.

By some instinctive gift of felicity, Diana's boys both found women who were, in very distinct ways, complementary to their own characters. Set against the long and mostly grim record of the royal roulette of marriage making, and in an age that no longer required arranged marriages, William and Harry both found, like the pastor said, that love was the only way.

CHAPTER 28

THE SUSSEXES
SAY GOODBYE

For nearly seventy years, the Queen had been exemplary in representing the institution, but she had often struggled to exercise the same sureness of touch with the royal family – a family that has become patently dysfunctional. As a result, towards the end of her reign there was a marked cooling towards the monarchy, particularly among those who will be the most influential of her heir's subjects, the millennials. A poll in 2019 by YouGov found that among 18–24-year-olds only 41 per cent are in favour of retaining the monarchy. (The Queen's own overall popularity rating was 73 per cent.)

Part of this cooling is a response to an institution that seems still to be unaware of its wanton profligacy. The Queen became one of the wealthiest women in the world, with a net worth of around £20 billion, much of it reflecting the acceleration in land and property values during her lifetime. This puts her in a very different financial bracket from the one her father had to manage. In 1931, when the world's economies collapsed as a result of the Great Crash, a new emergency coalition government demanded and got George V to cut his civil list allowance by £50,000, and Edward, then Prince of Wales, surrendered half of his revenues from the Duchy of Cornwall to the Treasury. The Queen's father, then the Duke of York, sold his six hunting horses to save money. Now, almost without anyone noticing, the royal family has acquired a wealth equal to that of the old landed aristocracy while at the same time they enjoy a lifestyle like the fattest Russian oligarchs – or the Romanovs. As Harold Wilson pointed out in 1969 to his Cabinet during the row over Philip's 'we're going broke' outburst, the family is loath to dip into its wealth to underwrite its public duties and does not practise the philanthropy common to families who feel a public obligation to recompense for their own good fortune.

At a time when the good stewardship of the planet advocated by Prince Charles requires sacrifices by everybody, the travel habits of the royal family remain unbridled. In order to conceal their excesses, they keep raising the cost threshold at which a trip should be publicly disclosed. Twenty years ago, the threshold was £500; by 2010 it was £10,000 and by 2016 had jumped 50 per cent to £15,000. In that one year the trick allowed 202 helicopter flights to go unlisted, as well as forty-three charter flights. Prince Harry, widely seen as a refreshing reminder of his mother's virtues, seems to have caught the habit. In 2018, he chartered a private jet for a short round-trip flight to Amsterdam at a cost of £20,000 and in 2019 spent the same amount on a flight home from Norway so that he could be with his wife on Valentine's Day.

All these contradictions and internal stresses in the family came to a head in 2019. At the age of ninety-three, the Queen suddenly faced two of the most severe family crises of her reign. Both had been simmering for a while without being faced up to. The first – and most contaminating – was caused by the cupidity and depravity of Prince Andrew. For years he enjoyed the hospitality of Jeffrey Epstein – who in 2008 was convicted of soliciting prostitution from a minor – taking many visits to various of Epstein's luxurious honey traps around the world. Epstein's black book of personal contact numbers listed sixteen for Andrew, including an ex-directory Buckingham Palace number, one for Balmoral and one for Sandringham. Andrew's priapic travelogue was already well documented before he decided to face Emily Maitlis, the coolly cogent BBC *Newsnight* interviewer, for a fifty-minute one-on-one grilling that was disastrous for him and for the family. It was apparent from the start that, at the age of fifty-nine, the stallion had given way to the ox, with a mind to match. Maitlis later disclosed that, just as the interview was about to begin, Andrew asked her if she had ever been interviewed by David Frost. 'It was not calculated to shock me,' she wrote, 'but it did. In his eyes, Frost is the convivial Sunday morning telly host … but in my head, Frost is the arsonist-in-chief of Frost/Nixon fame.' As it turned out, Andrew, under a vintage Frost-like interrogation, did not rise to the level of Richard Nixon, who was induced to apologise to the American people for his crimes. But the repercussions of the interview were every bit as sensational as those of the Frost/Nixon joust. Andrew displayed the coldness of a sociopath. There was no hint of remorse or apology, no answer for the well-documented trail of Epstein's largely underage victims, no concern for them at all. One alleged victim, Virginia Giuffre, had told a Florida court that she had sex with Andrew when she was eighteen at one of the two small islands Epstein owned in the Virgin Islands. She said this occurred during an orgy involving much younger girls. (Her first encounter with Andrew, she alleged, had been when she was seventeen.) The circumstantial context, at least, of her story, if not the specific charge against Andrew, was borne out when, in 2020, the Attorney General of the Virgin Islands cited evidence that scores of underage girls were kept as sex slaves and virtual prisoners on the islands. Andrew provided Maitlis with a totally disingenuous explanation of why he accepted the hospitality of a convicted paedophile – it was a 'convenient' place to stay. Epstein, he said, had given him opportunities that were 'actually very useful'. Maitlis said that, for her, that moment was pivotal: 'This is a man – a prince – who did not come to repent. He came to earn back his right to tell the story his way.'

And that was the big point afterwards. Why did Andrew submit himself to what was widely described as a car crash? Why did the palace (code for the Queen) consent to it? If Andrew had no sense of his own moral squalor, surely those around him did? Was the whole gamble based on a belief that controlling the damage was more important than conceding the infamy of the behaviour?

All these questions lead to the Queen and her relationship with Andrew. Even when the extensive reporting about Epstein had already swept up Andrew in its net, the Queen defiantly supported her second son by awarding him the insignia of a Knight Grand Cross of the Royal Victorian Order, for 'personal services to the Queen', in a private ceremony at Windsor Castle in 2011. At no time was there any sign of reproof from either the Queen or Philip. But their indifference could not survive the fallout from the *Newsnight* interview. Within a week Andrew was forced to close his office at the palace, all the charities associated with his name dropped him, his scheduled public appearances were ended and the Queen cancelled his birthday party. Errant priests are excommunicated with more consideration and less haste. The severity of the response was said to have been insisted upon by Charles, who obviously saw that the contamination of the monarchy was far more dangerous than the Queen had imagined – and that his own future could be jeopardised.

The whole thing brought to a head a split between the brothers that had simmered for decades. For a long time, Charles had resented what he saw as the favouritism shown towards Andrew by his parents, while he felt strongly that they (and the whole world) misunderstood him. That problem really went back to the issue of royal parenting and Charles's unwillingness (or inability) to be a stereotypical male heir. In any case, no matter what actions were taken to distance Andrew from the day-to-day affairs of the family, the Epstein scandal hung dangerously over him, simply by association. This was emphasised when

Ghislaine Maxwell, who introduced Andrew to Epstein, was indicted in New York on a charge of recruiting and grooming young women for Epstein's orgies.

This sordid story has actually overshadowed the cupidity issue, which is in its way just as damning. For ten years, beginning in 2001, Andrew cultivated a network of wealthy business contacts, mostly in the Gulf states and central Asia, working in the official role of the Special Representative for International Trade and Investment. One of the British diplomats who saw his performances in the Gulf said that he became known as HBH, His Buffoon Highness, because of his combination of swagger and ineptitude. He always travelled on a taxpayer-funded private jet with a team of six, including a valet who, among his duties, had to carry a special royal ironing board. Behind the buffoon, however, was a greedy mercenary. More shamelessly than any other royal, Andrew knew how to leverage his status as a Windsor prince. There are no available official records that would set the costs of his missions against the value to the country of any trade deals that were made, but his network of fat cats often helped to produce fat profits for himself – like Timur Kulibayev, the billionaire son-in-law of the then President of Kazakhstan, who paid Andrew £15 million for Sunninghill Park, the house given to him by the Queen when he married Fergie, a sum that was £3 million over the original asking price when there were no other bidders. The house was never occupied and was demolished in 2016.

While the extent of Andrew's entanglement with Epstein was drawing headlines across the world, Harry and Meghan, the Duke and Duchess of Sussex, were going through a crisis of their own; it had none of the moral depravity of Andrew's, but it was sweeping away all memory of the exultant joy that flowed from their wedding at Windsor in 2018. More seriously, they were finding it impossible to sustain the idea that they were harbingers of a new enlightened spirit in the family that finally embraced the twenty-first century. Of course, that was really as delusional as a version of the same idea had been when it was applied to the marriage of Margaret and Tony. And it was not just a problem for Harry and Meghan: it involved the whole volatile brood of Windsors. The first public sign of what was actually a far deeper degree of the Sussexes' disenchantment was when Harry declared open war on the tabloids. He began legal actions against *The Sun* and the *Daily Mirror* that referred back to a whole history of phone hacking, reminding people that a legal blackout had been in place for years over hundreds of hacking cases that were being quietly settled without reaching court, at enormous costs to the papers. The Murdoch group, covering *The Sun* and the *News of the World* (which had been killed off by the scandal), had paid out £400 million by 2019 and the *Mirror* group £75 million. By joining those cases, Harry was not only going to add to the costs – he was renewing the sense of public outrage. He said:

> Though [my] action may not be the safe one, it is the right one …
> I've seen what happens when someone I love is commoditised to
> the point that they are no longer treated or seen as a real person. I
> lost my mother and I now watch my wife falling victim to the same
> powerful forces.

Harry knew there was evident public sympathy for this particular *cri de coeur*. He had used it before – indeed, it expressed an uncontainable primal pain that ran through his youth and into his adulthood, the coda of the everlasting Diana tragedy. But it was only half the story. The pursuing swarm of paparazzi set in motion the tragedy, but they did not alone kill Diana on that warm summer night in Paris. The specific human cause was a drunken chauffeur, along with the fact that she was not wearing a seatbelt. But he was but a small part of a far more engulfing pathology: celebrity. Diana played with it, courted it, exploited it, recoiled from it, but could not give it up and it finally consumed her as one of its greatest hits. She appeared on the cover of *People* magazine, the most polished of the American celebrity weeklies, fifty-eight times, and the issue covering her death was the second-best seller of all time, exceeded only by the issue covering the 9/11 terrorist attacks.

Harry never seemed to be able to allow that it was so complicated, with multiple causes. It was too unbearable for his kinetic nature to acknowledge – too nuanced, too open to debate. Harry lived with his own condition of The Furies and there was always one clear cause of it: the tabloids. 'Now watch my wife falling victim' extended his experience of the scourge to Meghan, and she followed Harry's legal actions with her own, against the *Mail on Sunday*, alleging breach of copyright and privacy in publishing a letter she had written to her estranged father, a case that would inevitably be fought over the rights of public access to the lives of very public people.

But Meghan was less absolutist about her adversaries than Harry. Her career as an actress made her more aware of celebrity's transactional truths – as Sam Goldwyn said, 'There's no such thing as bad publicity' ... although she wouldn't go *that* far. In an interview with ITV, she confessed to being warned what was in store for her if she married Harry: 'When I first met my now husband, my friends were really happy because I was so happy. But my British friends said to me, "I'm sure he's great. But you shouldn't do it, because the British tabloids will destroy your life."' She was experienced enough to make a distinction between intrusions of privacy and the legitimate scrutiny that came with privilege, fame and wealth: 'That completely tracks for me if things are fair.' And it was surely fair to look critically at some of the Sussexes' extravagances, like the casual use of private jets and the fact that their decision to move out of Kensington Palace to the ten-bedroom Frogmore Cottage on the Windsor royal estate required £2.4 million of refurbishment and substantial increases in the cost of providing security. As for Harry, those episodes in his wild oats years, like believing that it was OK to treat a Nazi uniform as fancy dress for a party or playing naked billiards in Las Vegas, should have taught him that judgement and self-control are good policy for not providing tabloids with front-page material. That said, though, there were plenty of signs of a bias against Meghan. *The Guardian* reviewed 843 stories about her that were published in fourteen newspapers between May 2018 and January 2020. The bias was assessed by the tone of the headlines: 43 per cent were negative, 36 per cent neutral and 20 per cent positive. These numbers were then compared with the coverage of Kate Middleton in the same period – she had been the subject of only 144 stories (perhaps a message in that). Of those 144, 45 per cent were positive, 47 per cent neutral and 8 per cent negative.

In fact, from the moment Meghan was officially engaged to Harry, there was an undercurrent of racism in much of the tabloid commentary. It was never explicit – that is not usually the way it works. In the subtle, tribal bigotry of the tabloids and the pubs, as well as in the drawing rooms of the aristocracy, racism burbles out by inference and insinuation like a bacillus permanently cruising in the bloodstream. In one typical instance, Meghan's own bloodstream was cited: 'If there is issue from her union with Prince Harry, the Windsors will thicken their watery, thin blue blood and Spencer pale skin and ginger hair with some rich and exotic DNA. Miss Markle's mother is a dreadlocked African-American lady from the wrong side of the tracks…'

This is Rachel Johnson, sister of Boris – whose own DNA has a healthy Turkish component – writing in the *Mail on Sunday* in 2016. It was also an opportunity for the 'don't get me wrong' switch – 'mixed race has nothing to do with it, she's *American*', which comes closely followed by 'she's an actress and that makes her too pushy'. Little

Englanders tend to apply a proprietorial sniffiness to their affection for the royals, resisting, on their behalf, the 'outsider' as a naturally corrupting force, even though the Windsors have had Nazis among their kin. So this phobia, in its turn, flows seamlessly into a gratuitous apology for Harry's perceived misdemeanours. She made him do it etc.

All this established a rumbling subterranean discontent with the Sussexes before the seismic eruption in January 2020, when they jointly announced that they had enough. They were, they announced, no longer willing to serve as 'senior' members of the royal family. They wanted financial independence and they wanted to move to another country, Canada, for a large part of the time. The response was insane, on several levels. *The Sun* called it 'Civil War'. The *Daily Mirror*, complaining that the couple made the announcement before informing the Queen, seemed to take it personally as an insult. The Queen, however, at least in public, was far more considerate: 'My family and I are entirely supportive of Harry and Meghan's desire to create a new life as a young family,' she said, as she and her advisers sat down to find a way to make it work. Watching all of this from New York, I was soon aware of a divide opening up between the responses on each side of the Atlantic. In Britain, the mood became one of a resented loss, a defection that was beyond the pale for many of Fleet Street's daily ranters. In America, there was a sense of gain and sympathy – not just that the Sussexes were relocating to North America (with a probable branch office in Hollywood) but that, as the *New York Times* put it in an astonishing full-page editorial, '[Harry and Meghan] should be celebrated as the heroes of the next installment, as modern royals renouncing some level of privilege to seek their fortune in the real world. May they live happily ever after.' Tellingly, the phrase 'next installment' alluded to the Netflix version of the monarchy, *The Crown*, which informed many Americans' view of the royal family. In Britain, the monarchy was lived with daily as an actual institution; in America, it was top-rated entertainment from another world, providing a kind of surrogate First Family that was, for all its dramas, far more attractive than the real one. Indeed, Harry and Meghan were now being relished in America as the leads in the next season, or beyond, until *The Crown* ends its run. So there you have it: reality and fantasy were becoming interwoven in a way that made them virtually indistinguishable.

At the same time, there loomed an ethical issue. Harry and Meghan were trying to create a new reality for themselves while trading on the market value of the fantasy. Months before they announced their exit on Instagram, they were building a website with a trademarked logo, Sussex Royal. When it went up, it broke the Instagram record for pulling 1 million followers – in less than six hours. They hired a branding agency. The marketing teams smacked their lips: they reckoned that Sussex Royal could make at least £500 million in its first year of business. In terms of product placement, Meghan hardly needed to make an effort. After her first public appearance with Harry, at the 2017 Invictus Games in Toronto, the line of sunglasses she wore instantly shot to 80 per cent of the designer's sales. By January 2020, Harry and Meghan had at least 11 million followers on Instagram and a research firm reported that Meghan's search volume was nearly three times that of Beyoncé. The irony was too blatant to ignore – while on the one hand a super-charged celebrity franchise was being created, on the other hand its two stars were desperate for a new level of privacy.

One of their most aggressive steps was to withdraw their participation in the royal rota, the pool of reporters approved by the palace for the coverage of royal events. In 2020, the pool included the *Daily Express, Daily Mail, Daily Mirror, Daily Telegraph, The Times, The Sun* and the *Evening Standard*. This was a catholic spread of titles at all levels of the press that covered royalty, but for *The Guardian*, which was avowedly republican. The best this arrangement could achieve was a shaky consensus on where to draw the line between information and intrusion, and it did nothing to inhibit those who didn't know the difference between the two. As the Sussex crisis unfolded, the palace briefings, through the rota, struggled to guide the narrative, hampered by the fact that the family itself was in turmoil over how to control the outcome. But the statements issued in the Queen's name were not the usual bromides. Two phrases, in particular, felt personal: 'Harry, Meghan and Archie will always be much loved members of my family' and 'I am particularly proud of how Meghan has so quickly become one of the family.'

With the rota gone, Harry and Meghan set out on the Sussex Royal website their own rules for collaborating with reporters. They were, they said, prepared to 'engage with grassroots media organisations and young, up-and-coming journalists; invite specialist media to … give greater access to their cause-driven activities; provide access to credible media outlets focused on objective news reporting'. It seemed to me either extraordinarily naïve or, worse, an attempt to establish an alternative journalism on entirely their own terms. It's the kind of 'soft' censorship that corporations use in their public relations, where chosen journalists are expected to accept the company's rules in return for access, an arrangement that no self-respecting editor would for one moment consider. How would this work? Where were the 'young, up-and-coming journalists' who were ready to obey?

This was not a good way to earn sympathy for the story they wanted to tell. It disaffects reporters looking for their virtues – of which they have plenty. Apart from product placement, the power that Harry and Meghan brought to the marketplace was their almost unequalled ability to influence the support of charities and non-profit organisations. One of their early ideas was for a 'global philanthropy brand' that would support organisations working in areas where their own interests are already clear, including mental health; ecological and wildlife

conservation, particularly in Africa; child welfare; and wellness programmes for communities ill-served with guidance on diet and child
nutrition. Given those priorities, it seemed gratuitously offensive that
they were bracketed by some commentators with puerile 'influencers'
like Kim Kardashian and Gwyneth Paltrow. Potentially, the Sussexes
have a different model to follow – the Obamas. Meghan and Mi-
chelle Obama have already established that they are kindred spirits.
They have shared interests in Africa and on children's nutrition. As
things turned out, at the end of March 2020, when they officially
began their non-royal lives, Harry and Meghan had to drop Sussex
Royal as their brand name, but by then it hardly mattered. Their name
recognition was virtually unequalled.

It is worth remembering that the idea of monetising the monarchy did not begin with them. It was already well established, going
back to that moment in 2008–09 when Duchy Originals ran into
financial trouble, ending with a loss of £3.3 million. One of the original investors in the business was an American banker, Joe Allbritton. In 1993, Allbritton resigned as the CEO of Riggs Bank, based
in Washington DC, after losses it suffered in the collapse of a series
of savings and loan banks in California and other western states, a
scandal that ensnared a number of leading politicians. The bank was
unique in the nation's capital as a place that handled the finances of
both American political dynasties and foreign embassies; several of
its officials had connections to the CIA. The Allbritton family continued to run it until 2005, when the bank pleaded guilty to failing
to prevent money laundering by Augusto Pinochet, the former dictator of Chile. They paid $16 million in fines and the business was
taken over by a much larger firm, PNC. Meanwhile, Joe Allbritton
personally invested around half a million pounds in seed money for
Duchy Originals and, despite the banking scandal, had so effectively
ingratiated himself with Prince Charles that in 2007 he and his wife

rode in the fourth carriage behind the Queen at Ascot. When the world financial crisis hit and Duchy Originals went from profit to loss, Charles once again tapped Allbritton to help, in exchange for the American rights to the line of royal delicacies. In the end, the loan was not needed because Waitrose stepped in and, once its marketing skills were applied, Charles found himself with one of the most successfully branded businesses in Britain.

And it turned out that the profits from Duchy Originals would help to underwrite the 'financial independence' that Harry and Meghan said they wanted. The bulk of Harry's income would come from Charles, through the Duchy. The Sussexes agreed to repay the costs of renovating Frogmore Cottage. There was no risk of them ever being financially strapped in their new life: Harry's share of the inheritance from Diana, which came on his thirtieth birthday, had, through investments, grown to well in excess of £10 million and Meghan's TV work playing a paralegal on *Suits* had been lucrative. But the layers of fog that covered the whole family's financial affairs meant that it was impossible to say who would end up paying how much to whom and from where it would come, depending on who kept the books.

To me, the most unreal expectation of the Sussexes was that they were striving for a new normality of some kind that was never going to be attainable, a position that was described as half-royal. I was reminded of the two previous attempts to make a getaway from this family. Margaret was never half-royal, and she had no interest in being 'normal'. She managed to cut loose on her own terms and to dabble with wild abandon in bohemia without making any personal sacrifices in comfort or wealth. The suggestion of 'financial independence' was beyond her imagination. Diana, making the reverse journey from outside the glass cage to inside it, discovered that having royalty thrust upon you rather than being born with it didn't mean that it was any easier to shake it off once you wanted to. Instead of shaking it off, she reimagined it in her own image and, thereby, gave it a new kind of contagious power that proved fatal to her and a curse to the family.

Diana would have been distressed to see her sons caught by the same curse. Long before Harry declared that he wanted out, it was suggested that the brothers were barely on speaking terms. There were plenty of indications. When Harry and Meghan self-ejected from the Kensington Palace compound to Frogmore Cottage, it was clear that they didn't share or enjoy the same world as the Cambridges. However, this need not have implied ill-feeling between the brothers. They were never meant to have identical lives, any more than Margaret and the Queen had identical characters, interests or lives. Kate and Meghan had wholly different backgrounds and life experiences, but that ought to have enlivened their relationship, not soured it. In any event, this story – like so many others about the Windsors – was being largely narrated in the limited demotic of the tabloids and nobody really knew how much of it was true – except, of course, the servants. Stories of a breach between the brothers reached a new level of emotional power with reports in two Murdoch papers. *The Times* alleged that 'bullying' of Harry and Meghan by William was part of the reason for their actions. The *Sunday Times*, citing an anonymous source, quoted William as saying:

> I've put my arm around my brother all our lives and I can't do that anymore; we're separate entities. I'm sad about that. All we can do, and all I can do, is try and support them and hope that the time comes when we're all singing from the same page. I want everyone to play on the team.

It rang true, but only to the extent that it supported the unverifiable story arc promoted in the tabloids over the previous months. And William and Harry decided enough was enough. They authorised a statement saying, 'Despite clear denials, a false story ran in a UK newspaper today speculating about the relationship between the Duke of Sussex and the Duke of Cambridge. For brothers who care so deeply about the issues surrounding mental health, the use of inflammatory language in this way is offensive and potentially harmful.'

Harry and Meghan and son Archie's first haven on the other side of the Atlantic was on Vancouver Island, an extraordinarily beautiful offshore piece of British Columbia that much resembles the western islands of Scotland. It was ideal as a place for decompressing after the media circus in London, but I could not see how it could ever work as a permanent home. It was a natural idyll, not a place where their future careers could be launched and managed. And sure enough, early in April, as the coronavirus calamity was closing the border between Canada and the United States, it emerged that the family had quietly left Canada and moved to a secluded estate in Los Angeles, Meghan's true hometown, where, in due course, they signed a lucrative deal to produce programming for Netflix – the very people who, with *The Crown*, have done more than anyone to merge the real and fantasy lives of the Windsors.

CHAPTER 29

THE MONARCHY IN THE TIME OF APOCALYPSE

On balance, it seemed to me that, whatever the destiny of Harry and Meghan turned out to be, the monarchy would hold together on its own terms for a while, in the person of the woman who headed it.

I wrote this in a column for the Daily Beast on 24 June 2017:

This is part of what a 91-year-old woman did for a day job in the last week: She rushed to comfort people who were hurting after their homes were lost in a catastrophic fire at the Grenfell Tower and spent 45 minutes talking to them, sometimes close to tears; she spent two hours reviewing an immaculate military ceremony saluting her birthday and then decreed a minute's silence in the honor of the fire victims; she rode in an open carriage on one of the hottest days on record in a glamorous ritual marking the opening of one of her favorite sporting events; she read a fatuous speech that she had nothing to do with composing to open the oldest parliament in the world. She did all that and for every other minute of her life she still had to behave as was expected of her, as the queen of the United Kingdom.

This was not the same Queen who held back for a week before visiting the grieving parents of Aberfan, or the Queen who remained at

Balmoral while her people demanded her presence in London after the death of Diana. Her arrival at Grenfell Tower, where seventy-two people had needlessly been trapped and died, followed a visit by the Prime Minister, Theresa May. May's appearance was perfunctory and impersonal – it was, said the *Evening Standard*, 'another moment of not rising to the occasion as a leader with vision would do'.

I wrote that 'the queen's role sometimes seems conflicted, between archaic ceremony and natural spontaneity'. What was striking about her visit to Grenfell Tower was that her spontaneity was natural and it showed a human warmth that had rarely been glimpsed before. Prince William was with her, and together they signalled something else: at this moment the monarchy had skipped a generation and in some way found a more inspiring form in the combination of the two of them.

Oddly, too, I felt that we already knew William as a person while the Queen still withheld that knowledge from us. The reason was that she had always subjugated personality to duty. She understood the role and purpose of the monarchy in the abstract, what it could do and what it could not. One of the most persuasive examples of this came in May 2011, when she made the first visit by a reigning monarch to Ireland for a century. The decision to make the trip was thought to be something of a gamble. It made sense to follow up the achievement of the Good Friday Agreement that brought peace to Northern Ireland by promoting the idea of a new comity between the Irish Republic and the United Kingdom, but there was so much bad history to overcome. The genius of enlisting the Queen to do it was that instead of it appearing to be a political embrace between heads of state it became a meeting of the peoples, in which the Queen spoke for the people of the UK. Hardliners on both sides were cool. But when the Queen rose to speak at a state dinner at Dublin Castle and apologised for 'things which we would wish had been done differently or not at all' she received a standing ovation. The *Irish Times* led a cascade of praise from the Dublin media: 'Queen Elizabeth is welcome as a remarkable woman in her own right, as a figure to whom a significant minority on this island give allegiance and, above all, as a symbol of mutual affection and common interests of two separate but closely connected countries.'

So, for the Queen's generation, being the Sovereign was, in the end, about playing a role, not about being a person. She had to learn the part early. She was the understudy suddenly taking over the lead in a demanding production. John Colville, who was her private secretary before she came to the throne, between 1947 and 1949, noted that she 'has the sweetest of characters, but she is not easy to talk to, except when one sits next to her at dinner; and her worth, which I take to be very real, is not on the surface'. The drama coaches – in this case the courtiers – closed in on her and sternly rehearsed her according to their own strict interpretation of the script. Someone who watched her closely for a long time said she had always had the approach of a diligent head girl at a school. She tried very hard to fill out the part, but she had limits – as Lord Altrincham so mercilessly identified in 1957. But behind the coaches in the court another presence informed her in ways that they could not – her father. He would always be there, and she often sought his guidance, trying to imagine what he would advise. 'What would my father have done?' she sometimes said, aloud.

It was a very testing role that never let go – she was always very alert to how it should be played in public because she understood that the role required her to embody so much more than herself. '*L'état, c'est moi!*' declared Louis XIV, and although the Queen was not an absolute monarch, the symbolism of her throne meant that she was duty bound, like the Sun King, to uphold an *idea* of how her nation should be seen and even how it should behave. President Charles de Gaulle also appropriated Louis XIV's ownership of the nation for himself, but few knew that behind this pose he was far less assured. He confided to an aide:

> In reality we are on the stage of a theatre where I have been keeping up the illusion since 1940. I am trying to give France the appearance of a solid, firm, confident and expanding country, while it is a worn-out nation, which thinks only of its own comfort, which doesn't want any problems...

There is no evidence that the Queen was ever capable of being as starkly honest with herself as this. But at the beginning there was so much for her to master so quickly, and she did get so deeply, so absolutely into character, according to the way she saw it, that it and she fused into one, like a thespian who morphs permanently into his greatest performance. However, the longevity of the performance brought a serious problem: she lacked any sense of the institution's obsolescence.

The Queen became so certain of what was unchangeable about the monarchy *as embodied by her* that she was never really able to concede the need to change. In fact, there is clear evidence that she fought against change for so long and so hard because she distrusted the case for it – and its advocates – as facile. In 2002, marking her fiftieth year on the throne, she spoke to both Houses of Parliament in the Great Hall at Westminster. In a key line, she warned, 'Only the passage of time can filter out the ephemeral from the enduring.'

She clearly felt that no matter how much everything else changes there should be something constant in a nation's sense of itself – a stable core of identity and national exceptionalism that she, above all, had to preserve. In that same speech she said:

> We in these islands have the benefit of a long and proud history. This not only gives us a trusted framework of stability and continuity to

ease the process of change, but it also tells us what is of lasting value … What endure are the characteristics that mark our identity as a nation and the timeless values that guide us.

With those words she was handing out another dose of the national hallucinatory drug that has been freely prescribed as an antidote to what, in reality, has been decades of a steady and inevitable decline as a world power. The original prescription was written by another great actor who left a permanent mark on the Queen's sense of destiny: Winston Churchill. The Churchill of the 1940s was a discrete historical creation of his own will and the nation's courage – and a kind of foundational legend. For the remainder of his life, Churchill lived off the receipts of that legend. And for many people, the power of that legend has barely diminished. Margaret Thatcher's later years of office were in thrall to it. Tony Blair recklessly talked of a Britain 'that punched above its weight'. And – somewhat more cynically – Boris Johnson invokes the same texts as a basis for Brexit. It is not surprising, therefore, if the Queen, instead of seeing herself as a stubborn reactionary, believes that she is an essential custodian of that view of greatness and constancy and has done her bit in the spirit of the Blitz to 'filter out the ephemeral'.

There is something admirable about her obduracy. Some of the changes she resisted were, indeed, more about fashion than lasting systemic reforms: 'Swinging London' and 'New Labour' turned out to be ephemeral promises rather than permanent advances.

* * *

After all the family dramas the House of Windsor (and we) have endured, it is surely a point of wonder that the Queen was the one person in the family who had never really been burned by the tabloids. She remained the calm stoic at the centre of many storms.

And the greatest storm of her life since the Second World War came, as it did to all of us, stealthily, invisibly and lethally. With her government and her country struggling to contain and defeat a ravaging modern plague, the coronavirus, the Queen was called upon to bring her own uniquely calming qualities to her people. On Palm Sunday 2020, sitting in a room at Windsor Castle at a measured distance from a lone BBC cameraman wearing full protective clothing, she more than rose to the occasion – she embodied the full span of her years as the connecting tissue between one time of mortal terror and another, in a speech to the nation of 523 firmly spoken words. 'Together', she said, 'we are tackling this disease, and I want to reassure you that if we remain united and resolute, then we will overcome it.' Then, invoking something of the tone of Churchill at the time of Dunkirk, she continued:

I hope in the years to come … those who come after us will say the Britons of this generation were as strong as any. That the attributes of self-discipline, of quiet good-humoured resolve and of fellow-feeling still characterise this country. The pride in who we are is not a part of our past, it defines our present and our future.

The image of the Queen then cut away to a black and white photograph of her with Margaret in 1940 when, again at Windsor Castle, they spoke on the radio – 'to children who had been evacuated from their homes and sent away for their own safety. Today, once again, many will feel a painful sense of separation from their loved ones. But now, as then, we know, deep down, that it is the right thing to do.'

And finally a sentence with a calculated echo of wartime morale-boosting popular songs: 'We should take comfort that while we may have more still to endure, better days will return; we will be with our friends again; we will be with our families again; we will meet again.'

It was an impeccable performance, a deft fusion of bluntness, emollient familiarity and just enough patriotism to stir the most resistant soul. Indeed, it so stirred the soul of an erstwhile critic of the Queen and of the conservatism of the monarchy, Alastair Campbell, that he wrote in the *Daily Telegraph*, 'I think it is possible to make the case that the Queen is one of, if not the, most remarkable people on the planet.' He also said something that I had no argument with: 'She is one of the most written about people on earth, [but] we don't really know much about her beyond what we see.'

I found a compelling video snapshot that exquisitely captured this quality. While the Andrew scandal erupted, Prince Philip was briefly hospitalised in London. Meanwhile the Queen, knowing that Philip hated being visited in hospital, headed for Sandringham on a regular commuter train from Liverpool Street. In the video, arriving at Sandringham, she steps briskly down from the train to the platform without support, wearing a pink coat and a headscarf – the headgear she has favoured all her life when not required to be more formal. The video is shot in such a way that the Queen is virtually indistinguishable from the rush-hour crowds around her. Her minders are discreetly keeping their distance, as if by protocol. If you didn't know who it was, you would think it was just a neatly dressed country lady of the Miss Marple breed, still healthily independent of movement and coping contentedly with age – not that she is a 93-year-old monarch. The video lasts for thirty seconds. I kept replaying it and I thought about the frustrations of not really knowing this woman any better after studying her for so long. Indeed, as the narrative of this book evolved, it felt to me that she was being extremely unhelpful to the dramatists who attempt to bring her to life. The most obvious case of this is *The Crown*, a very superior soap opera about a very superior soap opera. Peter Morgan, the creator, is a gifted and inventive dramatist, but as the series reached the Queen's middle age even he could not conceal the hole at the centre: while the rest of the cast were absorbingly delinquent, the Queen really had nothing much to do other than be Queen with boring efficiency, albeit occasionally issuing stern homilies to the rest of her brood about the need for them to be boring, too. Clearly, they are not listening.

AFTERWORD

*'Buckingham Palace have had several centuries to learn the difficult art
of scandal burying. MI5 have only been in the business since 1909.'*
PETER WRIGHT, IN *SPYCATCHER*

When Peter Wright was interrogating Anthony Blunt, he was,
as we have seen, warned off raising any questions about
Blunt's 1945 mission to recover documents recording communications
between the Windsors and their German relatives during the 1930s, as
well as records of the Duke of Windsor's encounters with Hitler and
other leading Nazis. I have reconstructed as much of that particular
scandal as is possible from the existing sources, but without the support of official records the picture is incomplete. Having incomplete
documentation is almost as bad as having none. Almost. It removes the
account from the witness of the actual participants. It deletes the 'felt'
context of the time – the experience and atmosphere of the moment
in the kind of detail that could reveal pressures that we cannot, from
this distance, feel ourselves. Unfortunately, this calculated filtering of
the historical record as it applies to the royal family persists to this day.
There were some reforms made after a review of public records policy
carried out by Paul Dacre of the *Daily Mail*. The National Archives at
Kew, a place staffed by diligent and conscientious public servants, are
speeding up the pace of releasing key historical documents. The vast

Royal Archives at Windsor Castle are, however, regarded as private, under the control of the monarch. And their influence is still felt at Kew. When I first began searching for the records of the Duke of Windsor's relationship with the Nazis, some decades ago, the obvious and substantial gaps in the files were explained simply as having been 'weeded'. The indefatigable freelance auditor of the royal family, Norman Baker, found that there are still more than 3,600 files on the royal family at Kew that remain closed. (Interestingly enough, one of the subjects is the long-running feud over the change of the family name to Mountbatten-Windsor as recorded in correspondence with Downing Street.) The Royal Archives policy is not to release anything relating to the present Queen's reign. And there is no indication of what might happen when that reign ends – whether the weeding will have done its work to avoid more scandals, at what pace files might later be released, and what subjects will remain closed for as long as the palace dictates. The monarchy is not one family's property, although they act as though it is; it belongs to the people, who pay for it. Their history is our history, and their suppressions and deletions undermine the balance of the historical record of the nation in a damaging way. If the monarchy is to survive as an acceptable national institution, it should be as acceptably transparent as the other national institutions are – even though they are not perfect. There is no evidence that palace officials accept this principle; they have resisted every step towards a modern democratic concept of the freedom of information (which, in Britain, has never approached the standard accepted in the United States). As with all censorship, the question is: what are they so keen to hide?

SELECT BIBLIOGRAPHY

Bedell Smith, Sally, *Elizabeth the Queen* (Random House, 2012)

Bouverie, Tim, *Appeasing Hitler* (The Bodley Head, 2019)

Bower, Tom, *Rebel Prince* (William Collins, 2018)

Brown, Tina, *The Diana Chronicles* (Broadway Books, 2007)

Carpenter, Humphrey, *That Was Satire That Was* (Victor Gollancz, 2000)

Costello, John, *Mask of Treachery* (Collins, 1988)

Davenport-Hines, Richard, *Enemies Within* (William Collins, 2018)

De Courcy, Anne, *Snowdon* (Weidenfeld & Nicolson, 2008)

Dempster, Nigel, *HRH The Princess Margaret* (Quartet Books, 1983)

Donaldson, Frances, *Edward VIII* (J. P. Lippincott, 1975)

Greenslade, Roy, *Press Gang* (Macmillan, 2003)

Higham, Charles, *The Duchess of Windsor* (McGraw-Hill, 1988)

Lownie, Andrew, *The Mountbattens* (Blink, 2019)

Picknett, Lynn; Prince, Clive; Prior, Stephen, *Double Standards* (Sphere, 2002)

Vickers, Hugo, *The Quest for Queen Mary* (Hodder & Stoughton, 2018)

INDEX